Project Rescue:

Avoiding a Project Management Disaster

About the Authors

Sanjiv Purba is CEO of Purba Computer Solutions, Inc. He has over 20 years of progressive experience managing projects of all sizes and complexities and in many different industries. He has worked for the "Big 5" consultancies, for boutique consulting firms, and for Fortune 100 organizations around the world. Some of his clients include IBM, Deloitte Consulting, Goldman Sachs, Perrier, CIT, Microsoft, Sun Life, the Royal Bank, Blast Radius, MetaPCI Corp, BMW, Nintendo, MasterCard, The Hospital for Sick Kids, Legends of the Game, The Hudson's Bay Company, TD Waterhouse, TD Bank, and CIBC Mellon. Sanjiv has written over 15 books and hundreds of articles for such publications as the *Globe and Mail* and the *Toronto Star*. He is a recognized authority in delivering large, complex projects successfully and has been retained to successfully salvage many troubled projects. Sanjiv is a frequent lecturer at universities and colleges. He can be reached at spurba@rogers.com.

Joe Zucchero has over 24 years of solid experience in project and program management and the execution of highly complex IT engagements. He was named Executive Vice President of The Casey Group in December 2002 when NetigrateZ, a company he founded in April 2001, was merged with The Casey Group. Prior to founding NetigrateZ, Mr. Zucchero held executive positions with IBM, Ernst & Young LLP, and Keane, Inc. He is recognized as an industry leader in e-business, IT governance, program and project management, and IT services management. Mr. Zucchero, who has qualified to sit for the Project Management Institute's PMP (Project Management Professional) exam, began his career in information technology at AT&T. His work has been published in *Wall Street & Technology, CFO IT,* and *Financial Executive.* Mr. Zucchero holds a B.S. in Education from Villanova University.

About the Technical Editor

Al Santucci is a Project Management Institute (PMI) certified Project Management Professional (PMP) with over thirty year's of information technology experience. His background includes large scale system development for automobile manufacturing, consumer product distribution, telecom systems, and web-based systems. The last fifteen years have been in the consulting industry providing software sales, delivery, methods development, and internal project support. A significant number of years were spent as a Project Officer and auditor. Currently, he is the Director, Project Management Services, for The Casey Group, Inc Tampa, Florida. He provides IT management consulting services and PM training and coaching to clients, and assures internal project methodology compliance.

Project Rescue:

Avoiding a Project Management Disaster

Sanjiv Purba
Joseph J. Zucchero

Osborne/**McGraw-Hill**

New York / Chicago / San Francisco
Lisbon / London / Madrid / Mexico City / Milan
New Delhi / San Juan / Seoul / Singapore / Sydney / Toronto

The McGraw·Hill Companies

McGraw-Hill/Osborne
2100 Powell Street, 10th Floor
Emeryville, California 94608
U.S.A.

To arrange bulk purchase discounts for sales promotions, premiums, or fund-raisers, please contact
McGraw-Hill/Osborne at the above address. For information on translations or book distributors outside the
U.S.A., please see the International Contact Information page immediately following the index of this book.

Project Rescue: Avoiding a Project Management Disaster

1234567890 CUS CUS 01987654

ISBN 0-07-225537-4

Vice President & Group Publisher	Mike Hays
Vice President & Publisher	Scott Grillo
Director of New Program Development	Gareth Hancock
Project Editor	Kenyon Brown
Acquisitions Coordinator	Jessica Wilson
Technical Editor	Al Santucci, PMP
Copy Editors	Nancy Rapoport, William McManus
Proofreader	Linda Medoff
Indexer	Jack Lewis
Composition	Dick Schwartz, Apollo Publishing Services
Illustrators	Melinda Lytle, Kathleen Edwards, M. Sieben & Associates
Series Designer	Peter F. Hancik
Cover Designer	Pattie Lee

This book was composed with Corel VENTURA™ Publisher.

To my wife, Kulwinder,
my children, Naveen, Neil, and Nikhita,
and my mother, Inderjit.

—Sanjiv Purba

To my wife, Ginny, and daughter, Kristen, who understand
and support me when I'm away and to my mother,
Margaret, who always believes in me.

—Joe Zucchero

Contents at a Glance

Contents

Acknowledgments

We would like to acknowledge the support or encouragement received from the following individuals: Tony Small, Sandy Sicilia, James Fehrenbach, Gareth Hancock, Jessica Wilson, Kenyon Brown, Nancy Rapoport, Bill McManus, Susan Certoma, Brett Turner, Gautam Lohia, Paul Saunders, Cathy Tait, Ian Tait, Gord Shields, Chad Davidson, Claudette Taylor, George Ross, Nancy Stonelake, Rich O'Hanley, Wayne Thomas, Zool Samji, Wayne Martin, Katie Comerford, Ido Gileadi, Bharat Shah, John Wyzalek, Steve Litwin, Terry Stuart, Sue Banting, Victoria Tomalik, Bob Elliott, Michael Simonyi, Sandy Sicilia, Mario Perez, Richard Casey, Al Santucci, Wayne Pollard, Joan Barnes, and Mary Piccirillo.

Introduction

What course of action should a team follow when a project gets into trouble and is at risk of missing a key metric such as a deadline or cost to deliver? What if the situation is worse and it appears that the project is going to be a total disaster? Can the project be rescued? How much of the project can be salvaged? When is it too late to turn things around?

Even projects that can be described as well managed in terms of following general principles can end up hurtling toward failure. In fact, project management requires balancing so many different factors that it is not unusual for some risk to sneak past the mitigation strategies. Avoiding problems altogether is an ideal goal, but reality has shown us that it is also vital to recognize and deal with problems as they begin to manifest on a project.

Purpose of this Book

This book provides a four-phase rescue framework that serves two primary objectives. The first, as the title implies, is to rescue a project that is troubled and/or heading toward certain failure. The second objective is to serve as a guide for improving the value delivered by any project. The same project rescue framework serves both of these functions. It can be applied when problem symptoms are encountered. It can also be used at project checkpoints in any project to assess how well it is progressing toward its goals.

Managing the successful delivery of projects involves a combination of science and art. The science part focuses on tools, techniques, and methods that can be applied to every situation. Working from this perspective is sufficient as long as things go well. However, in real-world situations, things do not always proceed according to plan. Decisions are made for political reasons. Users cannot make up their minds. Budgets get chopped with little or no warning. An ideal response, such as delaying project delivery, may not be viable for any number of reasons. This is where the art portion of project management takes over.

A properly executed project rescue always leaves a project in a better state than when the rescue effort started. The sooner a project rescue is applied in a project cycle, the better the results that can be achieved. However, it is never really too late to apply a project rescue to salvage some success from every initiative.

Intended Audience

This book is intended for anyone who has a role in projects. This includes those working on the projects and those directly benefiting from the results. This encompasses a wide range of roles and responsibilities, including: project sponsors, executives, directors, project managers, program managers, project leaders, business users, consultants, and other resources on a project team.

This book can be read and applied by beginners and experts alike. However, we do assume that the reader has some knowledge of basic project management concepts. This includes understanding the basic definitions of terms such as project, project success, and metrics. We also assume familiarity with techniques for creating project plans, conducting team reviews, and writing status reports. We make these assumptions so that we can focus on the more advanced and subtle points of successfully delivering projects and turning runaway projects around. Readers unfamiliar with the basic project management concepts can review some of the books in the bibliography or material from the organizations discussed in Chapter 15.

Organization of the Book

This book contains 19 chapters that are divided into six parts, as described next. The publisher provides a web site for downloading templates described in the material—instructions are provided at the end of this introduction.

Part I: Troubled Projects

This part of the book describes the tools and techniques needed to identify projects that may be suitable candidates for a project rescue. Seeing any of the symptoms described in this part of the book should launch an intervention to save your project. The chapters in Part I also provide material to use in general project checkpoints to determine how well they are progressing. Chapter 1 discusses how to spot the warning signs. Chapters 2 and 3 describe the four-phase rescue framework that can be used alongside other development or management methodologies. Chapter 4 provides a list of questions to ask members of a project team to ascertain the extent of the troubles facing the initiative.

Part II: Assessment

Conducting a thorough assessment of the situation is the first phase of the rescue framework. This part of the book describes the techniques to use and the questions to ask to accurately diagnose the situation, in order to be able to understand what the project was trying to accomplish and what went wrong. Chapter 5 provides a step-by-step process for thoroughly understanding and analyzing a project. Chapter 6 examines the key areas to consider when revising the risk assessment. Chapter 7 lists the questions to ask when conducting the assessment processes.

Part III: Planning the Intervention

The second phase of the rescue framework is to plan the intervention. This part of the book describes how to create the infrastructure and how to define a new approach for improving the project results. Chapter 8 describes the requirements of a control office to track detailed progress. Chapter 9 looks at some of the alternate approaches that are available for rescuing the project. Chapter 10 examines the details that specifically need to be included in a project rescue plan and how they differ from traditional plans.

Part IV: Execute the Intervention

The third phase of the rescue framework is to execute the intervention. This involves following general project management principles in a highly energetic rescue environment. Of utmost importance is the ability to adjust the new approach to new situations that can arise during the intervention. Chapter 11 examines the new management activities related to the project rescue. Chapter 12 discusses techniques to keep the project rescue on track. Chapter 13 provides a list of questions to evaluate how well the project rescue is proceeding.

Part V: Post-Intervention

The fourth and last phase of the rescue framework is to conduct a detailed post-intervention analysis. This is to learn what went well, what could have been done better, and how the organization can benefit from the rescue experience. Chapter 14 provides a formal structure for conducting a post-mortem on the rescued project. Chapter 15 explains how to reduce the intensity of the project rescue intervention following the achievement of important milestones. This chapter also explains how to capture key lessons from the rescue experience and how to build these into an improved project management framework for future projects. Chapter 16 contains a list of questions to help drive the activities in this phase.

Part VI: Intervention Techniques

This part of the book describes some of the intervention techniques that are required to overcome the interpersonal and performance issues that exist on projects that are being rescued. The most important of these is building consensus between all the different groups that are involved in the project, as discussed in Chapter 17. Chapter 18 provides a list of tools that can be incorporated into a project rescue toolkit and ultimately form the basis of a project management toolkit. Chapter 19 presents the key lessons learned on different projects.

The Downloadable Online Forms

Throughout the book you will find examples of forms, the bulk of which have been used by the authors with great success on consulting engagements for Fortune 100 companies. All of the forms discussed and illustrated here are available for download in Microsoft Word format from the McGraw-Hill/Osborne web site. Visit www.osborne.com, click the "free code" link in the upper-left corner of the page, then scroll through the list of titles to find this book's link. The forms are sorted according to the chapter of their first appearance in the book.

Troubled Projects

## CHAPTER 1

Recognizing the Warning Signs

Following generally accepted project management principles does not always deliver successful projects. Competing factors, such as the need to optimize profits while creating the highest quality deliverables, lead to a narrow margin of error that is easily consumed in the real world. Other factors, such as unexpected external events, ineffective risk mitigation strategies, human errors, and the constantly evolving technology infrastructures, also damage projects. This is despite the best intentions and competence of everyone involved in an initiative.

There comes a point on many projects when the team and the stakeholders have lost control, but everyone remains in denial—rejecting the possibility that the worst case scenario could actually happen. But history shows us that once a project gets into trouble, we often see it spiral out of control at an escalating rate regardless of the fixes or patches that are applied. Beyond this *project breaking point,* a dramatic intervention is required to redirect the project activities and to rescue the project from ending in complete failure. This book is concerned with the effective facilitation of such action to maximize project benefits, returns, and outcomes.

Launching a project rescue, a loud unmistakable call to action, requires a structured, proven approach to redefine a project that is already underway and to deliver against a renegotiated set of acceptable criteria. While still following generally accepted project management principles, a project rescue is very effective in persuading everyone impacted by a failing project to focus only on priorities to recover whatever they can with the time and resources they have remaining. The process ends with a stronger project team, proven capabilities, and an infrastructure that can be leveraged to deliver subsequent phases of the original and revised set of deliverables.

A project rescue is about making tradeoffs and persuading everyone involved in a project to regroup and to follow the revised prioritized direction in order to provide the maximum possible value to the organization while starting from a compromised current situation. To be successful, a project rescue requires strong and clear leadership. An experienced project manager, with a successful track record for a similar sized project, asking questions similar to those shown in Figure 1.1 is often a good champion to determine when and how this process should be launched.

Defining Acceptable Project Outcomes

After hitting the project break point, a project rescue is required to evaluate the current status of the initiative and to guide it to an outcome that is acceptable to the business stakeholders while adding value to the organization as a whole. It is

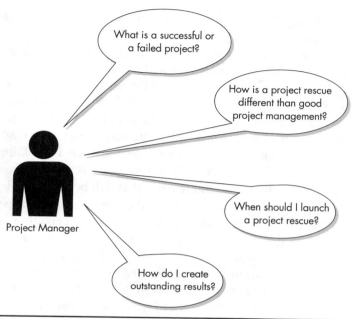

Figure 1.1   Launching a project rescue

also a recognition that following the status quo would mean that the project is not going to meet any meaningful objectives (for example, deliver any significant ROI) or that there is going to be a significant difference between what is going to be delivered by the project team and what is expected by the stakeholders or those paying for the project.

Providing strong and clear leadership is the most important prerequisite to launching a successful project rescue. Before we get into the specific requirements of a project rescue, let's examine some potential project outcomes. Project problems or troubles can lead to undesirable results, including failure—which in itself does not have a straightforward definition.

A project has a start date and an actual end date, during which time deliverables, or some other form of value, is created for the sponsors. Degree of success or failure becomes a relative continuum using this generic definition. For example, failing to deliver by a certain deadline (such as a launch date or a shutdown deadline for a plant) may be construed as a failure, while overspending on the budget may not. Another way to describe this is to consider the terms in Figure 1.2, Objectives Exceeded, Objectives Met, Key Objectives Met, and Some

Objectives Met, and a list of more undesirable outcomes that produce negative value for the company.

Planned objectives are the specific goals that are defined by the owners of the project and are usually captured in a project charter, statement of work, or requirements document. The Ideal Objectives, shown in the Figure 1.2, refer to value above what is requested by the business users and the project team. This could include creating reusable components, functionality that supports future requirements, or something else that no one has thought about. Of course, this begs the question of whether investing today in building for the future is an appropriate business decision. Trying to overachieve from the beginning introduces risks, costs, and rewards that will be discussed later in this book.

These terms add more clarity to the concepts of project success or project failure, which in most cases cannot be viewed as an all-or-nothing proposition based on a proportion of the project objectives achieved since all of these do not necessarily provide the same value to the organization. In fact, something interesting begins to happen as the deadline continually gets closer.

As shown in Figure 1.3, the threshold for measuring failure drops over time on many projects, as the team and stakeholders go through different expectations and emotional states regarding what can realistically be achieved with the resources that are available. This includes several distinct emotional states that can be identified by the following thought processes: "Everything is possible," "It

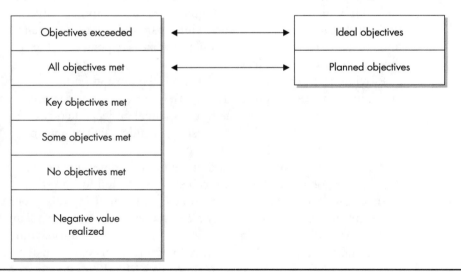

Figure 1.2   Project outcomes

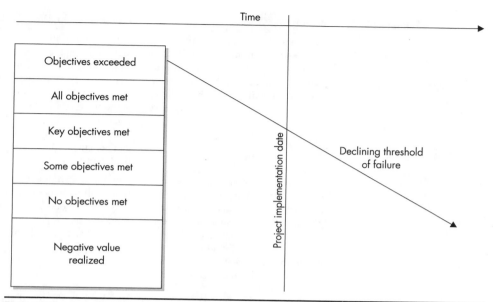

Figure 1.3   Acceptable outcomes change over time.

cannot possibly get done," "What were we thinking," and "Maybe what the organization really needs is the following." The correct answer is somewhere between these points.

Each emotional state offers an opportunity to add value to the project under the right conditions. Table 1.1 describes the common emotional states that are encountered on most nontrivial projects along with the potential benefits that can be enjoyed during that state.

Emotional State	Description	Potential Benefits
Irrational exuberance	Competitive professionals tend to jump into new ventures with a lot of excitement but without forming a thorough understanding of the true situation. There is no collective knowledge of the risks, challenges, obstacles, or true costs of the initiative. Everyone is filled with enthusiasm and expects that the project will run smoothly. The overriding idea is "just do it" without focusing on the details.	Without imposed limitations, the team and stakeholders have an opportunity to think out of the box and set high goals. They need to be reminded that the "how to" has not been rationalized yet.

Table 1.1   Emotional State Transitions

Emotional State	Description	Potential Benefits
Knowledgeable realization	Members of the extended project team start becoming aware of the true complexities of the initiative they are pursuing. Suddenly it becomes clear that many details or aspects of the solution have not been considered yet.	Expectations will be easier to manage given that there is a realistic understanding of the constraints and challenges faced by the project team. The "wish-list" that was created in moments of immense exuberance can now be reassessed using cold practicality. Priorities can be chosen and benefits to the organization can be determined.
Desperation and panic	Team members realize that the project is more complex than originally thought, and the project plan and resources suddenly appear to be totally inadequate to deliver on the objectives. Genuine fear, panic, and desperation creeps into the team members. This is the beginning of the sleepless nights.	Anyone involved with the project is more willing to compromise now that they know about the possibility of failure. This temporarily removes a lot of the team politics from the situation.
Fateful resignation	People connected with the project start dusting off their resumes.	Opportunity to inspire and focus the team by showing them how value can still be created for the organization by focusing on the critical path and priorities.
Realistic reassessment	Professionalism and experience begin to refocus the team. The nature of the project outcome is dependent on the leadership that brings everyone together to deliver value.	Build a realistic project plan with realistic expectations and resources. Project stakeholder expectations will be lower on the line shown in Figure 1.3.
Grim determination	The team begins to work night and day and on weekends to deliver the project. People on projects with strictly defined end dates frequently develop a very strong work ethic. Some members essentially make the project their life until it is delivered. Giving them the right priorities means that the right work is getting done.	Less resistance arises from interpersonal problems. There are fewer changes to requirements and certainly a greater willingness to make them a future priority.
Passionate relief	This depends on the culture of the organization. There may be incriminations, disappointment, celebrations, or determination to improve on the next project.	An improved corporate culture and pool of knowledge from the experience and lessons learned.

Table 1.1   Emotional State Transitions *(continued)*

However, it doesn't have to be this way. Table 1.2 describes how to deal with the negative aspects of an emotional state while simultaneously building on what can provide positive value for the project and organization. Project managers should also take note of the Desired Duration column as an indication of how long the state should last relative to the overall project life cycle, as well as what they can do to move things forward.

Almost every nontrivial project experiences a period of emotional resignation as team members begin to learn that the project is more complex than they initially thought it would be. Project managers should try and move things along as fast as reasonably possible to get to this stage and then spend ample time in the Grim Determination state to actually build things.

Emotional State	Mitigation Strategy	Desired Duration
Irrational exuberance	Collect ideas without commitment to direction. Make it clear that a final project charter plan will determine what is possible and what is not.	Short
Knowledgeable realization	Resist the temptation to reduce the project scope before a detailed project plan is made so that a balanced view of interdependencies is known. Create a list of items that can be reintroduced to the scope if time permits.	Medium
Desperation and panic	Focus the team on the idea of measuring project outcome and value instead of trying to reach a Boolean success or failure.	Short
Fateful resignation	Focus on getting agreement on new priorities.	Very Short
Realistic reassessment	Because the true constraints are well known across the project team and to the stakeholders, adjust the project plan and milestones for realistic targets—or risk achieving very little.	Medium
Grim determination	Focus on the project plan exclusively. Hold status meetings every day or several times a day to ensure that there are no obstacles affecting the project. Be ruthless about prioritization and change management.	Long
Passionate relief	Learn from experience without trying to find a scapegoat.	Short. Get on with the next challenge after learning from the lessons and celebrating the conclusion of the initiative.

Table 1.2   Mitigation Strategies for Emotional States

Using Value to Position Project Outcome

Project outcome can be measured and explained by determining the value of individual business requirements to the organization or stakeholders. Value can be measured in hard terms such as impact on net revenues or reduced stock level, or softer ones such as gaining competitive advantage or a happier workforce. A value-based approach demands ruthless evaluation and prioritization of project objectives and business requirements with the clear understanding that delivering the higher priority items will have a greater weight when assigning the overall success or value of the project.

Figure 1.4 shows a relatively simple approach for measuring and comparing value to support a different priority for the project objectives. The graph shows elapsed time as a function of work effort and cost for every objective in the project charter. Stakeholders can then prioritize each objective in terms of any of these parameters: value to the enterprise, delivery date, or the cost of the function.

For example, Figure 1.5 shows three groupings of the objectives based on value delivered. Because the highest value objectives are included in release 1,

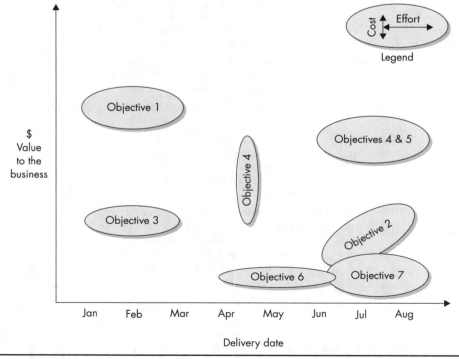

Figure 1.4   Objectives, costs, work effort, and value

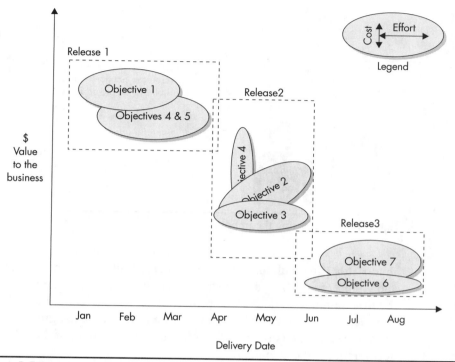

Figure 1.5   Prioritized objectives

the business may find it acceptable to focus all team resources into delivering these first—perhaps even adding resources temporarily. Even if all the objectives provide value—which presumably they would or why include them in a project charter in the first place—your goal is to find an order of delivery among the most critical of the important.

Traditional Project Levers

Using value as a reference point to prioritize the objectives of a project also has the advantage of removing an all-or-nothing way of looking at the deliverables. It's not unusual for a project manager to be asked to deliver an expansive set of functionality on a short timeframe and budget, as shown in Figure 1.6. This situation is probably the norm.

At some point, the strategy shifts from explaining how to get the best return on investment to explaining impact and repercussions of trying to do too much

Figure 1.6   Expecting the impossible

in too little time with insufficient resources. A project manager can use the levers
shown in Figure 1.7 to demonstrate what this means to stakeholders—namely,
the time required to deliver the project, what's included in the project scope,
and the budget that is available to acquire resources. Changing the level of any
of these requires a corresponding change in one or both of the other variables to
accommodate the change.

Increasing the scope of a project requires additional budget, a longer timeline,
or both. Reducing a budget requires a smaller project scope. Shrinking or expanding
the timeline may not be much help in compensating for the increased scope because
resources will be required proportionately to any changes that are made. Shrinking
a timeline requires an increase to the budget, a reduction in scope, or a balance of
both strategies. These relationships can be explained mathematically and are an
important part of a manager's toolkit to help other people involved in the project
understand the impact of changing any of the core variables.

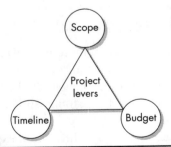

Figure 1.7   Traditional project levers

Now if you add very talented resources, or get team members to work additional hours without charging for them (this has its own Human Resources (HR) and morale implications) it is possible to modify the impact of this equation to a certain degree, but the reliability is still suspect. How long before overworked team members burn out? What if the talented resources do not accept responsibility to deliver against new requirements that are delivered while a project is well underway? What if the additional pressure drives them away? You are effectively increasing risk to the project by relying on these strategies. The results cannot be guaranteed.

These three variables are not enough to represent the tradeoffs available on modern projects. In fact, you should add three additional levers to a project manager's toolkit, as shown in Figure 1.8. These are people, quality, and, reusability.

In this context, the morale, coaching, and personal development of team members can be allocated a direct cost during the project, but they offer a longer term benefit to the organization as a whole. The project manager must be cognizant of the effort invested in this area versus the need to deliver on time and on budget. Is burnout worth meeting a deadline that does not offer a concrete benefit? What is the impact of a one-week delay to the project schedule?

Quality is important on every project, but there is a big difference in the effort required to achieve "absolutely no defects," "hopefully no defects," "no defects," "no show-stopping defects," "no major defects," or "clean up after launch."

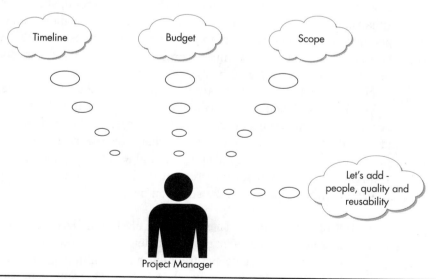

Figure 1.8   Additional project levers

Resources allocated to quality control are taken from somewhere else. As projects get into danger, the acceptable quality level also tends to decrease over time, pretty much parallel to the acceptable outcome line that was shown previously in Figure 1.3. This raises the question about what is really the true acceptable quality level for a project?

Nobody wants to or should start a project from the ground up. Regardless of the industry, reusable components (for example, staircases, auto parts, code modules) help the project get a tremendous head start and also contribute to efficiency, quality, and scheduling. However, building, assembling, collecting, or integrating these reusable components has a cost that needs to be absorbed into an existing project. This has to be compared to the cost of building without reusability in mind—which can often require less time.

Recognizing Projects in Trouble

When a *project break point* is reached, the chances of putting a project back on track without relying on a significant intervention decreases dramatically with each passing day. Following the behavior shown by an exponential curve, problems continue to multiply, team behaviors deteriorate, and mistakes are compounded and repeated.

Of course you're free to follow a project rescue approach on every initiative. However, a project rescue involves setting a pace, mood, and tone that will both exhaust and exhilarate a project team. A project rescue may not be needed, or perhaps may be required only to get over a few hurdles. There are some telltale signs that can be used to identify a project that needs the focus, discipline, and prioritization that is offered by systemic project rescue.

No matter what you call it—troubles, problems, obstacles, hurdles, or realized risks—in the end you are describing a project that is not close to proceeding according to plan. Almost every nontrivial project will experience troubles, or at least the project team should expect that to be the case, but some of these problems may just require adherence to tighter project management principles.

Figure 1.9 identifies several areas of focus for the project manager, who needs to get a sufficient handle on the situation before hitting the panic button.

- **Telltale symptoms** These act as an alert to realized risks or problems in a project. This is what the project team and stakeholders can see as the manifestation of the deeper troubles that are hitting an initiative. The project manager must decide whether the symptoms are sufficient enough to warrant project correction, a full blown project rescue, or a limited project rescue.

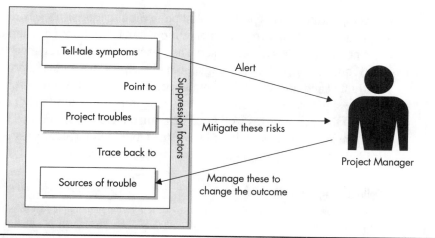

Figure 1.9   Spotting project troubles

- **Project troubles**   This is a standard list of project problems that plague most initiatives. These serve as a checklist for the risk assessment process that precedes the launch of a project. Not all of these will be realized, so the symptom is what shows that the problem has occurred. These need to be managed and controlled on an ongoing basis.

- **Sources of trouble**   Project troubles or problems can be traced to these common sources. These need to be addressed when the symptoms show that problems are occurring on a project. A catalogue of sources can also provide an input into risk identification and assessment through a checklist.

- **Suppression factors**   There are specific behaviors or events that suppress or hide the fact that a project is experiencing problems. This is the reason many projects that fall into trouble are not diagnosed properly and end up in a downward spiral that leads to costly project outcomes with little of the projected benefits.

Telltale Symptoms

Observing certain specific symptoms on a project should trigger a project rescue intervention. It's important to separate symptoms from the sources of troubles. A source of trouble will not necessarily derail the project. For example, a lack of solid business requirements is potentially a source for future troubles. However, depending on the chemistry of the project team, they may be able to work effectively with users to compensate for this problem. Although the situation is not desirable and it would benefit from a project rescue intervention, it may get through without one.

Specific telltale symptoms serve as a warning system to suggest that further details are required and that a manager should dig deeper to decide if a project rescue is warranted and how extensive it will need to be. Table 1.3 shows some of the types of telltale signs that you should watch out for, important modifiers or caveat(s) to further qualify the symptom, as well as some immediate considerations. These are discussed in more detail in the text that follows the table. If you recognize any of these signs, it is likely that your project requires additional scrutiny.

Telltale Symptom	Modifier	Considerations
Missing deadlines or no deadlines	Without good or compelling reason(s) being articulated.	Are people just looking to justify bad management practices?
Changing requirements	Without reflecting changes in the budget, timeline, or the project scope.	Are people trying to hide a lack of discipline in really deciding what they want built, integrated, or constructed? Is there an effective change management process?
Final decisions not being made	Is this because there is no clear ownership or is no one stepping up to the plate to make the important decisions?	Is there enough information to make a decision with any degree of certainty?
Project completion is stuck at 90 percent done	There has been no corresponding change to scope, budget, or timeline. There is a lack of continuous progress regardless of the percentage complete.	Can you relate completion percentage to interim, measurable deliverables? Can each team member accurately articulate the "estimate to complete" for outstanding tasks?
No problems being reported	No deliverables are being signed off either.	Problems and issues are normal on projects. Does the team have a handle on the true requirements? Is there an agreeable acceptance management process?
Lack of key project deliverables	A good rule of thumb is to produce measurable deliverables during frequent intervals to allow tracking of progress and reduction of risk. Relying only on a major deliverable at the end of a long project (anything over three elapsed months) is an enormous risk, which should be mitigated by interim delivery points.	Are deliverables being created but without explanation on where they are going to be used or how they are going to influence the final result? This is a serious waste of time and can ruin the motivation of the project team.

Table 1.3   Telltale Symptoms of Project Troubles

Telltale Symptom	Modifier	Considerations
Interpersonal problems	People issues and interpersonal tensions are overwhelming the project schedule. The extended project team members do not appear to put the interest of the project ahead of their personal needs.	Are too many personal needs of team members being sacrificed for the project? Is there a risk that key people will leave the company before or at the conclusion of the project?
Excessive quality problems	This is even after testing cycles (for example, unit, functional, system) have been completed and a test plan has been executed.	Begin the project with a clear definition of the quality expected, number of errors that are tolerable, and the tests required to prove that the solution is acceptable. Is there an effective quality assurance process in place?
Unknown factors	Constantly hearing the terms "will find this out," "we are assuming," "to be determined," or "to be confirmed." Each of these terms are imprecise, making accurate planning impossible.	Not every unknown can be identified, but the plan should be robust enough to accommodate surprises by identifying clear check points. There is a danger of analysis paralysis if you try and go too deep in this analysis. Is there an effective risk management process in place?
Lack of management reporting tools	Specifically a lack of an integrated project plan that is being used regularly to track progress, as well as clear communication channels to all the team members.	Is there too much overhead involved in complying with management reporting? Conversely, are people just trying to document and report everything to protect themselves? Are project status reports fact-based or opinion-based?

Table 1.3   Telltale Symptoms of Project Troubles *(continued)*

Missing Deadlines or No Deadlines

Project deadlines are always going to be missed for a multitude of reasons that include poor planning, unforeseen events, and business complexity. You can make the statement that deadlines *must* be met because they are important—but you would be fooling yourself. However, not sticking to a deadline, or continually pushing it off, results in highly undesirable team behaviors. If your team is missing deadlines repeatedly, what makes you think this behavior is going to change? Are the problems typical of the entire project or are they limited to one or more of the earlier phases only? Where's the accountability? Having no deadline also shows a lack of discipline.

Always break deliverables down so that something of value and something that is measurable is produced within two-week increments—sooner if the risks on the project are deemed to be very high. Manageable deliverables make monitoring simpler and enable risk to be addressed on a consistent basis.

Changing Requirements

There are many reasons for project requirements to change, despite everyone's best efforts. New ideas are brought forward; something was not considered in the original plan; business users/stakeholders simply change their minds. Indeed, technology often fosters additional change. The key is to differentiate whether the requirements are changing, being augmented, being added to, or being replaced, or even whether they are stable and mature. If somebody is repeatedly changing his mind, does he really know what he wants? This symptom can be a sign that something deeper is wrong with the project as it is set up. Maybe the expectations are not clear or the true decision makers have not been involved. Maybe the true stakeholders have not been identified or consulted properly.

Changing requirements are a fact of life on every project in any industry. They result from a desire to keep the client and users satisfied. However, a properly planned project is built around an initial project charter that contains a timeline based on specific business requirements. The math is very straightforward. Changing a requirement impacts the timeframes and costs, so the plan needs to be updated and some initial deadlines may slip.

Start the project by clearly identifying how a change process is going to work and when it will be invoked. Create an expectation that future requirements may lead to additional releases in the project. Always talk about the cost, benefit, and impact to the project whenever the requirements begin to change. Let the users or stakeholders make the decision based on these facts.

Final Business Decisions Not Being Made

Incomplete or wavering business decisions are a sign of some really terrible things with equally terrible consequences. While this seems intuitively obvious, many projects from the small two-person team to the $50 million mega-initiative may be based on a high level business vision with multiple unfinished scenarios and business rules. In this case, project teams start to build what they are certain about, while business decisions are made. This can take you only so far before a lack of business clarity means a lot of rework later in the process. Here are some examples of critical business decisions that require answers early in the project lifecycle:

- Who is the business owner—who determines the final acceptance criteria?
- What exactly should the final product look like?

- How many defects are acceptable?
- What are the performance and operations criteria of the final solution?
- What are the business rules? Which are key? What is the relative priority of the ones that remain? What will users accept?

Project Completion Is Stuck at 90 Percent Done

When a project manager first hears that a project is 90 percent complete there's a lot of excitement and euphoria. This level of completion is presumably achieved through gradual increases, week over week, and reported on regular status reports or at status meetings. There are several potential problems with a completion number. It is usually generated by imprecise qualifications or a gut feel on the part of a project manager or a project coordinator. The complexity of the remaining 10 percent is also unclear and the small number may be misleading.

Indeed, projects have a tendency to remain in this state. Dig deeper when a percentage complete value does not change between successive status periods. Another warning sign is a sudden deceleration in percent complete. For example, say the project complete value is moving at a clip of 20 to 30 percent a week and then all of a sudden you're seeing only a 1 or 2 percent change. The project team may be coming to grips with the true requirements of the initiative and may have been too optimistic in earlier status meetings.

A final consideration is when a percent complete goes down. This could also be caused by an introduction of new requirements, but it could be a result of bad reporting in earlier status segments. Usually a number that is brought down may not be low enough, due to additional wishful thinking from a project team. The problem may be much deeper than reports suggest.

No Problems Reported

All nontrivial projects encounter some sort of obstacles or problems at one time or another. Many of these may be easy to overcome; nevertheless they do occur. If these are not being reported, the team has either not dug far enough or is not communicating all the relevant information. Project managers may want to start detailed walkthroughs of the current project status and deliverables to ensure that the right questions are being asked. If the project is truly proceeding well, then a celebration may be in order upon the completion of key project milestones.

Lack of Key Project Deliverables

Key project deliverables, sometimes referred to as milestones, are not just what is produced at the end of an initiative, but also interim deliverables that are necessary to ensure a smooth conclusion. A lack of key interim deliverables or end deliverables is a sign of troubles to come. If asking for these is causing chaos, a project rescue is required.

Subsequent chapters of this book identify some of the interim project deliverables that are required on information technology, strategy, or industry initiatives.

Interpersonal Problems

Interpersonal considerations are unavoidable on projects. However, managing them poorly can result in an employee retention problem, employees threatening to leave, immense unhappiness, poor morale, bullying, people trying to protest themselves, arguments that do not resolve anything, and politics at all levels.

The presence of interpersonal problems is an alert for a deeper investigation. Extensive problems will begin to manifest themselves in some of the other symptoms that are discussed in this section, including poor quality and missed deadlines.

Excessive Quality Problems

Quality, or the lack of it, can be obscured during normal development phases because things that are not present or working properly can be argued to be delivered in the future. However, a line must be drawn at some point. Quality issues are obviously a problem, but there comes a time to either hit the rescue button or accept that the problems being encountered are within expectations.

Quality expectations and quality assurances processes need to be defined at each phase of the project, with an answer to the following questions: What types of errors are acceptable? How are errors prioritized and resolved? What tests need to be run to find the errors?

Unknown Factors

From the project management trenches, there is no way to anticipate, predict, and mitigate every project variable—without a substantial increase in the cost and timeline of the project. However, employing an effective risk management process that regularly reviews high probability, high impact risks will help the extended project team understand the expected behaviors when a risk comes to fruition. Events that cannot be accommodated in a project plan need to trigger a project rescue.

Lack of Management Reporting Tools or Culture

How many times have you heard someone say "We don't waste time doing status reports; we actually do the work." The underlying sentiment is noble and can apply to any number of project management tools or procedures. However, there are some things to consider before dismissing these entirely. First, if anything goes wrong, these tools are needed to recover. Second, without the tools, you will not know something is going wrong until it is too late to do anything about it.

Absence of management reporting tools guarantees that there are problems in the field that are not being reported or communicated to the extended project team. Catching these early enough may allow them to be accommodated. However, a lack of management reporting tools will generally mean that signs get neglected until it is too late.

Common Project Troubles/Risks

While the symptoms discussed previously are a strong signal that a project is getting in trouble, they are not the focus of a rescue effort. The symptoms point to underlying problems or risks that have emerged. As a project management industry, we have amassed enough knowledge and best practices to catalog the common troubles or risks that are frequently encountered on different types of projects. Table 1.4 identifies some of the common ones. We go into more detail in subsequent chapters as specific questionnaires are provided to delve into these areas.

Sources of Project Troubles or Problems

We've moved from the topic of symptoms of project troubles to the common categories where these problems can occur (as seen in Figure 1.4). These in turn

Problem/Risk Category	Potential Problems
Project team	Lack of training, lack of skills, morale
Requirements	Lack of clarity, lack of agreement, lack of priority, contradictory, ambiguous, imprecise
Planning	Insufficient details, missing items
Technology	Incompatibilities, new technology, incorrect usage
Expectations	Too high, unrealistic, or just not managed
Priorities	Resources being taken by higher priority projects
Timelines	Too tight, unrealistic, overly optimistic
Budgets	Lack of allocation, unrealistic, cut during the project, insufficient
Project governance	Lacking, ineffective, different priorities, no clear involvement
Vendors	Too small, poor customer service, unable to deliver on time, go out of business
User Training	Untimely, too high level, not to the correct audience, not enough
Methodology/ framework	Inappropriate for project, incorrectly applied; not enough test points and quality gates

Table 1.4 Problem Categories

can be traced to a list of common sources of project problems. Unfortunately, many of these problem sources cannot be eliminated because they are usually part of meeting the project objectives.

Awareness of these sources allows a project manager to control and moderate their influences throughout a project lifecycle. Notice that the existence of a problem source does not mean a manifestation of a problem in every case. For example, stakeholders can be a source of problems due to unrealistic expectations, delay in signing off, or changing priorities. However, each of these can be managed to a certain degree. Table 1.5 provides some of the common sources of problems on projects.

Problem Source	Explanation
Lack of leadership	Leadership that keeps all parties focused on a common purpose and common objectives is crucial. Missing leadership at any level, especially the project management, stakeholders, or sponsor level is devastating to nontrivial projects. Lack of leadership often manifests itself as a lack of clarity.
Poor communications	Project communications are often incomplete and irregular. The lack of a formal project plan and the discipline to adhere to it result in inconsistent communication and an increase of speculation and rumor.
Lack of clarity	The bane of many project teams is a lack of clarity in any area that impacts what a project is intending to deliver. This includes what is being built, who needs to accept it, and even why it is being built.
Politics	Although some level of politics is expected and unavoidable as soon as you have more than one person involved, personal agendas can begin to take precedence over the project outcome. Beyond the interpersonal level, organizational culture and departmental politics can also have a major impact on a project.
Planning for the best case	This can be an example of misplaced optimism. Project planning assumes that everything will go according to plan. No contingency is left for things to go wrong. Tasks are estimated with best case scenarios. This is an example of team members believing that they always do things right the first time because they are the best but they don't realize that mistakes do occur and new factors do emerge. Good management is the ability to respond to these factors.
Parallel thinking/ ignoring dependencies	Assuming that all the work segments can be done in parallel and that there are no dependencies between the deliverables. In other words, as soon as a user thinks about what a report looks like, the development team will already have it built.
Ignorance/habit	People connected with the project simply do not understand what they are involved in. Others connected with the project want to do things their way without understanding or recognizing that it may not be the right way in the current context.

Table 1.5 High-Level Problem Categories

Problem Source	Explanation
Incorrect assumptions	Some people rightly hate the word "assumption" and bristle whenever it is used. "Don't assume," they insist. "Research, get the facts, and act on them." This is wise advice, but people can make assumptions implicitly without even realizing it. For example, we expect professional behavior from at least some members of a project team. We don't expect simultaneous power failures in our primary and backup sites. We don't expect all our backup tapes to go bad. Implicit and explicit assumptions can go wrong.

Table 1.5   High-Level Problem Categories *(continued)*

Using the problem categories from Table 1.4, you can do a similar analysis and identify some major sources of problems as shown in Table 1.6. The table also shows a major cause for each of the problem categories discussed. These will be discussed in more detail later in the book.

Problem/Risk Category	Common Source of Trouble
Project team	Misalignment between personal objectives and needs and the project needs.
Requirements	Improper translation of the desired requirements with what is actually being built.
Planning	Planning without validation.
Technology	Integration issues between different types of technology solutions.
Expectations	Expectations are formed without any justification or backing.
Priorities	Losing resources to projects that have a higher priority in an organization.
Timelines	Letting other pressures and wishful thinking to drive the timelines of the project.
Budgets	Trying to fit into a number that is allocated without justification.
Project governance	Not providing meaningful and timely information.
Vendors	Vendors who are more interested in their own performance metrics (e.g. bottom line) than yours. They are also interested in selling their tool or solution.
User training	Misalignment of current employee skills with what is going to be required.
Methodology/Framework	The methodology or development framework is incomplete or inappropriate.

Table 1.6   Sources of Trouble by Problem Category

Suppression Factors

A *suppression factor* manages to hide the dire or true status of a project from those who could take drastic action to change a negative outcome. Specific suppression factors can themselves become enablers of project troubles. These factors keep the project team, especially the project manager, from pinpointing the worsening situation on a project and taking the drastic actions required to correct the problems before they lead to an unacceptable solution. The following list identifies some suppression factors that may be hiding the truth on one of your projects and you may not know about it until it is too late to take meaningful corrective action.

- **Denial**   A refusal to accept reality; also known as wishful thinking.
- **Fear of being blamed**   This is really a fear of punishment.
- **Fear of looking foolish**   Project team members may suspect something is going wrong but are not sure and do not want to raise alarm bells only to find out that nothing is wrong.
- **Laziness**   An unwillingness to invest the effort to turn things around.
- **Negative incentives**   This is similar to a fear of punishment, but there may be specific incentives to deliver a project or specific result under a set of conditions.
- **Unwillingness to admit wrong**   There are specific behaviors that suppress or hide the fact that a project is experiencing problems. An enormous reluctance to accept that there is a problem.
- **Someone else's problem**   The idea here is to end the project in such a way that it becomes someone else's problem.
- **Self-fulfilling prophecies**   The belief in the infeasibility of a method, approach, or idea ultimately leads to reduced effort and to the realization of the prophecy that the method or tool cannot work in a given situation.
- **Not made here syndrome**   A need or belief that all components must be built in-house when other valid ones can be leveraged instead.

Closing Perspective

A project rescue is a phased responsive approach for dramatically altering the direction of a project that is in a state of decline. A project rescue requires that you make certain compromises in order to realize specific gains. Observing the symptoms in this chapter is an indication that a project rescue intervention may be required. The questions, which are answered in the next chapter, are what type of project rescue is required, what can be salvaged, how much will it cost, and when should you launch it? The longer you delay in launching a project rescue, the less you can benefit by the proposed deadline.

## CHAPTER 2

Four-Phase Intervention Framework

In the previous chapter, we defined a decisive point on an initiative that, when reached, signals an inevitable downward spiral toward project failure. We call this the *project break point,* and you can recognize it through specific symptoms that point to deeper problems with the initiative. When you reach this point, you need to make a choice. For example, the project team could choose to continue operating within the same boundaries and using the same assumptions that led to the project break point. Conversely, it may be time for a dramatic intervention. In fact, most real-world projects that reach the break point continue the direction of the former, without considering the following:

- Only by changing the fundamental, underlying reasons (root causes) of the symptoms that are being observed, can the troubled project get back on track.

- Time or money is of the essence on most projects and you're probably running out of both at this stage of the life cycle.

- Trying to do everything with limited resources is impossible and it's time to make choices that will provide critical value to the business.

A dramatic, but well-planned and well-defined intervention can reverse the downward spiral of the failing project by systematically challenging the status quo and enabling project team members to make the difficult decisions that are necessary to salvage the initiative. Launching a project rescue is a call to action that registers the urgency of the situation and the need to do things better and differently.

Launching a Project Rescue

Formally launching a project rescue gives permission to the project team to begin to think out of the box in order to reverse the decline of the initiative. It often brings to bear ideas that members of the project team were afraid to surface for various reasons but now can be liberated by the out of the box approach. A salvage operation on a sunken ship provides a sound metaphor for a set of guiding principles:

- **Start right away**   The sooner you get started, the more you can save before the ship is carried away by the currents or pirated.

- **Careful planning**   Do as much research and upfront planning to ensure that there is enough oxygen and time to satisfy the objectives.

- **Clarify and prioritize**   Locate and save the important items first. Go back and rescue more if there is time.

- **Make your stake**   Avoid confusion among the extended team by showing that a rescue mission is underway and that your plan is the one to support; otherwise resources will get divided and diverted.

While the symptoms of problems have allowed someone in the project team to act as a "champion" in convincing stakeholders that a project rescue is warranted, it is unlikely that the precise problems are identified or understood at this stage. There are generally many intertwined causes and effects that make it unclear what came first, second and so on. For example, Figure 2.1 shows two circles that represent the amount of work effort required and available to the project team.

The larger circle represents the amount of effort required to complete all the functions within the scope of the project. The smaller circle represents the amount of effort available in terms of the resources that are working on the project. Is the problem really a shortage of available resources as Figure 2.1 suggests? Or is this just the symptom? Which problem led to this symptom? The answer is not obvious at all.

For example, maybe the smaller circle was the result of several team members resigning because the company's pay scale was severely uncompetitive and they were all raided by the same headhunter. Perhaps team members quit because they found a coworker or a stakeholder to be unreasonable to work with. Maybe team members who lived a long distance from work got tired of the long commute.

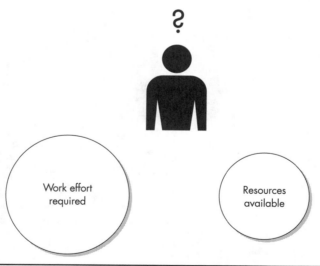

Figure 2.1   What's the real problem?

Maybe the problem was something totally different. Maybe a change in technology architecture made the skill sets of the project team temporarily obsolete.

While the situation is analyzed, the clock is still ticking, money is being spent, and the deadlines keep getting closer. The salvage operation needs to begin while you are still trying to identify all the problems, without getting into further trouble.

Figure 2.2 shows the invocation of an intervention process when the break point is reached. After the rescue is completed, your goal is to learn from the experience and to return to project management best practices (for example, those espoused by the Project Management Institute). The intervention can be done at any time during the project life cycle. Iterative and agile methodology approaches, which are discussed later in this book, are removed for this example. The closer it is to the end of the life cycle, the less time remains available to recover and the less that can be salvaged.

Figure 2.2 also shows two *rescue champion* roles. Rescue champion 1 takes the lead in the *rescue evaluation* phase to show the need for a project rescue. This requires showing that a project break point has been reached—usually to the

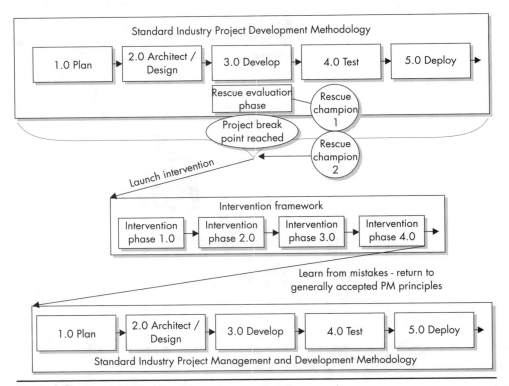

Figure 2.2   Invoking the four-phase intervention framework

project stakeholders or executive management. This person could be the project sponsor, someone on the project team, another executive, or the project manager.

After getting agreement on the urgent need for an intervention, rescue champion 1 could continue to play that role, or more commonly will assist the executives in identifying a second rescue champion that will complete the process. Ideal candidates for this role are external project managers, project managers from a different part of the organization, or consultants who bring a history of success and no baggage to the project. They are accountable to the future and not the past.

The rescue champion must work closely with the initiative's regular project manager. The organization must also resist the temptation to punish the regular project manager. The key objective here is finding the root causes that triggered the project break point so effective remediation can take place to get the project back on track. The idea here is not one of replacement, but of working alongside each other. Depending on the size and complexity of the project, the rescue champion may also bring along a small group of dedicated resources. This can include, for example, project controllers, architects, or quality specialists.

Types of Project Rescue

If you start early enough in the project life cycle you may be able to salvage much of the original scope of a project that is failing. Project rescue interventions, however, are likely to be started late in a project development life cycle because of the growing awareness that substantial deliverables are not being built. Figure 2.3 shows that in the best case, you're generally well into the development phase before a case can be made to formally launch an intervention. Some projects get well into the testing phase before the inevitability of a failed project is accepted by the project team.

The lesson here is to be open minded and objective in viewing progress on any project. You must discern whether problem symptoms are anomalies or trends. By accepting that problem symptoms are really bad trends earlier in the life cycle, it is possible to make low cost, small adjustments or less dramatic interventions to bring a project back on track. With this mind, consider the following types of project rescues, which increase in the extent and complexity of the intervention as you read further down the list:

- **Adjustment**   Low cost intervention designed to streamline the business requirements and the scope of the project. May require three to five days to complete.

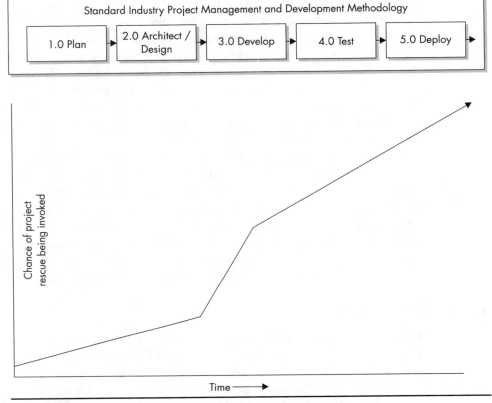

Figure 2.3   Likelihood of launching a project rescue intervention

- **Realignment**   Low-medium cost intervention that examines the assumptions of the project, goals of the business, and organization to identify the critical path. May require one to three weeks to complete.

- **Stop-Gap**   Recognition that the project is getting further out of control and heading toward disaster. This is also acceptance that the project objectives cannot all be met as originally envisioned. Requires a shifting of the methodology and resolution of the realized risks. May require one month to complete.

- **Partial Salvage**   The project is heading toward disaster. Larger functional items will need to be postponed. Redrafting of the project documents is necessary. May require one to two months to complete.

- **Complete Salvage** The project is heading toward disaster. The project must be reprioritized from the ground up. Project documents will need to be reworked. May require one to six months of rescue team involvement to resolve.

Table 2.1 shows the type of rescue operation that is usually invoked at different times of the project life cycle. The Primary Rescue Type column identifies the normally expected type of rescue. The Other Rescue Types column identifies second and third common choices of rescue at that point of a project life cycle. Your objective is clearly to use the *rescue assessment phase,* to launch adjustments whenever a break point is detected.

Project Rescue Considerations

A project rescue is essentially a defined process that is invoked when a project break point is reached on an initiative. The intervention framework replaces the original methodology for a period of time whereby disaster is averted, the project team skills are enhanced, and critical business functionality is implemented. At that point the project rescue framework is used to realign the initiative with the project methodology in use in the organization.

This section examines from a project rescue standpoint, the guidelines for an intervention.

Launching a Project Rescue

While a project framework provides a reusable process, each rescue intervention is unique. There are different personalities, deadlines, business pressures, tools,

Phase	Primary Rescue Type	Other Rescue Types
Plan	Adjustment	None
Architecture/Design	Adjustment	Realignment
Early Development	Realignment	Adjustment
Mid Development	Realignment	Stop-Gap
Late Development	Stop-Gap	Realignment, Partial Salvage, Complete Salvage
Early Testing	Partial Salvage	Stop-Gap, Complete Salvage
Mid Testing	Complete Salvage	Stop-Gap, Partial Salvage
Late Testing	Complete Salvage	Stop-Gap, Partial Salvage
Early Deployment	Complete Salvage	Stop-Gap, Partial Salvage
Mid Deployment	Complete Salvage	Partial Salvage
Late Deployment	Complete Salvage	Partial Salvage

Table 2.1 Project Rescue Types

and resources. The number of combinations and permutations arising from these makes an intervention part science and part art.

Although convincing people to start a project rescue is an art, the launching of a project rescue is definitely science. There is no doubt that most of the people involved in the project have begun to feel pressure because they know the project is hurtling towards a disaster. Some may have already given up; some may feel very jaded. A project rescue must be done right to overcome this negativity.

Furthermore, a successful rescue launch is not sufficient in itself. The launch must result in a successful rescue that includes a set of best practices that can be leveraged by the organization to improve project delivery capabilities in the future.

The project champion or the project rescue team must provide clarity around the following items at this time. Each of these items will play an important role throughout the intervention framework:

- **Leadership**   Demonstrate that the executive is not going to force repetition of processes and practices that have not worked and is willing to do what is right.

- **Decisions**   Make decisions regarding the project scope, costs, and resources. Launch the rescue with a clear demonstration that difficult decisions will not be avoided. Show how (for example, who is empowered) a decision will always be reached especially when there are politically charged deadlocks, or the related item will be removed from the critical path.

- **Clarity**   It is no longer anyone else's problem. Describe every part of the project with clarity or move it off the critical path.

- **Energy**   Understand that, yes, there have been problems; people have worked long and hard, and the project is still heading for disaster. The project rescue cannot suppress enthusiasm and effort for the new direction. It is a new direction and an opportunity to help everyone involved in the initiative. Time for celebration and rest will come after the rescue is completed. Kick off the project rescue with a formal event (preferably with food!) to show appreciation for the effort to date and over the rescue period.

- **Confidence**   Don't pretend to know everything. It's impossible and project participants know it. However, showing the project participants what to expect, both positive and negative, and providing a strategy for dealing with what could arise will build the confidence of the team.

- **Prudence**   Keep the fact that the project was headed for disaster in front of everyone to ensure that the project moves forward in a practical manner.

Project Rescue Risk Assessment

After a new project plan is developed, another set of risk assessment activities needs to be done. The rescue champion can lead this exercise. The project management team should begin with a review of the original risk assessment and examine what went wrong. The new risk assessment needs to be built with this information. If certain assumptions proved to be inaccurate (for example, we believed erroneously that new employees do not require technical training), they need to be incorporated into the new risk assessment.

This activity can result in some hurt feelings if you allow the process to be taken personally by anyone on the project team or blame is assigned to a particular person or group. Keep it objective by removing references to people or roles wherever possible. Risk assessment will be revisited repeatedly throughout this book due to its high impact on project success and realized value.

Four Phase Intervention Framework

A basic four phase intervention framework is the basis of a project rescue as shown in Figure 2.4. Table 2.2 describes each of these phases including major objective(s) along with a key consideration.

This section provides a further breakdown of major phases into their subphases. Input deliverables and output deliverables for these are discussed in Chapter 3. We will also provide a list of suggested interview questions in subsequent chapters. Although the subphases are shown in a sequential fashion, parallelization and iteration can be used to reduce cost and time to implement. This must be determined on a project by project basis by the project manager based on resources available, the size of the original project, and other dependencies.

Phase 1.0: Assessment

The first phase of an intervention is to assess the initiative from soup to nuts. The project rescue champion and team do most of the information gathering and review. This phase consists of several major activities: document gathering, interviews, review, and assessment.

Figure 2.4   Four-phase intervention framework

Phase	Phase Name	Objective	Remember To
1.0	Assessment	Investigate the project background and analyze the current status.	Listen, understand, investigate. Verify, test, and confirm.
2.0	Intervention planning	Work with the extended project team and sponsors to identify the critical path. Revise the project plan and documentation.	Make decisions. Build consensus with every decision-maker. Lead. Encourage.
3.0	Intervention execution	Ensure that the new plan is properly executed and adjusted with new information that is gathered..	Check status every day or several times a day. Communicate information. Stay on the critical path. Record and classify all issues.
4.0	Post-intervention review	Implement the rescued solution. Share lessons learned, celebrate, and move quickly to the next phase of the project. Plan to remove the rescue infrastructure.	Learn and grow. Do not allocate blame. Celebrate successes.

Table 2.2   Four-Phase Intervention Framework

The critical skills in this phase include the following:

- **Document gathering**   Locating documents in the organizations (for example, intranet repositories) and knowing who to get them from (for example, from people who have left the team and kept personal files).

- **Interviewing**   Setting up an interview, running an interview, building cooperation and consensus. Recognizing when you are hearing the truth, double checking answers, separating personal objectives and agendas among the interviewees.

- **Listening skills**   Listening without making or at least sharing judgements. Building rapport so that interviewees will want to share information with you.

In this phase, you are likely to find some of the following emotions:

- **Anger**   People don't like to be wrong.

- **Fear**   Recognition that the project is spiraling out of control and personal livelihood is at stake.

- **Frustration**   Enough progress is not being made. Additional feelings of trying to find someone to blame for the project failings.

- **Desperation** This can quickly turn into enlightenment. Willingness to cooperate fully so as not to be associated with a project disaster.

Figure 2.5 shows five major subphases in this unit of work. You'll find a description of each in the sections that follow.

Subphase 1.1: Review Project Documentation
The first part of the assessment involves reviewing all the documentation that has been produced in relation to the project. Many different types of documents can be included in this mix. An effective approach is to ask the project team members for the documents they have (electronic or hard copy) and to build a catalog that can serve as a checklist. You should also locate anyone else that was involved in the project and see if they have any documentation that is relevant and not catalogued.

Some document types that must be included in the review if they exist include the following:

- Project charter
- Project plan
- Risk assessment
- Business requirements
- Technology architecture
- Designs
- Project deliverables
- Acceptance documents

Subphase 1.2: Interview Stakeholders
The list of stakeholders for a project includes anyone who has a business or financial ownership or influence on the initiative. There is usually a hierarchy within the stakeholder group. For our purposes, there are two categories of

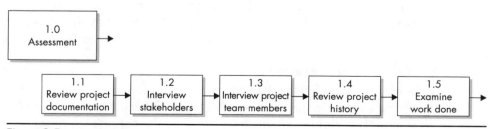

Figure 2.5 Assessment phase

stakeholders: decision makers and other stakeholders. The first group is the more relevant of the two. It is imperative to identify the key decision makers from among the larger list of stakeholders. The key decision makers are the ones who can change the scope and boundaries of the project. It is not uncommon to have a single key decision maker, but there may be several. The other stakeholders are influencers who are responsible for running some portions of the business.

Finding the key decision maker(s) can sometimes be an elusive task. It may not always be the person paying for the project. First, look for the Executive Sponsor or the Project Sponsor named in the Project Charter or Statement of Work. If no formal sponsor is documented, a good way to proceed is to identify the most senior executives who have the most to lose or gain from the initiative.

The project rescue champion and the project manager, if they are separate resources, must understand what the key decision makers are thinking to build a rapport with them and to build trust and confidence that their problems are going to be solved. That is what the decision makers care about. That is what the decision makers are being measured on. At this stage, the key decision makers have accepted the need for a project rescue and probably realize that their jobs and careers are on the line. They are looking for a way out.

Subphase 1.3: Interview Project Team Members

Every member of the project team has an experience to share and a perspective on what is happening on the project, what has happened on the project, and what could be done better if there was another chance. It's useful to schedule a one on one meeting (individual) with different members of the project team to get these perspectives.

The project rescue champion will either have an outsider advantage or a new mandate to get at truthful perspectives, without placing blame. This provides a greater chance of getting the truth, helping you to avoid the "how can I tell this to my boss without getting fired" syndrome. The project rescue champion must be clear that a witch hunt is NOT in process, but rather a rescue initiative to help everyone associated with the project and for the organization as a whole.

Individual meetings should also be used to corroborate statements from different sources. It's not that people are being untruthful, but individual perspectives can clearly cloud judgments. Always validate what you are hearing.

Subphase 1.4: Review Project History

In addition to reviewing the documentation, interviewing stakeholders, and interviewing team members, it is helpful to focus on the detailed history of the project. This particularly includes previous attempts at the project, ones that may have failed or been terminated for some reason. Documentation, lessons learned, and post mortem information for each of these attempts should be recovered and reviewed.

Some of the leaders or even the people who were beat up in the previous attempts at the project may have hard feelings. These people are such a fountain of information, however, that you need to find a way to interview them and to understand their perspective of what went wrong. During these conversations it is important to project the following:

- Your desire to get the project done for the sake of the organization
- A nonjudgmental approach
- Your humility, appreciation, and willingness to incorporate any help that is offered
- A strong desire to help the organization learn from the experience

Subphase 1.5: Examine Work Done

By this point in the phase, the rescue champion should have developed a good understanding of the following:

- **Business drivers**   Why the project was launched
- **Project objectives**   What the people paying for the project are expecting for their investment
- **Key decision makers**   How their performance is being measured by their bosses
- **Acceptance criteria**   How the business determines that the work is completed and acceptable
- **Project charter**   Overall project resources, timelines, and deliverable contents

You also need to review all the status reports, issue logs, and minutes of meetings to get a perspective on what has been completed and how it is being perceived in the organization. The rescue team also needs to understand the outstanding tasks and the associated effort to complete them. Begin to form your conclusions at this stage.

Phase 2.0: Intervention Planning

The major activities in this phase are to analyze, plan, communicate, and update. The actual intervention can be planned after understanding the history and status of the project. All the information and relationships learned in the previous phase need to be leveraged here. Here are some guidelines to consider:

- Information from the past is relevant in ensuring that troubles are not repeated again.

- Contrary to the popular belief that professionals should always aim to exceed expectations, you need to take a *minimalist* approach here. This means that you need to determine the minimal critical path to satisfy the least functionality that the business is prepared to accept, using the following direction:

  - What is the most important performance metric? A specific delivery date? Amount of money spent? Functionality delivered? Even if they are all important, which is the most important and which is the least important? In the unlikely event that they are all equal, what order must the functionality be delivered in?

  - What is needed by the business to move forward? Are there external requirements, legal requirements, new product launches, or stock valuations that must be delivered by a specific date?

  - Once the minimalist critical path is defined, what items are of the maximum value? What effort do they require? What are the risks?

The critical skills in this phase include the following:

- **Negotiation skills**   You need to persuade people at all levels to stick only to the critical path.

- **Organizational skills**   A detailed plan that can be tracked on a daily basis needs to be built.

- **Problem solving skills**   You have to deduce the underlying problems as the rescue is being planned so that they are not repeated

In this phase, you are likely to find some of the following emotions:

- **Confusion**   Current resources may compare, unsuccessfully, everything being proposed to the way things were done before the rescue started.

- **Resistance**   Minimalist approaches are counterintuitive to many and some team members will resist by citing the need to deliver maximum value to the business. Realistically, unless a different approach is implemented right away, the business may end up getting nothing.

- **Hope**   A fresh approach empowers some team members.

Figure 2.6 shows four major subphases in this unit of work. A process description is defined for each in the sections that follow.

Subphase 2.1: Document Critical Path

We all want to under-promise and over-deliver to our clients—internal or external. When you're in early planning meetings, you'll find one of two extremes. There may be a willingness to accept everything that the business users propose. Or there may be resistance to everything that the business users ask for. Neither is the right approach. The first one tries to do too much at the risk of delivering too little. The second approach delivers too little by definition.

The objective of the minimalist critical path is not to under-deliver, but to ensure that you deliver what the business needs, and then to over-deliver from there. This approach removes a lot of noise from the system and optimizes resource usage. It gives you high value of return for what is invested.

Use this rescue opportunity to rate all the deliverables that are within scope of the project. Are they really required? When are they really required? For what reason? Who asked for them? What is the business value in terms of increased revenue or decreased costs? The second point is imperative because this document can be used to get buy-in from the decision makers to stagger deliverables if they all cannot be delivered in the timeframe, but a stakeholder is unrelenting.

Subphase 2.2: Revise Project Documentation

With a new minimalist critical path defined, a revised set of the project documentation that reflects the new direction needs to be driven out. This includes the following:

- **Project objectives**   Objectives should be broken down into timeframe by phase. For example, if the original project objectives were for *a, b,* and *c* by

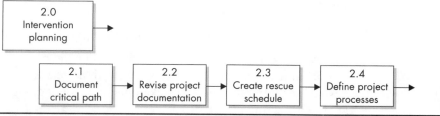

Figure 2.6   Intervention planning phase

date *x*, the revised project objectives will be *a* by date *x1*, *b* by date *x2*, and *c* by date *x3*. Here there are three phases or segments: *x1*, *x2*, and *x3*.

- **Project priorities**   Dates when each functional item or feature needs to be delivered.

- **Architecture**   The core architecture must support the full solution, but there will be several iterations of it as it scales up to support future releases.

- **Organization chart**   A detailed organization chart that describes roles and responsibilities for anyone connected with the project. Poorly structured organizations are a major source of problems, so take care to remove redundancies, inconsistencies, and inefficiencies here.

- **Communications plan**   A formal communications plan addressing each person in the preceding organization chart must be defined and communicated to the extended project team. This plan describes how and when each person and organization will receive written and oral communications from the project manager.

- **Acceptance criteria**   Criteria should be divided into the phases or segments that are defined.

- **Key metrics**   This should document what can be modified as the project unfolds and gets off track again. In other words, prepare for the next adjustment as a precautionary measure.

- **Risk assessment**   This should document what went wrong in the project thus far and the mitigation strategies for avoiding the problems in the future.

- **Project charter**   Charter needs to be updated with the new dates and phases.

Subphase 2.3: Create Rescue Schedule

Rebuild the project plan given the definition and boundaries of the new phases or segments (for example, x1, x2, and x3, which were described previously). This document is going to be needed to convince everyone involved in the project to buy into the new direction of the initiative. The plan must have the following attributes:

- **Detailed**   You should break tasks down to a maximum duration of half a day.

- **Clear**   This should be easy to read and understand. You are going to use this document as a tool of conversation with project team members, the business community, and key stakeholders. It is *not* going into a drawer after being written.

- **Trackable**   This will need to be updated frequently, sometimes several times a day, to follow the project.
- **Modifiable**   The plan will need to be modified and adjusted to reach the target as new information is learned.

Subphase 2.4: Define Project Processes

There will not be much tolerance in the timeframe or budget for errors. The following processes need to be defined, documented, and communicated:

- Communication
- Management tracking
- Organizational adjustments
- Resource requests
- Testing
- Deployment
- Review and signoff

See Chapter 3 for details of these processes.

Phase 3.0: Intervention Execution

This phase goes much more smoothly if the proper amount of diligence and planning is done previously. It executes against the project plan with constant tracking and verification. The processes identified earlier are used to ensure that the project does not get bogged down again.

One important difference between a project rescue process and other methodologies involves the frequency with which the project plan is tracked. Instead of weekly meetings, a rescue calls for daily or even intraday checkpoints. Consider two types of checkpoints: *executive checkpoint* and the *project checkpoint.*

The executive checkpoint process involves the key decision makers, key business owners, the rescue champion, and the project manager. Their checkpoint meeting is used to review the overall direction of the project, immediately resolve any obstacles, and eliminate inter-team conflicts. These checkpoints should be held once a day, at the beginning or the end of the day.

The project checkpoint involves the project leaders, project managers, and the rescue champion to discuss the project direction at a detailed level. This often involves a review of the complete issue log and the project plan. These checkpoints can be held once a day or intraday.

The critical skills in this phase include the following:

- **Negotiation skills**   You need to persuade people at all levels to stick to the critical path.
- **Organizational skills**   You need to build a detailed plan that can be tracked on a daily basis.
- **Tracking skills**   You need a constant snapshot of the project to know how things are proceeding.
- **Reprioritization skills**   You need to guide fast decision making when the project moves off track. At the rapid pace of a project rescue, this should be identified and done within hours of each other—not the days, weeks, or months it took earlier.
- **Coaching skills**   You need to be able to help people who have never been in a closely scrutinized, high-visibility situation. Plan to spend a lot of time encouraging those team members that are having a difficult time, especially in the beginning of the rescue effort.

In this phase, you are likely to find some of the following emotions:

- **Enthusiasm**   To get things done.
- **Skepticism**   Is this really going to work?
- **Hope**   That the approach will work.

Figure 2.7 shows that there are six major subphases in this unit of work. A process description is defined for each in the sections that follows.

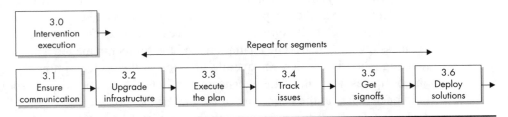

Figure 2.7   Intervention execution phase

Subphase 3.1: Ensure Communication

Start the execution phase by conducting the previously mentioned kickoff meeting with all the project participants in attendance. Walk the extended group through a shortened version of the revised project deliverables. Explain the communications plan and how the team will execute it. This could be some combination of the intranet, networks, memos, reports, voicemail, and e-mails.

Subphase 3.2: Upgrade Infrastructure

Do not allow the infrastructure—information technology, premises, or other equipment—to stand in the way of completing the project. Why is this considered to be a "subphase" in itself? There is a huge discrepancy in the real world about the consequences of spending in this area. It can be surprising how much time is wasted in getting a computer for a new resource or upgrading an existing machine. The same is true for office space—although it is not as frequently discussed. The following infrastructure items are on the critical path and should be available with almost no notice:

- Baseline test environment—to validate what is being built on an ongoing basis
- Personal computers (desktops or laptops)
- Software licenses
- Access to work premises around the clock (24/7)
- Deployment tools

Subphase 3.3: Execute the Plan

If the other subphases have been completed correctly, execution becomes routine even though it is still complex. Be prepared to make adjustments as the plan is executed. Leverage the key decision makers to remove obstacles as they arise. Share information freely and openly. Deal with issues as they come up. Be prepared to do any of the following:

- Make or guide decisions to meet the key metrics of the project
- Remove, or at least transfer, problem resources
- Keep your project objectives clear
- Reprioritize
- Call multiple status meetings in one day

- Work with the decision makers to change the scope again
- Consider new information
- Encourage the team

Subphase 3.4: Track Issues

Aside from keeping the key metrics upfront, how you manage issues that arise will be critical for continuing to enjoy the confidence of the extended project team. If stakeholders or team members feel that important elements are being ignored or avoided, they will begin to mistrust the process.

Instead, capture every issue that is raised electronically in a shared medium and prioritize it according to importance, value to the planned launch, and the timeframe when it is needed. For example, apply the following codes to every issue:

- **Showstopper**   Must be done before the project is implemented.
- **Critical**   Must be reviewed with the project sponsors and reclassified as a showstopper or downgraded to major status. The latter change means that this issue is no longer stopping the project from launching.
- **Major**   Can be done in a cleanup stage after launch.
- **Minor**   Should be done only if time permits.
- **Nice to have**   These are not going to be done, let's face it, during a project rescue.
- **Enhancement**   Functionality for a future release.

Subphase 3.5: Get Signoffs

With the rapid pace of the project, you may not be able to get a formal written signoff from every stakeholder using a usual process of review, update, incorporate, distribute, and get signoff. Instead, you need to define the process. This could involve group presentations, verbal acceptance, implicit acceptance, or electronic signatures. Whatever is agreed to must be included in the updated project charter. Define who has acceptance authority. Keep it simple with a minimal number of approvals for a deliverable.

Signoffs are not guaranteed, so you may need to negotiate what needs to be changed, updated, or postponed in order to continue the project. You also need a signoff from the project decision makers or their designate on the acceptance criteria before proceeding to the next subphase.

Subphase 3.6: Deploy Solutions

Deployment is what all the previous steps are about. The process here is to get the solution into a production status and then to start with the cleanup work or the next phase. Set expectations here by reinforcing that there will be cleanup involved. Critical deliverables include the following:

- Training for users affected by the deployment.
- Ensuring that infrastructure is in place.
- Ensuring that testing of the infrastructure and the solution has occurred.
- Security lockdown.
- Availability of 24/7 contact numbers for users, developers, and anyone else affected by the solution. Publication of help desk contact information.
- A universal message that summarizes the deployment activities in memo form.
- A ticket system to record the results, which have been demoted to a "major" priority.

Chances are that there is an issue log that contains a number of critical issues, along with all the others. There should be no showstoppers in the list at this point. Signoffs are not guaranteed, so you may need to negotiate what needs to be changed, updated, or postponed in order to continue.

Phase 4.0: Post-Intervention Review

Project rescues are iterative processes that are intended to support the business and add value to the organization. This phase provides the opportunity to reward the hard work of the extended team, to share learning from past mistakes, and to launch the next phase of development in a timely fashion.

The critical skills in this phase include the following:

- **Celebration skills**   The team needs to feel good about what they have accomplished.
- **Self-assessment skills**   The team needs to understand what went right, what went wrong, and what could be done better.
- **Self-starting skills**   The team needs to push forward with the next piece of work.
- **Relinquishing skills**   The rescue champion or rescue manager needs to learn how to let go if the project team is capable of proceeding without additional support.

In this phase, you are likely to find some of the following emotions:

- **Exuberance**   A project that was heading toward disaster has been saved.
- **Denial**   It was never a problem.
- **Exhaustion**   Fatigue from all the long hours and hard work. People need to take time off to recover.

Figure 2.8 shows four major subphases in this unit of work. A process description is defined for each in the sections that follow.

Subphase 4.1: Communicate Rescue Results

The results of the project rescue intervention should be summarized and communicated to the rest of the organization for several reasons. The previous project, and previous attempts at the project, may have created a lot of skepticism and negativity in the organization. A publicized success will help to offset this. There should also be a quick celebration in honor of the hard work that has just been done. Resources that have worked long hours should be encouraged to take time off, preferably without dipping into their vacations. A party is also useful.

At this point in time, personal agendas will likely return, and some of the original thinking that got the project into trouble in the first place will begin to reappear. Some of these are natural, such as competitive behavior, while others may be nasty such as personal jealousies. The next subphase offers a hedge against this.

Subphase 4.2: Incorporate Lessons Learned

An organization must learn from its mistakes and build value into its processes and people through continuous improvement and learning. This subphase is intended to share this information through various presentations, meetings, and discussion papers. These lessons will be valuable in the future when similar

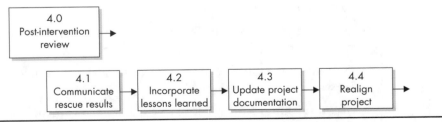

Figure 2.8   Post-intervention review phase

habits begin to reappear. All the lessons may not be implemented, however, and future project rescues may be required. The key is to ensure that the organization is better off now than it was before the intervention. This includes the skills and maturity of the project teams, stakeholders, sponsors, and decision makers.

Subphase 4.3: Update Project Documentation

Despite the celebration and good cheer, the work must continue, beginning with an update to the project documentation. Because there is cleanup and additional work to be done, this involves generating another version of the documentation for future work. Be sure to capture all standards that have been defined through the rescue effort. Also, task actuals should be kept in an estimating repository for future projects.

Future iterations of the initiative should begin to see the gradual elimination of the project rescue role, along with any other specific roles that were created for the intervention. The project rescue is officially completed when these roles are completely phased out or handed over to the permanent project team. Information and documentation should continue to be shared with these resources in the event that a project rescue needs to be invoked again.

Subphase 4.4: Realign Project

The project could have gotten into trouble for any number of reasons, including lack of project management principles or other uncontrollable factors. Once the project rescue exercise is completely done, this subphase is used to realign the project with the organization's standard project methodologies and project management principles.

Closing Perspective

This chapter defined a four-phase intervention framework for rescuing troubled projects. The phases were discussed at the subphase level. The following chapter examines the detailed processes and deliverables within each phase. These will be augmented with detailed questions to get to the root of the problem(s) in subsequent chapters.

## CHAPTER 3

Rescue Deliverable Framework

The preceding chapter defined a project rescue framework that is based on the following four phases:

- 1.0 Assessment
- 2.0 Intervention planning
- 3.0 Intervention execution
- 4.0 Post intervention review

This chapter augments this basic framework in two ways. The first involves identifying a set of key themes or threads that the project rescue manager uses to monitor and retain control over the direction of the fast-paced rescue effort. The second way is to identify a set of key deliverables that are either used, created, or maintained in the rescue framework. This list represents the minimum set of deliverables that is needed to support a successful project rescue.

Enhancing the Rescue Framework

We are going to add more much needed flesh to the rescue framework in this chapter. The phases show the direction of activities to understand and resolve a problem-plagued project. However, working or managing exclusively by activities can be highly cumbersome. There are any number of correct activities and any number of correct sequences.

A better approach is to focus on threads and deliverables. The many-to-one relationship (for example, many activities or tasks required to produce a single deliverable) can lead to extensive arguments on a project team about what should be done in what order and using which technique. Focusing on what is being produced, instead of how it is being produced, although still complex, is still better for building team consensus. It is also easier than leveraging the traditional Work Breakdown Structure (WBS), which still relies on process discussions that require a discussion of "how" instead of "what."

Threads

Threads provide a horizontal aggregation of related activities across the phases of the intervention framework. As you can see in Figure 3.1, threads generally stretch across the entire project life cycle. The threads shown in this figure—communication, resources, suppliers, quality assurance, risk, scope and requirements, and planning—are the minimum set of threads required to control and direct project rescue efforts.

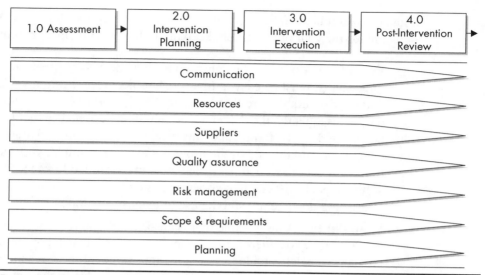

Figure 3.1   Threads to watch

More details on how the rescue manager can use threads is provided after the introduction to deliverables.

Deliverables

Deliverables can be an area of much discussion on projects, and the discussion often focuses on the following types of questions: What is the appropriate format of the deliverables? What is the appropriate content? What is the optimal number of deliverables required to properly manage a project using a generic development methodology? How about for a project rescue?

The project rescue framework identifies a minimum set of deliverables that is required to support the rescue process. These deliverables provide the level of detail that is required to track and adjust to events that occur during a project rescue. We've provided some standard templates as examples of what deliverables should look like. These can be downloaded from the publisher's web site as discussed in the Preface of this book.

Of course the deliverable formats shown in this chapter are not the only correct versions. Many other formats are just as effective. Some may be more effective in a given environment. When deciding on a consistent format for the set of deliverables for your organization, keep the following principles in mind:

- **Ease of processing** The deliverables must be easy to create and, more importantly, must be easy to modify. A project rescue initiative demands that the deliverables are frequently updated—perhaps several times in one day. Consequently, the deliverables should be designed so that they can be changed easily. In practice, this means avoiding fancy layouts and constructs until the end of the project cycle. For example, you want to minimize complex documents that contain embedded links to different software packages (such as spreadsheets embedded directly into word processing documents) and the use of extensive colors.

- **Readability** A deliverable that is clear, crisp, and readable means that it is ready to be considered as a corporate standard. Instead of rearranging the contents of a deliverable to suit a previous notion of how it should appear, be objective and assess whether it is readily readable in the current format. Working to build a consensus on degrees of readability and clarity will consume more time than the benefits.

- **Standardization** Based on the two preceding criteria, standardize on a single format for all the deliverables used during the project rescue. Some or all of these may have already been established during the project before the rescue was invoked. The ones that satisfy these requirements can be adopted as standards. Empty templates and a working sample should be centrally located and shared to ensure that the standards are known to the extended team.

- **Access** The deliverables need to be centrally located on an intranet, extranet, and in paper files. Instructions for access also need to be distributed to the extended project team. Remember to mark each deliverable as "confidential and proprietary" to protect the intellectual property. It may take some members some time to become familiar with the new formats/standards, but it will save a great deal of time later in the process if all the documentation fits neatly together.

- **Content** Deliverables need to be judged by the value of the content they provide. Focus on this when evaluating the effectiveness of a deliverable.

The biggest return on your effort to define the deliverable formats for the rescue initiative will be realized by focusing on these considerations and using these rules to resolve any disagreements that arise. If a format feature does not add value to one of these criteria, it should not be a consideration in the decision making.

Key Threads

The importance of activities such as "risk management" and "communication" to project management efforts has been well documented for decades. What is often overlooked, however, is how these activities transition from one phase to another. A risk assessment that is completed in the first phase needs to be revisited in the other phases. Producing and storing it is not enough. This section explains the key threads that are required by managers to stay on top of a rescue initiative. Note that the project rescue was probably initiated due to a problem in one or more of these threads. The early part of the assessment phase needs to focus on trying to identify the sources of these problems.

Communication

The communication thread refers to all the information that needs to be shared with all the different members of the extended project team. This includes the project sponsors, project stakeholders, the project team, and related third parties. Dimensions of interest to the project manager include the accuracy, timeliness, and responsiveness to the communication. You need to specifically consider the What, When, Who, and How of communication.

What to Communicate

Lots of information needs to be communicated, but it is better for the rescue manager to focus on sharing a couple of key pieces of information. Selected properly, these sources will drive out the construction and content of other key deliverables. For example, the following deliverables are good anchors for driving the remainder of the deliverable set:

- **Acceptance criteria**   Also drives the development of the business requirements and testing plans.
- **Roles and responsibilities**   Also drives several important processes such as fast responses to issues or obstacles. Fast turnaround during a project rescue requires strong clarity around this. A single point of responsibility or accountability is preferred during a project rescue.
- **Obstacles**   Also drives the risk management and quality management deliverables.
- **Timelines**   Also drives identification of the resource requirements and the detailed project plan.

- **Status report**   This collects the status on all the other deliverables, especially the issues log and the percentage complete of activities on the project plan. Another approach, for those who are not fans of percentage complete, is to use Estimate to Complete (ETC)—in hours, days, or some other unit of measuring work. This latter approach can tend to be a bit more accurate in terms of effort left to completion. ETC can also be used to derive remaining cost and schedule information.

When to Communicate

A daily touch point (for example, a face to face meeting) and a daily status report should be used during a project rescue. The length of each can vary from time to time, but keeping to a daily schedule like this keeps the team focused. People tend to do most of their work when faced with an immediate deadline.

Communicate to Whom

This includes the entire extended project team: sponsors, stakeholders, project team members, end users, and interested third parties.

How to Communicate

Real-time, interactive contact with members of the project team is vital. Both reports and meetings/workshops need to be used to communicate the essence of the deliverables. Foregoing one of these will not produce the desired results. Rescue managers need to resist calls from team members to let them focus on work by skipping meetings or workshops.

Distribution lists for e-mails, voicemails, pager numbers, and home contact numbers should be built right at the start of the rescue initiative. There should be several groupings, such as a project management distribution list, extended project team distribution list, stakeholder distribution list, executive sponsor distribution list, and core team distribution list.

This information should be documented in a formal communication plan and be approved by the Executive Sponsor. Once approved, the lists should be distributed to all project stakeholders—probably at the rescue kickoff meeting.

Resources

This broad thread encompasses both human and material resources. This thread identifies the requirements and availability of the resources through the project rescue plan. In particular, you need to ensure that all barriers that prevent the resources from becoming available in a timely manner are removed.

Project teams are often screaming for additional resources that can be justified, but obstacles such as cumbersome processes, disconnect between finance and the team, or fulfillment capabilities stand in the way. Conducting the project rescue without getting these out of the way will infuriate the project team and derail the initiative. These resources must be documented in the project plan. Any hurdles encountered in acquiring the resources in accordance to the plan should be managed by the project's management and change management processes.

Suppliers

Suppliers, such as those providing human resources, software, hardware, or other materials are managed as a thread. Streamline the process of working with suppliers by building your nondisclosure agreements, contracts, expectations, and service level agreements. The expectations and service level agreements need to clearly communicate your requirements and important deadline dates. Also ensure that there is an acceptable remedy if the supplier does not perform as per the agreement.

For contractor employees, you need to establish training and skills expectations. Project rescue periods are going to require extensive working hours so ensure that the contractors are willing to be part of the team. Are they willing to be contacted around the clock during a crisis—or even just to ensure that the deadlines are met?

Quality Assurance

Because a successful project rescue is all about making tradeoffs for the greater good, quality expectations need to be reconsidered. Are they too lax or too rigid? What are the minimum quality expectations for acceptance? Who is going to make this determination?

Risk Management

Risk management cannot stop at the end of the first phase. The basic risk management process can begin with an assessment that identifies the following key information:

- Risk category
- Risk
- Impact

- Probability of occurrence
- Who's affected
- Mitigation strategy
- Costs (optional)

Scope and Requirements

Pool all the statements, conversations, and modifications into one shared scope and requirements document that everyone on the project team can buy into. If a requirement is not recorded in this document, it is not within the scope of the project. This thread acts as a pressure release valve that needs to be managed to add or remove requirements, with appropriate buy-in, to meet the initiative delivery dates.

The requirements must have a formal approval by the Executive Sponsor to establish a scope baseline. Any requirements that are added, changed, or deleted should be handled by the project change management process.

Planning

In a rescue initiative, the project plan is used and modified constantly to track every deliverable and activity. Any slippage should flag an immediate response to correct the remaining steps to meet the delivery dates.

The project plan should be updated weekly or as often as daily depending on depth of the crisis.

Key Project Rescue Deliverables

This section identifies the key deliverables belonging to each of the four phases in the project rescue framework. The subsections describe the important information on each deliverable and any special items you should be looking for. Templates for deliverables that need to be specifically created in the project rescue are included in this chapter.

These deliverables are inherited from the project that is being rescued, reviewed, updated, and transformed. They can also be created using any number of different techniques such as iterative development, parallel development, or agile methodologies.

Assessment Deliverables

Because the objective of this phase is to assess the status of the current project, the rescue manager and project team need to review all the deliverables that were created to date. Figure 3.2 shows the minimum set of deliverables that we recommend you review in this phase. If some of these were not created during the project, they should be built as part of the rescue process. This could be a reason for the project rescue being needed in the first place.

Project Charter

This deliverable describes the vision, objective, and costs of the project initiative. Look for specifics around how the objectives map to the vision. Very often, the objectives may try to achieve more than is required to satisfy the vision.

Organization Chart

The organization chart should identify the key sponsors, stakeholders, project team, and any other resource groups that are involved in the project. Look for clarity around the roles and responsibilities and reporting relationships. Are there any gaps? Is there accountability? Who can remove obstacles that the rescue will encounter? Are they ready to help?

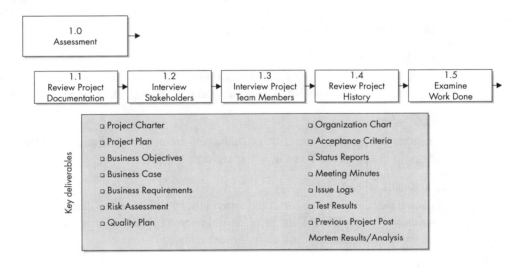

Figure 3.2   Assessment phase key deliverables

Project Plan

This can be a Gantt view of the project plan at the activity level showing resource requirements at the task or activity level. You need to review this plan to understand the original project dates. Were there enough interim dates? Was the schedule reasonable to begin with? How was the time allocated?

Business Objectives

Understand the high-level business objectives and try to assign an impact of each to the business. As the project rescue manager, you need to understand whether the business objectives are achievable. You may also want to consider whether, in your judgment, they are valid objectives for the business. Do they really result in added business value? Were they a problem to begin with?

Business Case

This is an important document as it describes the business need for the project. The more important it is to the business, the more the company will be willing to invest to make it successful. Use this to identify the key supporters of the initiative.

Business Requirements

Compare the business requirements to the business objectives from the project charter. Look for inconsistencies, vagueness, and ambiguities. How complete and relevant are the business requirements? Are they clear and ambiguous? Too often, objectives are confused with business requirements.

Risk Assessment

Focus on understanding the identified risks, the mitigation strategies that were defined, and what was actually done. Identify any risks that were obviously missed.

Quality Plan

Who is the quality champion or manager? How did the quality requirements hurt or help the project? Were they too rigid or too few?

Acceptance Criteria

Create a detailed statement of the criteria that will be used to determine if the project solution is acceptable. Must be clear and related to the business requirements. If this cannot be articulated, it is a sign of more ambiguity to come.

Status Reports

Examine all the documents and notes related to how the project was being tracked. This should include the formal status reports, but also the informal emails, notes, and minutes of meetings that were shared between the team members.

Meeting Minutes

A lot of useful information never makes it onto the regular status reports. You need find the formal or informal meeting minutes and memos to build a more complete background of what has occurred on the project.

Issue Logs

Review the outstanding issue logs for several important pieces of information. What types of issues were being identified prior to the project rescue being invoked? Are these to be expected? Were they getting resolved or at least addressed in a timely manner? Are there any personal issues coming out?

Intervention Planning Deliverables

In this phase, you are going to either update the project deliverables that were identified in the previous phase or create new ones. Information may be inaccurate or missing in these deliverables. This could have been a source of the problem in the first place. You may also need to create any of the deliverables on the "must have" list if they do not exist. These documents feed the generation of a new set of deliverables for the project rescue. Figure 3.3 shows the smaller set of deliverables that must be created during this phase of the rescue.

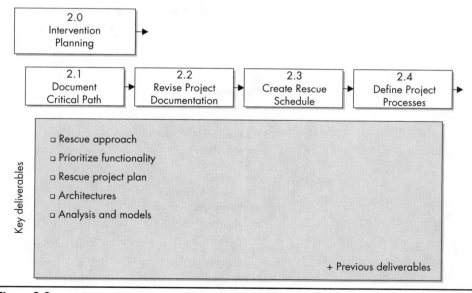

Figure 3.3   Intervention Planning phase key deliverables

Rescue Approach

This deliverable mirrors the project charter and is intended to persuade everyone involved in the initiative to contribute to the project rescue. This document should show the cost of several different approaches and recommend a direction in which to proceed. It should also identify processes and procedures for the project rescue initiative. Figure 3.4 shows the major content areas to be included in this document.

Prioritized Functionality

This is a list of the functions or units of work that must be completed to satisfy the rescue objectives with associated priorities and "must have" dates. You will need to work with the sponsors and several stakeholders to go through the original project charter and business requirements to determine what is critical or not, and in what sequence it should be delivered.

Some stakeholders will want everything on the requirements list, but remember that the alternative is to deliver nothing. If you are new to the project in the role of the rescue manager, you will be better positioned to negotiate in these meetings as you cannot be blamed for past problems on the project. You should build a list similar to the one in Figure 3.5.

Rescue Project Plan

This is a detailed project plan that facilitates regular walkthroughs with different members of the extended project team. This may require several versions of the plan. One version could show the major activities and milestones using a monthly or quarterly time scale so that the entire plan fits onto a page. This document helps

```
Background
Project objectives
Project benefits and cost of non-completion
Project scope
Project deliverables
Proposed schedule
Project budget
Organization
        Executive sponsor
        Steering committee
        Project team
Rescue approach
Risk management
Quality plan
```

Figure 3.4   Rescue approach

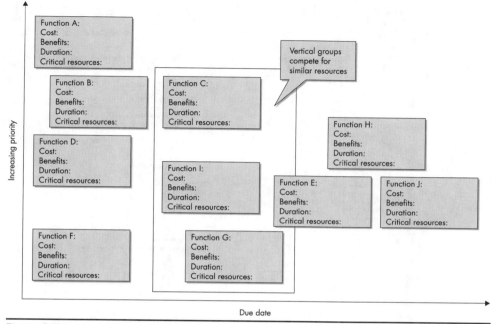

Figure 3.5   Prioritized functionality list

to position the business user's understanding by providing meaningful reference points. The other view of the plan could show activities broken into days, so that an early morning meeting can be used to track the progress of the day before. The plan could also be updated at the end of the day to ensure enough progress was made before team members go home. Figure 3.6 shows a sample of this deliverable.

Architectures

An integrated architecture is needed to show how all the different pieces of the solution fit together—and whether they actually do fit together. Architectures are useful for understanding and explaining the big picture, to support building the details into the project plan, and to help in calculating the resource costs.

Three architectures are of interest in this phase: the Application architecture, the Data architecture, and the Technology architecture. Figure 3.7 shows samples for these.

Analysis and Models

This deliverable analyzes the business requirements and produces models (for example, object models, storyboards, creative mocks) to support detailed design

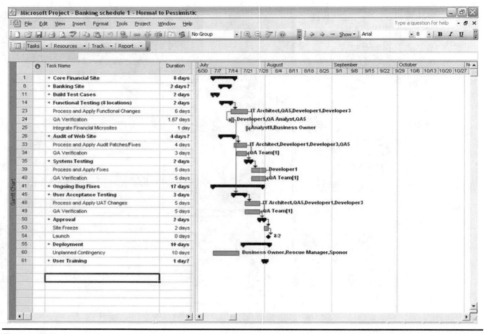

Figure 3.6   Rescue project plan

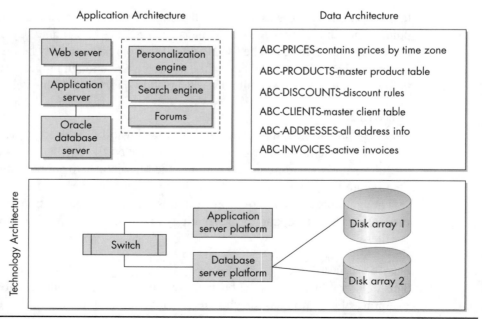

Figure 3.7   Architectures

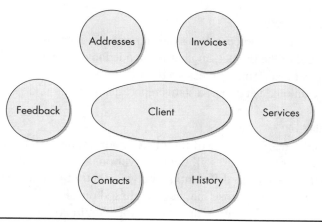

Figure 3.8   Analysis and models

and specifications for the solution. This deliverable can be produced in parallel to the architectures. Figure 3.8 shows sample models that can be adopted.

Intervention Execution Deliverables

The bulk of the deliverables produced during the project rescue are done in Phase 2. If the planning is done well, this phase essentially implements the solution, producing deliverables that monitor the situation, track progress, identify problems, and produce resolution. Figure 3.9 shows the smaller subset of deliverables processed in this phase. The deliverables in the previous phase also need to be maintained to reflect any changes on the ground.

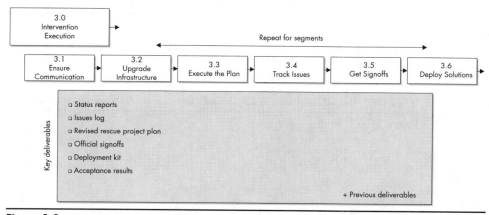

Figure 3.9   Intervention Execution phase key deliverables

Status Reports

There are several types of status reports. One type is intended to be a permanent record of the project, another is intended to convey information to the project team, and a third format serves as a daily discussion document. Figure 3.10 shows a highly streamlined version of a status report that is easily understood and maintained.

Issues Log

The issues log is one of the most important documents during a project rescue initiative. It captures all the observations from the extended team and uses priority codes to differentiate between activities that need to be done to fulfill the rescue and those that can be phased out. Figure 3.11 identifies the major pieces of information that such a log should contain.

Change logs should be included to document all changes to scope along the way.

Revised Project Rescue Plan

This is a daily update of the rescue project plan that was created in the previous phase. This needs to be updated with percentage complete or estimates to

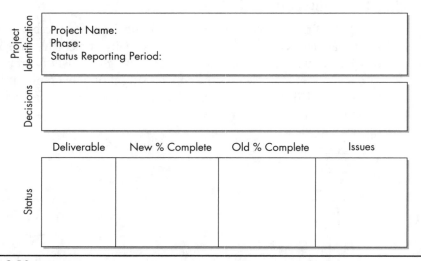

Figure 3.10   Status reports

Priority: Showstopper

#	Issue	Description	Assigned To	Due Date	status
1					
2					
3					
4					
5					
6					
7					
8					

Priority: High

#	Issue	Description	Assigned To	Due Date	status
1					
2					
3					
4					
5					
6					
7					
8					

Figure 3.11   Issues log

complete frequently (for example, at end of day). Figure 3.12 shows an approach for representing percentage complete.

Official Signoffs

During a project rescue, it is sometimes difficult to get that final signoff from a stakeholder and owner. This could occur because of a lack of availability, final nervousness, or simply fear. It would be awful to be ready to deploy an application but miss the delivery date by days because a signature is not forthcoming.

You need to establish the process for getting a timely signoff. Perhaps an oral acceptance is permitted. This would certainly support a faster process, but what record is there of such a notice being given. Project rescue managers need to

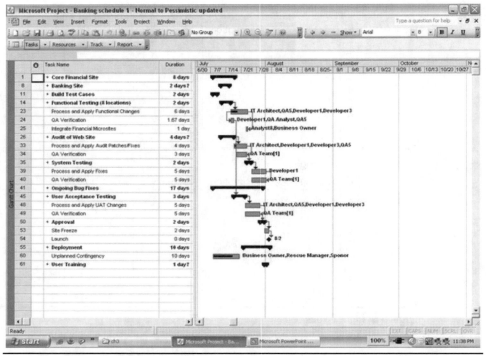

Figure 3.12 Revised project rescue plan

document the acceptance process and detail what is considered to be acceptable, and distribute this in an e-mail to the stakeholder. What do the corporate lawyers say is acceptable? Figure 3.13 shows a sample page that could be a cover to all the deliverables that need to be signed off before deploying the solution.

Deployment Kit

Deploying a solution is a project in itself. Figure 3.14 shows the components of the deployment kit that needs to be produced, tested, and distributed well ahead of implementation.

The components include the following:

- **Deployment plan**   Also drives the business requirements and testing plans.

- **User training plan**   Identifies the type of training that is available, the users that require it, and a timeline when they are expected to receive it. Training is required for users of the solution, the technical team that

Please sign below and return by email of fax to xxx-xxxxx.

By signing you acknowledge that you have read the document and are agreeing with its contents.

Sponsor

Name _____

Title _____

Signature _____

Date _____

Rescue Manager

Name _____

Title _____

Signature _____

Date _____

Signoff Contingent On _____

Comments:

Figure 3.13   Official signoffs

supports the solution, and the help desk that is going to respond to user problems.

- **Contact list**   This is a list of all the key contacts and how to reach them around the clock during the deployment phase. This information will be required, so ensure that it is accurate and that the people on the list are well rested before the deployment process begins.

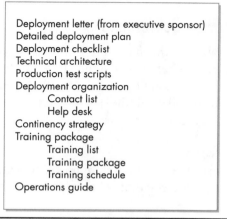

Deployment letter (from executive sponsor)
Detailed deployment plan
Deployment checklist
Technical architecture
Production test scripts
Deployment organization
        Contact list
        Help desk
Continency strategy
Training package
        Training list
        Training package
        Training schedule
Operations guide

Figure 3.14   Deployment kit

- **Letter to users**   Should come from the project sponsor and be sent to everyone affected by the launch, explaining the detailed process for the deployment.

- **Contingency plan**   Build and test the process that will be followed if the deployment does not go according to plan. The plan should identify the communication that is needed and the steps that need to be followed to make a decision to implement the contingency plan instead of the solution. The plan should also identify the cutoff time for when this needs to be started. This is an undesirable situation and, let's hope, you won't need to invoke it.

- **Post-launch test**   The system may have worked during the final test, but test it again after deployment and before the world sees it to ensure that nothing was missed. You may want to use a streamlined version of the acceptance test so that there is enough time left over after deployment to do this. The major risk factors involve ensuring that all the components of the application have been deployed into production and that the environment is properly configured.

Acceptance Results

This deliverable collects all the results from the different tests, especially the acceptance tests, to demonstrate the quality of the application. This package needs to be reviewed with the sponsors when you are getting signoff from them. Figure 3.15 shows a document that summarizes the relevant information to make this determination.

Post-Intervention Review Deliverables

The deliverables in this phase are intended to capture the lessons learned from the project rescue initiative and then to return the project back to the project team. Figure 3.16 shows the new deliverables that need to be produced. Typically, you would also update all the deliverables starting from phase 1 to reflect the situation after the project review.

Post Mortem Report

The purpose of the post mortem report is to learn from the project experience. This includes understanding what went well, what did not go well, and what

Project: name   Tester: name
Date: month day, year   Contact info: extension

Function: name 1

#	Test Name	Expected Results	Actual Result	Passed?/Comments
1				
2				
3				
4				
5				

Function: name 2

#	Test Name	Expected Results	Actual Result	Passed?/Comments
6				
7				
8				
9				

Figure 3.15   Acceptance results

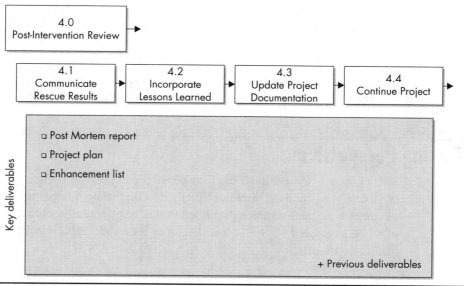

Figure 3.16   Post Intervention Review phase key deliverables

Dimension: name

#	Expectation	What Happened	Business Impact	Alternative Strategy
1				
2				
3				
4				
5				

Figure 3.17   Post mortem report

could be done better. Punitive post mortems create avoidance or defensive behaviors. It's better to have an objective "let's learn from the past and move on" session that is led by someone such as the project rescue manager. Figure 3.17 shows the contents of a sample post mortem report.

This step is often skipped due to project pressures, but that's a mistake. The post mortem report is protection that the same behavior that resulted in the necessity for a project rescue will not be so easily repeated.

Master Project Plan

The original project plan needs to be updated and modified to reflect the next phases of activities. Figure 3.18 shows a sample of this.

Enhancement List

Mine the issues log to find specific new enhancements and their costs, and include them on the project plan. Figure 3.19 shows a format for this list.

Closing Perspective

This chapter extended the basic four-phase project rescue framework by identifying specific threads and deliverables that the rescue manager needs to leverage. Both the threads and deliverables discussed in this chapter really represent a minimum of what is required on most project rescues for a successful conclusion.

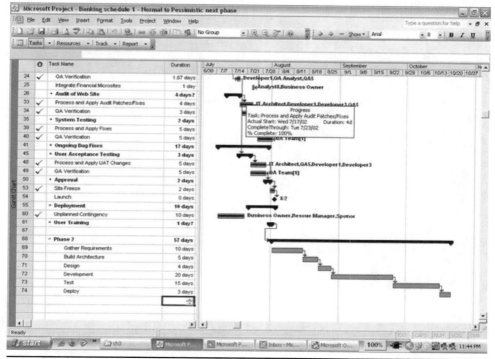

Figure 3.18   Project plan

#	Function Name	Requested By	Priority	Description
1				
2				
3				
4				
5				

Figure 3.19   Enhancement list

## CHAPTER 4

Early Detection Questions

Projects do not suddenly get out of control; there are always early warning signs that indicate a project is in jeopardy. In 1975 in *The Mythical Man-Month: Essays on Software Engineering*, Frederick Brooks asked the question "How do projects become two years late?" and answered it "One day at a time." This is true of all runaway projects, whether they are IT-related or not. To identify a runaway project (or one that can potentially become a runaway project) you must recognize the early warning signs that precede project failure.

Just like a major disease against the body, the key to correction is early detection and a proven treatment plan. Let's take the disease analogy a little further and say that the earlier the detection the less radical the treatment. Usually when a project is in trouble there is either too much data about the project being collected and distributed, often to hide the problems, or worse yet, too little data being collected and shared. Each of these possibilities contains its own set of problems. With massive amounts of project data flowing in, cutting through the clutter to get to the important data takes a trained eye and often a lot of time. On the other hand, hunting down project data can be time-consuming, especially if the project team members have not been trained to accurately track their time on each task they've performed. The goal is to understand a project is off course long before disastrous career and financial costs occur. In this chapter, we identify key symptoms and the subsequent key questions to ask if you suspect a runaway project.

Spending More Time

Anyone can recognize a runaway project when the cost and schedule are running three, four or ten times the original estimate. If the project budget and schedule have been grossly exceeded, you already know you have a project that is out of control. What you really want is to understand long before these nightmarish events just when your project is spinning out of control.

It is important to understand that the project schedule and related budget will not go exactly as planned. There will be tasks that are completed in more hours or fewer hours than the original estimates. Most likely, there will be scope changes that affect the overall schedule and budget. By taking a periodic look at the project's actual progress against its planned progress you will begin to see the early warning signs and trends that you have a potential disaster on your hands.

Key Question: What was the actual time spent on each task versus the original estimate?

There are some legitimate reasons for spending more time and money on a project than what was originally allocated. If you practice rigorous project change control, however, the schedule or budget "overage" should not be a surprise because it would have already been approved. Troubled projects tend to be victims of poor change control. Quite often, either the project manager is inexperienced in good change control methods or the project team members are constantly allowing "a tiny change" on a regular basis. Project scope can get out of hand quickly and severely.

By having each member of the project team complete the chart in Table 4.1 for every task they work, planned or unplanned, you can understand what happened before you ask why it happened.

Once you understand what happened and why the variances occurred you are on your way to knowing to what degree the project is out of control and whether the missed deadlines and requests for more money are anomalies or trends.

Project Definition Documents

The project charter and project plan are crucial to the success of any project. They should have been in place before the project began. Without them, no one is accountable for the runaway project.

Task		Planned			Actual			Variance	
No.	Name	Start Date	End Date	Hrs	Start Date	End Date	Hrs	Days	Hrs
1	Task A	mm/dd/yy	mm/dd/yy	nn	mm/dd/yy	mm/dd/yy	nn	nn	nn
2	Task B	mm/dd/yy	mm/dd/yy	nn	mm/dd/yy	mm/dd/yy	nn	nn	nn
3	Task C	mm/dd/yy	mm/dd/yy	nn	mm/dd/yy	mm/dd/yy	nn	nn	nn
4	Task D	mm/dd/yy	mm/dd/yy	nn	mm/dd/yy	mm/dd/yy	nn	nn	nn
5	Task E	mm/dd/yy	mm/dd/yy	nn	mm/dd/yy	mm/dd/yy	nn	nn	nn
6	Task F	mm/dd/yy	mm/dd/yy	nn	mm/dd/yy	mm/dd/yy	nn	nn	nn

Table 4.1 Task Variances

Project Charter

The project charter (also called the *Statement of Work* or *SOW*) is the defining document of a project. It serves as the project's operating plan and indicates things such as how the deliverables are defined and who has acceptance authority.

Key Question: How complete is the project charter? Does it have all the necessary components with a sufficient level of detail?

Most likely a weak project charter is on file somewhere because many people do them just because they have to. Generally, some defining document is required so the project can be funded. Runaway projects tend to have project charters with poorly written sections with ambiguous wording or, worse yet, missing key sections. To make matters worse, the project charter is usually tucked away and kept for historical purposes only. The project charter should be actively reviewed and maintained on a regular basis. Without a solid project charter, it is very difficult to hold people accountable for the project's success or failure. The following list contains the sections and content of a good project charter:

- **Executive summary**   A brief (one to three pages) summary that highlights the project from a business perspective. This section should contain the reason(s) the project is undertaken, cost, schedule, ROI based upon accepted company policies, intangible benefits, affected organizations, and the consequences of not doing the project.

- **Project scope**   Describes what the project is supposed to accomplish. This section starts as a snapshot of the project's function at the project's inception. It should be updated regularly as part of the change control function. The key areas in this section include the project's critical success factors, deliverables and known out-of-scope items and activities. This is one of the most likely areas that got out of control in a troubled project situation. The In-Scope section should be explicitly called out in the Scope section to quantify the items to support the project estimate (i.e. estimating assumptions). The quantified items also act as boundaries with which to invoke change control and limit scope creep.

- **Management approach**   Describes how you're going to manage this project. This section contains the project management methods that will be employed during project startup, execution and completion that will help keep the project on track. The key areas include the activities associated with change management, issue management, acceptance management, communications management, risk management and plan management. These activities and their associated tasks should be directly reflected in the project plan. Not following the methods in this section, especially change control, is clearly the leading cause of runaway projects.

- **Technical approach**   Describes the methodology that will be employed during the technical phase(s) of the project. This section contains the activities and tasks that will occur in order to produce the deliverables described in the project scope section. As with the management approach activities, these activities and their associated tasks should also be directly reflected in the project plan.

- **Quality approach**   Describes the methods to be used to ensure project management and technical quality. These methods include such things as the accepted standards regarding project charter content, estimating, status reporting, and project notebook content. Also, the timing and procedures for project reviews or audits should be stated here as well. From a technical quality perspective, methods such as structured walkthroughs would be articulated. Items related to the walkthroughs such as objectives, attendees, timing and procedures are included. Again, all of the tasks associated with this approach should be included in the project plan.

- **Roles and responsibilities**   Describes the function and authorities of the various project roles. This is not a job description of each project member team because a person can fill multiple roles and certain roles may be filled by more than one person. Key roles and responsibilities should include

  - **Functional business team**

    - **Executive sponsor**   Works with the technical project manager to act on behalf of the functional business team for accepting deliverables, authorizing change requests and resolving escalated issues.

    - **Project sponsor**   Works on a day-to-day basis with the technical project manager and assists in resolving issues, as well as designating, delegating and scheduling the subject matter experts' time as required.

    - **Subject matter experts**   Provide specific business and technical information to the technical project manager as requested and specified in the project plan. If necessary, identify key subject matter experts for clarity.

  - **Technical team**

    - **Project manager**   Responsible for the day-to-day management of the project and reporting status to the project sponsor and project executive sponsor.

- **Project architect** (also known as the technical project manager) Responsible for the technical viability and quality of the project.
- **Technical team members**   Various technical team roles such as business analysts, programmers, testers, technical writers, trainers, data administrators, database administrators and so on. It is very important to describe each appropriate role, especially if that role is to be fulfilled from an "external" organization such as a shared services group or outside consultants.

- **Project plan**   This will be explained in full detail later in this chapter.
- **Budget and staffing plan**   Describes the costs, both internal and external, including hardware, software and labor. The labor component is tied directly to the project plan and should reflect a reasonable ramp-up, peak load and ramp-down staffing level. Most project management software allows for material costs to be entered in the project plan as well as labor. If material costs are included in the project plan, those variances can be tracked and managed as well.
- **Project organization chart**   Displays the reporting and authority structure of the extended project team. The project steering committee should be indicated with all members. All direct and indirect relationships should also be noted. This section tends to have been omitted in troubled projects or there is an extremely complex organization chart. Keep it simple!

Key Question: How current is the project charter?

Every time there is a change to the project, that change should be reflected in the charter. The project charter should be the most current snapshot of the project's scope and business case. The audit trail for each generation of the project charter should reside in the project notebook. Most projects get derailed when the project team just sticks the project charter on the shelf and never looks at it again. Changes to the project charter reflect the need to change the scope of the project development boundaries. Scope changes are a big deal and when approved, require a complete recasting of the project plan estimates or a re-baselining of the plan to reflect the changes in the dates. Changes within scope—variances from the plan—are normally authorized through the Change Management process and do not require the entire plan to be re-baselined but only the changed tasks.

Project Plan

The project plan has its own set of key questions associated with early diagnosis. Although similar to the project charter key questions, these key questions will give you an insight into the day-to-day operations of your project.

Key Question: Does the project plan exist?

Without a doubt, the most important tool for managing a project is the project plan. The plan is the blueprint by which all project activities and tasks are performed. It's alarming that many multimillion-dollar projects are allowed to sail along without the benefit of a formal, documented project plan. Those projects are later known as multimillion-dollar failures and career enders.

Key Question: Are all the tasks accounted for in the plan?

The primary goal is to have a plan that includes all activities and tasks, including their dependencies and estimated effort that are needed to produce the deliverables described in the project charter. The plan should not only include the technical tasks, but it should also include the tasks associated with project management and quality management approaches in their respective sections of the project charter. As mentioned earlier, the primary reason projects get into trouble is team members don't adhere to the Management Approach, especially change control. The most prevalent root cause of excessive change is missing tasks.

Key Question: Are the task estimates based upon a known history or are they just guesses?

The next most prevalent root cause of excessive change is aggressive or even far-fetched estimates. Having a proven development methodology or a set of proven project plan templates with experience-based work effort estimates is the best way to avoid those two diabolical causes of catastrophe.

Key Question: Is each team member working only on the tasks specifically assigned in the plan?

Once you have a valid project plan, the project team members should be doing work according to that plan. This may sound like the most obvious statement one could make, but project team members very often work on other tasks, even those outside the scope of the project without informing the project manager. This especially happens with project team members who have responsibilities outside the project (for example, break-fix response for a production system). Having team members who are working on tasks other than those in the project plan is a sure sign that the project is not being managed properly and is headed for major problems—if it's not already there.

Key Question: Is the plan current with respect to the work effort and time to complete the project?
Another crucial point related to the project plan, even more so than the project charter, is currency. The project plan should be updated weekly. Updates include the following:

- Reestimating the effort to complete all open tasks.

- Reviewing the validity of the estimates for future tasks. For example, if you have future code reviews scheduled for 30 minutes each and the past review sessions have lasted an hour, you should plan on future review sessions lasting an hour each and adjust the plan appropriately.

- Tracking all variances (positive and negative) to determine if they are temporary anomalies or emerging trends. Every project has plenty of variances. In fact, some project managers believe managing variances is the key technique for managing a project.

- Rescheduling the project plan. Whatever project management tool you are using, it is a good idea to reschedule the plan on a weekly basis to help keep an eye on the estimated project end date.

A project plan that is nonexistent or is not up-to-date is a definite sign that a project is (or will become) out of control. If the plan is created because of a funding requirement and then put on the shelf to collect dust along with the project charter, you can be assured the project is being "managed" by opinions instead of facts.

As you can see, the project plan and the project charter are inextricably connected. You cannot expect to successfully complete a substantial project unless these two essentials are in sync. In the "building a house" analogy that is often associated with IT projects, the project charter is the architectural renderings and plan while the project plan is the blueprint specifications. You need both to achieve the intended results.

Project Staffing

Troubled projects can be well planned and well funded but poorly executed. Team experience and team chemistry play a major role in the success or failure of projects. The more important the project, the more you rely upon experience for success. Next we will take a closer look at how having the wrong people in certain key project roles leads to a project's downfall.

Project Manager

The project manager has the most critical role in rescuing a runaway project. This person's experience and skills form the foundation of the rescue.

Key Question: Does the project manager have the appropriate experience for your project's scope and size?

With all the project management tasks that must be executed well, it's easy to see why the project manager plays the key role in the success or failure of a project. Still, project managers are often assigned to projects in a haphazard way. In the best case, the project manager should be experienced in managing projects of similar size and scope. If that is not possible, it is extremely important to understand where the deficiencies may lie and prepare a support environment for that project manager to access in times of doubt or trouble.

For example, good technicians are often promoted to project management because they did a good job as a programmer, business analyst, architect, and so on. However, this doesn't always work out because the project management job and the technical job require different sets of competencies. It's like the difference between being the conductor and playing the violin. Good technicians know how to manage their tasks. A good project manager, however, must know how to manage the tasks of other people. Also, the project manager must be more empathetic to people than an individual contributor.

Another example of inappropriate staffing is having a project manager who has only managed a five-person project now manage a twenty five, fifty or one hundred-person project. Different skills and competencies are needed to manage small, medium, and large projects. The key competency is in the project manager's communication skills. With larger groups, the project manager needs more team meetings and good status reporting. To manage larger projects, the project manager must have more of a rigid structure in place in order to accurately provide a fact-based answer to the ever-present "Where is the project?" question from the project sponsor. Also, with larger groups, the project manager must be able to motivate managers instead of individuals and be a manager of managers, which requires yet a different competency. All of these factors must be considered when selecting a project manager in order to prevent the project from failing because of an inexperienced leader.

Project Sponsor

After the project manager, the project sponsor has the second most important day-to-day role in the project rescue effort. This person's ability to marshal the appropriate resources is clearly the key skill related to getting the right people on the project.

Key Question: Does the project sponsor have the authority, political clout and the willingness to use them for this type of project?

If the project manager has the key role in the success or failure of a project, then the project sponsor is certainly next in line. The project sponsor must have the authority and political clout to effectively get things done from the business perspective. This is especially important when dealing with projects that cross functional boundaries, which is more of the norm today. Often a project starts with an initial sponsor who is high on the food chain, such as a Vice President. This person does not have the time to be the sponsor for the entire length of the project because of other responsibilities. The project sponsor role is then handed to one of the original sponsor's lieutenants. The new sponsor should also be able to sign off on budgetary items and have ultimate approval and tie-breaking authority when the team cannot reach a consensus on some issue. The new executive sponsor must also have ultimate authority to approve deliverables and expenses.

Project Team

Of course, the project's success is not solely rooted in processes and techniques. The experience and ability of the project team members are critical in getting the project back on track and to ultimate success.

Key Question: Does each team member have the most appropriate experience for their respective role(s)?

Sometimes projects get staffed by the "who is available?" method. This is then justified by the "it will be a good learning experience" theory. In fact, the only lesson that may be learned is that this is the absolute worst way to staff a project. Unfortunately, this staffing method occurs in both the technical team as well as the subject matter expert team. The reasoning behind this method defies all logic. On the business side, the best people within the organization tend to be the people who have the knowledge needed for the project's success—the true subject matter experts. However, because the project is not viewed as "the real job" even though is has extreme strategic importance, functional heads will not release these people to work on the project. Managers often say, "You cannot get Billy and Susie, so I'll give you Crusty, Dusty and Rusty." The problem is that Crusty, Dusty and Rusty probably cannot accurately depict the business processes that need to be done; they are the ones who have been put aside and passed around because they couldn't cut it.

The technical management team often does the same thing. It assigns people that are available regardless of their technical skills (this sometimes applies to external service providers too, so beware). Also, external edicts such as "no new hires" or "no outside consultants" put boundaries around a staffing manager that reduce the number of effective options. Again, the logic is baffling when it comes to a multimillion-dollar, cross-functional project. You cannot expect a technician right out of training to be an expert. The optimal team should have a mixture of experience but never to the detriment of the project's success.

Many troubled projects have compromised on the experience of the technical and subject matter expert team. If the project is important, you've got to put the right people on it.

Quick Acid Tests

Plowing through reams of project data can be a daunting and frustrating task. Likewise, trying to scratch around for project data when it appears none exists can be even more frustrating. This area describes some quick tests you can conduct using key project data. If the data does not exist, the project manager should be able to look back in the status reports and get some idea of how to complete the data chart. If no data is being collected, start collecting it immediately! Each of these tests is designed to give you an initial clue that a project is in trouble. More due diligence is needed to discover the root cause(s) and take corrective action(s).

Work Ratio Model

How much work is left to complete the project? Are there enough resources to do that work? Often, runaway projects have more work to do for the number of people working on the project.

Key Question: Are there enough resources to complete the remaining effort?

The first rule of successful project management requires that the work effort not exceed the resources allocated to the project. This planning rule, expressed as a ratio of remaining work effort to the amount of resource hours, is called the *Work Ratio*. During all phases of the project and at any time in the project phase, this ratio must be less than or equal to 1. If the work ratio ever exceeds 1, the project is in jeopardy.

$$1 \geq \frac{\text{Remaining work effort (estimate to complete)}}{\text{Number of resources*work hours per week*number of remaining weeks to the scheduled end date}}$$

In this model, the work hours per week may not be the standard 40 hours; it may be less and usually is. It must be adjusted to accurately reflect resource productivity (for example, 80 percent) and availability of the resources (for example, 4 hours per day = 50 percent). An 8-hour day at 80 percent productivity and 50 percent availability yields 3.2 hours available for work (8*.50*.80). As this ratio becomes greater than 1, the initial tendency is to have people work more hours per week, starting the proverbial "death march" of the project.

Task Starts

Tracking the number of tasks that have been started versus the number of tasks planned to have been started produces some revealing trends.

Key Question: Is the number of project task starts going according to plan?

With properly planned projects, the number of planned starts plotted over time should resemble a smooth line rising on an approximate 45-degree angle from left to right (see Figure 4.1). Of course, no project will be an exact 45-degree line, but any planned "bumps" should be defensible by the project manager. Once the project manager plots the actual task starts, the data points should hover around the original "planned line" without excessive deviation. This indicates the project is running according to plan.

With troubled projects, the actual task starts chart will probably shoot up the y-axis and then flatten out (resembling a reverse hockey stick). This indicates that people are opening many new tasks ahead of schedule (see Figure 4.2). The initial reaction from a less-experienced project manager is that it's not a big deal; he or she assumes that the team simply got a better jump on the plan. Although that is certainly a possibility, more likely the team is waiting for others tasks to finish and opened more tasks to keep busy. This creates a problem when the open tasks require rework because some things are wrong.

The project manager will have too many open tasks to manage, a lot of work in progress and no way to know the true status of the project.

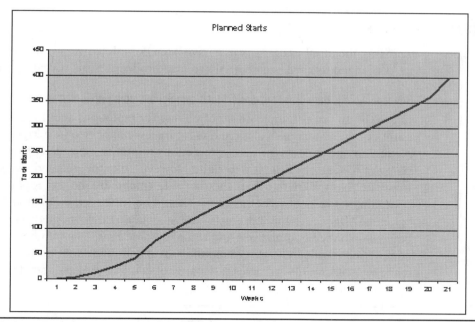

Figure 4.1 Planned task starts over time

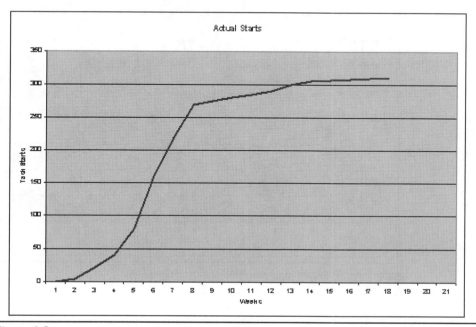

Figure 4.2 Actual task starts over time

Task Completions

Tracking the number of tasks that have been completed versus the number of tasks planned to have been completed also produces some revealing trends.

Key Question: Is the number of project task completions going according to plan?

In a well run project, the number of planned completions should resemble the number of planned tasks chart and lag it by a week or two (see Figure 4.3). Again, no one expects the task completions to plot in a perfectly smooth line rising at 45 degrees from left to right. However, like the planned starts, any irregular "bumps" in the chart should be defensible by the project manager.

Again, the respective completions should be small variances along the "planned" lines. Troubled projects almost always show a huge disconnect between planned completions and actual completions. The number of actual completions tends to hover around the x-axis and then shoot up (resembling a hockey stick). This indicates tasks are not being completed (see Figure 4.4).

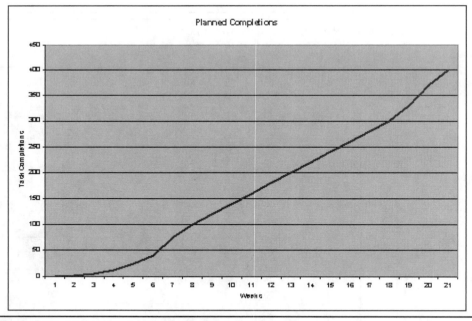

Figure 4.3 Planned task completions over time

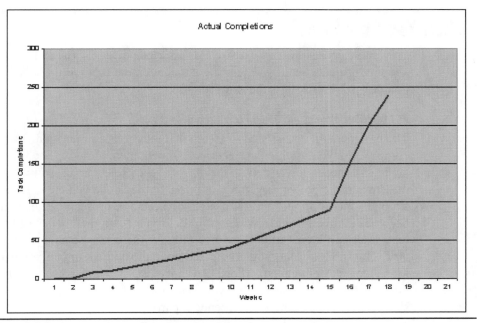

Figure 4.4   Actual task completions over time

There are several reasons why this occurs, but the result is usually the same—capital is being tied up in unfinished tasks and the budget is eroding at a frenetic pace. This is true only if the task durations are all relatively short and of the same magnitude. Capital will be tied up if you have long-running tasks. It is very difficult to gauge the status of a long-running task. Usually the person performing a long-running task does not realize the completion is in trouble until it is too late. A rule of thumb is to limit task durations to no more than 80 hours. The smooth time phasing of the tasks will then yield the type of curve described previously.

Again, the risk here is the huge number of open tasks and the uncertainty of their completion. With all this work in progress, there is no telling the true status of the project. The project manager may know the project is probably behind, but there is no way to tell the extent.

When You Should Ask

Preventive care is the best way to avoid serious disease. The same is true for keeping projects healthy. The project management method that corresponds to a doctor's checkup is the project audit.

Key Question: How often should I conduct a project audit?

The project audit is designed to assure that the project's management activities comply with your defined project management methodology. The focus of project audits is to accurately ascertain the status of the project and recommend corrective measures if the project is getting into trouble. It is not a vehicle to be used to punish anyone. Once a project audit is used to persecute or prosecute, the audit process becomes ineffective and a waste of time. Project team members will band together to hide any problems and the project will take the primrose path right over the cliff. The audit criteria should be based upon the defined organizational Project Management Methodology. If one does not exist, of course you have a fundamental problem that most probably got you in trouble in the first place. These audits should be conducted by an independent party—typically the project officer or a respected project manager without a vested interest in the project.

The Four Types of Audits

Different audits are required for different stages of a project. No audit type is more or less important than the other audit types.

- **Project startup audit**   This audit is performed at project initiation. The purpose is to review project planning and management at the front-end of the project. The objective is to ensure that, from a project management perspective, everything is in place for a successful project start.

- **Project periodic audit**   The purpose of this audit is to ensure that the project is progressing according to your project management methodology. This audit should be performed at least once every three months, depending upon the size of the project.

- **Full process audit**   This audit provides an extensive review of the project, identifies current or potential problems, and suggests specific corrective actions. This audit should be performed at the request of the technical or business unit management because of the impact on the project team resources in the data gathering activities. The intent of this audit is to determine the current status of the project and assess the project team and their ability to achieve the project goals. This audit is normally performed when evidence suggests that a project may be in jeopardy.

- **Post audit**   This audit is intended to identify what went well during the project and to pinpoint areas for future improvement. A full, written report should be produced at the completion of the review. In addition, the project manager should produce a "lessons learned" report.

Where the Answers Reside—The Project Notebook

Good project management practices dictate the creation and maintenance of a project notebook. The term "project notebook" may be misleading. It is not a three-ring binder sitting on the project manager's credenza. Rather, it is a series of files, both hard copy and electronic, that provides ready and easy access to all the defining documents and status reports for the project.

Key Question: How complete is the project notebook? Does it have all the necessary components with a sufficient level of detail?

Without a project notebook it is very difficult to gather information that may be needed to respond to a management query, to prepare for a status meeting, or to quickly answer questions that need an immediate response. The project notebook provides the main source of input for your project audit. The team will find it easier if the project notebook is established at the onset of the project and maintained on a weekly basis. The project notebook should contain the following sections:

- **Project charter**   All versions of the project charter should be included. If there is more than one version of an approved project charter, it should be accompanied by a change request.
- **Project plans**   Maintained on a weekly basis.
- **External agreements**   All agreements should be present in this section, including the nondisclosure agreements, services agreements, proposals, the proposal acceptance, and letters of intent.
- **Time sheets**   For each project team member.
- **Requirements definition**   All requirement definition documents and a requirements log.
- **Analysis documents**   All analysis documents: Unified Modeling Language (UML), Information Engineering (IE), Structured Analysis and Design, simple flowcharting, and so on.

- **Design documents**   All design documents and a design standards documentation memo.

- **Test plans, cases, and results**   All formal test plans, test cases, and expected results should be traceable to the requirements log.

- **Deliverable acceptances**   Acceptance forms for all deliverables as specified in the latest valid project charter along with the deliverable acceptance log.

- **Implementation documents**   All implementation documentation must be maintained in the project notebook including the transition plan to production, the staff requirements to maintain the project, data conversion requirements and system administration documentation.

- **Status reports**   All weekly and monthly status reports.

- **Risk management**   All minutes from the monthly risk management sessions.

- **Issues management**   The issues management log and minutes from the issues discussion meetings.

- **Change management**   All documentation regarding change management including the change management log and all individual change requests that have been submitted whether they have been approved or not.

- **Software configuration management**   Specifies the standards, tools, and protocols used to manage moving the project into production.

- **Miscellaneous**   All other noteworthy items such as meeting minutes when decisions affecting the project have been made.

Closing Perspective

This chapter listed several questions to ask to detect the symptoms of a runaway project. Additionally, we discussed principles of good project management. It is important to review a project at the onset, periodically and at completion to help you understand if the project is on course or headed for trouble. Concentrate on the project management process and the skills of the project team for a successful conclusion.

PART II

Assessment

## CHAPTER 5

Diagnosing the Situation

In the previous chapter we listed questions you can ask if you suspect you have a runaway project. We also discussed some basic principles of good project management on the planned path to successful completion. In this chapter, we discuss what you should do with the answers to those questions, how to interpret those answers, how to get to the root cause(s) of your runaway project and we suggest ways to get the project back on track. It should come as no surprise that we will structure the diagnosis and prescription around those good project management principles.

Admit You Have a Problem

As with any problem, the first step is to admit you have the problem. This step is one of the two hardest steps to take in the process. It takes a lot of wisdom, vision, courage, political clout and probably job security to admit that a highly visible, mission critical project is out of control. Some project sponsors and IT management people are like bad investors: they stick with the dogs (projects that are losing money) instead of cutting their losses. They think they can spend their way out of a bad project—throwing good money after bad.

Don't get bamboozled by optimistic opinion. This frequently occurs because many people say, "I'm this close. I just need one more month." This belief tends to have no grounding in fact and that last month never comes. If your team is still waiting for that last month, chances are they are only hoping it will come. It is not coming.

Stop the Project

Once you admit to having the problem, it's time to put a tourniquet on the bleeding. By continuing, you are burning more hours and cost against the project and you really don't know where you are going. Out of all the steps, stopping the project is the hardest and the scariest. Here is where that wisdom, vision, courage, political clout and job security will be tested. You will be challenged and presented with countless reasons why the project needs to roll on (remember there's only one more month to go!). Many will point to the considerable amount of money and time already spent on the project. They will fear that stopping the project will stop the momentum. This may appear to be true because you may be at a point when some tasks and deliverables are actually being completed or being declared completed. If you're working with a vendor, it may threaten to pull its team out because you are stopping the project and you fear that all that project knowledge will walk out the door. This may be true, but it will give you an insight into your relationship with that vendor. You probably don't want a partner that is there only during the good times (in other words it is getting paid regularly). You want a partner that has a vested interest in the project's success and your success as well.

However, if you don't stop, the results down the line will be even scarier. Because of the accumulation of time, cost, and aggravation, the project could reach its breaking point and collapse under its own weight; you have no choice but to stop. If you don't rescue the project, someone else (usually higher than you on the food chain) could come in and tell you enough is enough and that it is time to stop the hemorrhaging of money. Stop, replan, and then decide how or whether to move forward.

Conduct the Project Audit

Now that you're past the two most difficult, politically charged steps, it's time to conduct the assessment phase of the project audit, using the key questions from the previous chapter. We have also included a useful audit checklist in Chapter 18. Remember, the intent of the audit is to help you uncover the root cause(s) of the runaway project. It should not be used for ammunition to punish the guilty party. You will probably find that there is no guilty party; rather, most members of the extended project team have had a hand in the decimation of the project. If you use the audit as an execution tool, you will never again get the opportunity to use this critical tool for discerning project problems.

Often, the best way to conduct the audit is to use an outside service provider. By utilizing a trusted outside auditor, you send the message that finding the answers is important. After all, you are spending "real money" to do the audit. Also, the outside auditor usually has no political baggage to threaten the project team. The auditor should be well versed in creating an open, comfortable environment that is conducive to open communication, honesty and trust. No matter who conducts the audit, it's important to utilize different methods for assessment. A combination of individual interviews and facilitated sessions usually works well. Try to avoid the formal questionnaire because you will be asking the respondent to interpret the meaning of the questions. Face-to-face communication should always be your first choice. In the facilitated sessions, try to group the participants in peer groups. Conduct separate sessions for the technical team and the subject matter experts. To facilitate open communication, separate the management team from their respective worker-bee team. Finally, when documenting the results, try not to attribute any remarks or quotes to an individual.

Review the Project Audit Results

Once you have completed the assessment phase of the project audit, it's time to review the results and take corrective action. We'll use the key questions from the previous chapter as a guide for the diagnosis and prescription of our patient.

Key Question: What was the actual time spent on each task versus the original estimate?

You may find that the project team is not tracking actual hours spent on each task. This is a serious issue not only for the current project, but also for your IT group's ability to estimate future projects. There are a couple of ways to deal with this situation. First, the project team must understand that from this point forward, the effort associated with all tasks are to be tracked on a weekly basis and reported to the project manager. There will be initial resistance, but the team will get into the routine and realize the time associated with tracking the task efforts is actually very minimal.

From an organizational change perspective, this should be done with a compliance strategy—or "tell it" not "sell it." There is no time to wait for each team member to be sold on the benefits of tracking hours to tasks. You must make it clear that there is no choice in adhering to this practice as long as the project team member wishes to remain employed. Managing large projects is dependent upon the ability to manage variances—both positive and negative—and you cannot do that well without weekly updates on the effort.

Second, if feasible, go back to the weekly status reports and try to associate approximate hours for each task. Even though you won't get an accurate picture of the task effort, you will get an approximation that will allow you to determine if the remaining estimates are reasonable. If you cannot find the previous status reports or they do not give you the sufficient details of the tasks that were started and completed, consider interviewing the team members to get their recollections of the expended efforts. You can get a great insight to how the project got out of control once you understand how the project's hours have been spent. With this information in hand, you should be able to tell if the team members are working on the tasks they had been assigned. You may discover that the team members are working on other non-project related tasks such as current system maintenance, answering questions about items outside the project scope, working on tasks missing in the plan or making undocumented "little" changes. Your goal is to verify the remaining effort to successfully complete the project. Knowing the reasonability of the estimate to complete is a key factor. Once you verify what happened and why the variances between the original task estimate and the actual task effort occurred you will know to what degree the project is out of control.

Key Question: How complete is the project charter? Does it have all the necessary components with a sufficient level of detail?

The project charter is the defining document for the entire project. It should represent a snapshot of the project's logical scope, expected deliverables, cost, schedule and affected organizations. In the previous chapter, we gave a list of sections that should be included in a good project charter. With runaway projects, you will find various degrees of completeness with respect to project charters. In the worst case scenario you will not find a project charter at all. If you find there is no project charter, you should assemble the project management team (the project sponsor, project manager and application architect) and construct a new charter. By creating the charter you will get great insight to the necessity of the project. Getting concurrence on the scope, budget and schedule and then documenting these items will bring the project back into focus. Often, runaway projects no longer look like their original intention. Verifying today's project with the originally funded project will help people understand why the project got away.

If the project charter does exist but in varying levels of detail, you should again have the project management team come together to complete the missing or deficient sections so you can get a clear consensus of the project's logical scope, expected deliverables, cost, schedule and affected organizations. By completing the charter you will receive the same benefits as you do when creating a charter. In either case, you are closer to making a critical decision—let the project continue or pull the plug.

Key Question: How current is the project charter?

As we mentioned in the previous chapter, every time there is a change to the project, that change should be reflected in the charter. You may find you do have a project charter, but it is the original document probably used to justify the funding of the project. In this case it is extremely important to bring the project charter up-to-date to reflect the most current snapshot of the project's scope and business case. Again, it is time to assemble the project management team to review all documentation that may have affected the project's logical scope, expected deliverables, cost, schedule and affected organizations. Some places to look include

- Project change requests
- Interview notes
- Facilitated session notes
- Status meeting minutes
- General meeting minutes
- Correspondence
- E-mail
- Project notebook
- Change requests that may have never made it into the change management process

Once these project artifacts have been reviewed, the team should begin the process of reconstructing the project charter. Once the charter has been completed, it should again go through the approval process in order to gain consensus among the extended project team. After the new charter receives approval, you should put a policy in place that all scope changes go through the change management process and that process is not final until the project charter is appropriately updated. After the project management team has gone through this tedious reconstruction process, you will not have much opposition to this policy, if any at all.

Another way to ensure the project charter remains current is to have the entire project team read it once a week. Encourage the project team members to communicate any changes or obsolescence they see in the charter to the project manager so the project charter can then be updated via the change control process. This practice will also produce another beneficial result in that the project team will remain focused on the items within the charter and therefore the tasks they need to accomplish as well.

Key Question: Does the project plan exist?

Hopefully, at first glance, this question seems absurd. We've already stated the project plan is the most important tool for managing a project. However, if you find your runaway project is sailing along without a formal, documented project plan, you are in the deepest hole from which to climb. Don't panic—there is a road to recovery.

First, interview the technical team members and find out what they're doing. Those hours are piling up so something must be getting effort expended against it. Ask each team member to lay out their activities and tasks, hours expended on each task and their estimate to complete their open tasks. This will at least give you an idea of what has been done and maybe even what needs to be done.

Next, get a copy of a project template that includes all activities and tasks. The first place to look is you development methodology. If you do not have a development methodology, check with your on-site employees and consultants. Someone somewhere has a project template stashed away. It may not even be a good one, but it is better than trying to cobble a plan from scratch. Rebuild the plan with all tasks. Be sure to account for all deliverables in the project charter. Most importantly, make sure you have reasonable and realistic estimates for all outstanding tasks. This is not the time for planned heroics. Your goal here is to quantify the effort needed to complete the project. By knowing the hours needed for each task as well as the task dependencies, you can derive the cost and schedule. With this information in hand, you and your enterprise can make an informed decision with respect to stopping the project or continuing to move forward.

Key Question: Are all the tasks accounted for in the plan?

Most likely, if a plan exists and your project is still running out of control, your project plan is missing several activities and tasks. This tends to happen when project plans are built without the benefit of a project template or a methodology task plan. Most of these incomplete plans tend to have a fairly comprehensive list of technical tasks, but they also tend to miss the tasks associated with project management and quality management. The project gets into trouble when new tasks are discovered and added to the plan without utilizing the change control process. Often the project manager is embarrassed about missing these tasks and tries to hide the omission. The problem gets worse because there is no explanation or audit trail of how the additional hours got into the plan. This is a classic example of the infamous scope creep.

The path out of this mess is very similar to the path that must be taken when there is no project plan, but not as severe. Again, try to find a copy of a project template in your organization. That will help identify the missing tasks and their associated dependencies. Next, with the IT team, review the completed and in-progress activities and tasks to determine the hours expended on each of those tasks. Using this historical data, determine the reasonable and realistic estimate to complete all open tasks—those that were in the plan and the missing tasks that you had to add to the plan.

Finally, check that you accounted for all deliverables in the project charter. Again, your goal is to quantify the effort needed to complete the project so you can derive the cost and schedule.

Key Question: Are the task estimates based upon a known history or are they just guesses?

Probably the most difficult function in building a project plan is estimating the work effort. Most people tend to estimate on a "personal experience basis." Another term for this is "my guess." Personal experience, dead-reckoning or guesstimating work well if the estimator has the appropriate baseline definition documents and is doing the work personally. Quite often in a runaway project, a senior architect will have the responsibility for the technical estimate. This person tends to have a great deal of experience in performing the technical tasks to be estimated and produces an estimate based upon that experience. Unfortunately, the technical team tends to be less experienced than the architect—some times far less experienced. This results in aggressive estimates that do not get revisited during the project, which leads to a negative variance in time and effort. Slowly but steadily the project gets farther and farther behind. Left unchecked, more and more time and money are poured into the project and you have the classic runaway project.

An even worse scenario exists related to estimating has led to the demise of the well-intended project. In this case, the project team did all the right things and produced a defensible estimate of the work effort and subsequent schedule and budget. However, either the budget or the schedule or both was unacceptable to the project's executive sponsor, for real or perceived reasons. To make the project more acceptable, the estimate was reduced by an arbitrary amount without reducing the scope of the project. Unfortunately, these team members were only fooling themselves. The work is the work. Not surprisingly the project falls behind and is more in line with the original estimated effort, budget and schedule.

Once you get the plan's activities, tasks and dependencies in place, the proper way to estimate your project is to use a proven development methodology or a set of proven project plan templates with experience-based work effort estimates as the initial guide. These estimates are only a start to your estimating process. Working with the project team, determine the best case, worst case and most likely case as described in Table 5.1.

Task/Component	Best Case (BC)	Most Probable Case (MP)	Worst Case (WC)	Weighted Average (WA)	Standard Deviation (SD)
Totals	38	95	171	99	
4.0 Design phase					
4.1 Application architecture report					
Define physical architecture	2	5	9	5.20	1.17
Define operating system requirements	2	5	9	5.20	1.17
Define communication requirements	2	5	9	5.20	1.17
Define external application system interfaces	2	5	9	5.20	1.17
4.2 Data Base Design Report					
Define physical schema	2	5	9	5.20	1.17
Define population & conversion plan	2	5	9	5.20	1.17
Build test environment	2	5	9	5.20	1.17
Build production environment	2	5	9	5.20	1.17
4.3 Module Design Specifications					
Define module specifications	2	5	9	5.20	1.17
Reusable code design	2	5	9	5.20	1.17
Reusable code matching	2	5	9	5.20	1.17
Design inspection	2	5	9	5.20	1.17
Design rework	2	5	9	5.20	1.17
4.4 Test Plan Approach Report					
Define test plan strategy	2	5	9	5.20	1.17
Define test plan WBS	2	5	9	5.20	1.17
Define test plan personnel	2	5	9	5.20	1.17
Define test environment	2	5	9	5.20	1.17
Define expected results	2	5	9	5.20	1.17
Define test data	2	5	9	5.20	1.17

Table 5.1   Tasks and Components

Start by putting the template estimates in the Most Probably Case column and adjust it according to the experience of the planned resource. Next, working with the IT team, add the best case and worst case scenarios. Risk factors such as level of specification, physical resource availability, geographic location of the extended team, and so on will help derive the best case and worst case scenarios. Next calculate the weighted average using the following formula:

$$Weighted\ Average = (BC + (MP * 4) + WC) / 6$$

This gives the greatest weight to the most probable case, giving a 67 percent probability of the weighted average falling within +/–1 sigma. The Weighted Average represents probability that the task can be completed at or less than the Weighted Average. Of course, the real value here is the variance—the greater the variance, the greater the uncertainty of the estimator. The variance is what you want to reduce. The lower the variance the greater the estimator's confidence in the estimate and the more stable the overall project estimate will be. Use these weighted averages as the task estimate. Finally, refine the estimate by computing the standard deviation of each task using the following formula:

$$Standard\ Deviation = (((WA - BC)2 + (WC - WA)2) / 6).5$$

Review any components having a standard deviation greater than 2. This indicates a low level of requisite knowledge for that task and the worst case estimate should be used for that task instead of the weighted average. The new estimate for the project would be the sum of the refined task estimates.

Key Question: Is each team member working only on the specifically assigned tasks in the plan?

This situation is the silent killer of projects. For runaway projects, the project management team tends to assume that the project team is working on the tasks that are in the plan. However, on troubled projects, project team members very often are working on other tasks, even those outside the scope of the project, without informing the project manager. There are two primary causes for this problem. First, the plan is missing tasks needed to complete the project. We covered this scenario earlier in the chapter. The other problem occurs when your project is "sharing" team members, intentionally or unintentionally. A project team member working on two projects simultaneously works well when the two project managers are communicating with each other. Projects have heavy activity periods and lighter activity periods. By avoiding coinciding heavy activity periods, or at least planning for coinciding heavy activity periods, you can mitigate the impact to your project. Unfortunately, project managers tend not to communicate with other project managers that are not directly in the extended project team. This puts the onus on the team member to prioritize the competing responsibilities. More often than not, that decision is not communicated to the affected project manager and the trouble begins.

One example of the unintended sharing of a team member occurs when a project team member has maintenance and break-fix responsibilities for the production system. This team member was chosen to be on the development project because of extensive knowledge of the current system. However, that legacy production system is still working, still breaking, and still requires attention. Also, this key person may be fulfilling ad hoc requests from the business organization.

The best way to determine if your team is not working on the tasks in the plan is to track each team member's effort each week. By having each member track hours expended by task, you will quickly see if they are working on missing tasks or tasks outside the project. If team members cannot account for a full work week or the number of hours you expected for that week, you can assume they are working on non-project related tasks. In any case, you will need to start negotiating with the competing manager to make sure you get the time you need for your project. If you cannot achieve satisfactory results in the negotiations, then relieve that team member from as much responsibility as you can or remove that person from the project. If you let the situation linger, you will slowly kill your chances for success.

Key Question: Is the plan current with respect to the work effort and time to complete the project?

As with the project charter, the currency of the project plan is essential for a successful project completion. It is extremely important to keep the project plan up-to-date to reflect the most current status of the project's progress. If you find the only project plan you have is the one that was used for project funding, you will need to build the "go-forward" plan to help you track the project. Again, it is time to assemble the project team to bring the plan up-to-date. You will perform the necessary subset of the activities described previously to complete the plan's remaining activities, tasks and dependencies with their associated estimates.

Once the plan is recast, you must put a policy in place that requires the collection and posting of hours expended by task and estimates-to-complete open tasks to the project plan on a weekly basis. In addition to the benefits we've already mentioned, by taking this weekly inventory, the manager will now be able to recast the plan each week, get insight into estimate-to-actual variances and manage those variances. With this knowledge, the project manager will be able to raise issues in a proactive mode rather than react to schedule slippage and cost overruns. If your project manager is unable or unwilling to manage the plan on a weekly basis, then it's time for a change in project management.

Key Question: Does the project manager have the appropriate experience for your project's scope and size?

The lightning rod for a runaway project is the project manager. Although we have given many scenarios in which the project management process had been broken, you must examine whether you have the right person in the project manager role. The overall question you have to ask is "Does your project manager possess the competencies, experience, personality and management style necessary for the success of your project?" With runaway projects, all four of these areas are important. You can no longer afford to take a chance on a project manager that may not work out. If you answer no to any of these four areas it's time to make a change. The success of the project hinges on the right leadership—especially the project manager.

If you decide a change in project manager is needed, make the change immediately but be careful how you make the change. If the project manager is a valued contributor who was put in a bad situation, you need to handle the change with some style and grace. Explain to the outgoing project manager that his or her contributions are valued and he or she needs to look upon this experience as a learning opportunity. Try to keep that person on the project as a team leader where he or she can learn from a more experienced project manager and perhaps perform in the role successfully in the future. On the other hand, if the project manager was just incompetent and does not have a track record of success in your company, make the transition swiftly and cleanly.

Now that you have decided to replace the project manager, what do you look for in the replacement? The most important factor is experience. Look for a project manager that has successfully implemented projects of similar type, size and scope. For example, if your runaway project is a Customer Relationship Management (CRM) project, look for a project manager that has implemented that particular CRM software suite at a company that has a similar number of customers as your company. Try to get a project manager that has managed projects with a similar staff size. Remember it takes a different set of competencies to manage a five person, twenty-five person, fifty person or one-hundred person project. Different skills and competencies are needed to manage small, medium, and large projects. Most important, you now need someone who has experience in rescuing runaway projects on top of these other skills. Your new project manager must also fit the soft skills requirements of your company with respect to personality and leadership style. You don't necessarily need a true match. In some cases you may need a real driver in a laid-back culture. You just need to understand the implications of these soft skill matches and mismatches. The project manager must also have the ability to deal with the maddening level of detail required to drive a project plan. Often, a project administrator may be required on larger projects to handle the project accounting chores for the project manager. Project managers are expensive pilots and you don't want them being bookkeepers. You need to get a project manager that satisfies all of these factors. The project has already failed once—it's highly unlikely you will be given a third chance at success if it fails again.

Key Question: Does the project sponsor have the authority, political clout and the willingness to use them for this type of project?

If your project manager has the right stuff, the next place you need to look for problems is your project sponsor. Runaway projects sometimes have project sponsors that are not qualified to be in that position. Sometimes they are put in this role to just fill a funding requirement to name a project sponsor, but they are absentee sponsors. In other cases, they are thrust into the position because the initial project sponsor is too busy or has moved on to another initiative. If you're having trouble with your project sponsor, it is probably because that person lacks the authority or political clout to effectively get things done from the business perspective, or is unwilling to use the necessary authority and clout.

You have two choices when dealing with an ineffective project sponsor— shore up that person's authority or replace that person with someone who has the authority and clout. The first alternative is usually more difficult to do, but it usually achieves better results. However, do not use this alternative if your current project sponsor carries a very negative reputation that would require too much effort to repair, detracting from the goal of getting the project back on track. If it's a case of authority, get it for that person. If it's a case of judgment, replace the project sponsor.

Finding a project sponsor replacement will let you know exactly how important the project is to your company. If you are struggling to get a replacement and you are not getting senior management support, you can deduce that successful completion of your project is not high on the company priority list. This should weigh heavily as you decide to continue on or permanently stop the project. If your company decides to continue, insist the project sponsor has the ultimate authority to approve all project-related deliverables and expenses.

Key Question: Does each team member have the most appropriate experience for their respective role(s)?

After reviewing the suitability of your project manager and project sponsor, it's time to review each member of the project team. In each case you need to determine if the project team member has the appropriate skills and experience for their respective role(s) on the project. Availability can no longer be the staffing criteria. With a runaway project, you must eliminate all weak links. It's time to jettison Crusty, Dusty and Rusty because your best recovery plans will fail if you do not have the right people to execute them.

Replacing the inappropriate IT team members is easier than replacing the inappropriate business subject matter experts. You have more external options if your attempts to get the right internal people are not successful. You can hire new employees or secure the services of consultants. Just get the right people.

On the business side, the best people for your project are within the organization. These people have the knowledge of how the business is run and therefore have the knowledge of how the system should run—the true subject matter experts. You need to sharpen your negotiation and selling skills to pull these people onto the project. You will need to know exactly how much time they need to commit and when they need to commit that time. Now that you have a complete, reasonable project plan, you can provide those answers. You will also need to articulate the benefit of having those people on your project. People are leery of joining a runaway project. If you are unable to secure these people, you have a difficult, but not impossible, external alternative. You can get consultants that have implemented packaged software or have industry experience, but nothing replaces your company's true subject matter experts.

With runaway projects you cannot compromise on the experience of the technical and subject matter expert team. If the project is important, you've got to put the right people on it.

Key Question: Are there enough resources to complete the remaining effort?

In the previous chapter we discussed the work ratio—the planning rule comparing the remaining work effort to the amount of remaining resource hours. Runaway projects not only have huge amounts of expended effort, but they also tend to have huge amounts of remaining effort as well. When you discover your work ratio is much greater than 1, you probably have a project that is out of balance. There is a delicate balance within all projects of scope, schedule and resources. In a well-balanced project, the scope, schedule and resource blocks are all level like a child's mobile (see Figure 5.1). When you add pressure to one of the blocks, either one or both of the other blocks is out of balance and needs an adjustment. For example if you add more scope to the project without increasing the resources, the schedule will not be made. Likewise, if you cut the schedule without increasing resources you cannot deliver the scope. You must keep the project in balance if you expect a successful completion.

Key Questions: Is the number of project task starts going according to plan? and Is the number of project task completions going according to plan?

The negative answers to these two key questions are tightly coupled. When you have a project team that starts rolling along, the team members will not patiently wait to start a task while approvals for their respective current tasks are pending. Therein lies the most probable problem—approvals are taking too long or they are not coming at all. This creates a high-risk impact to your project regarding rework. The more open tasks you have waiting for approval, the more potential errors you have. Fixing these errors can have a huge impact on your project, especially if you did not plan a significant number of hours for rework.

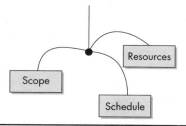

Figure 5.1   Project balance

A good analogy comes from a manufacturing model. Your work in progress (WIP) continues to build. Your capital is being tied-up in WIP. If you have a quality control problem with that WIP, your unplanned costs will soar as your unfinished inventory soars. It's the same with your runaway project. You have a large number of unfinished tasks that may have a quality issue. If there is a lot of rework to be done, your budget will erode at a very fast rate.

Key Question: How often should I conduct a project audit?

If you are conducting your first project audit as a reaction to your runaway project, you have been part of the problem. For normal projects, you should conduct an audit at project inception, then once a quarter and then at project completion. For runaway projects, your current audit replaces the project inception audit. Conduct audits every other month until you are convinced the project is back on track. Then you can fall back to the once-a-quarter schedule.

In any case, there should be a formal project review with the executive sponsor and the senior project management team every month. Remember these audits and reviews are for early problem detection and correction or prevention. Avoid the instinct to use them as weapons of punishment.

Key Question: How complete is the project notebook? Does it have all the necessary components with a sufficient level of detail?

Discovering you have a skimpy or missing project notebook gives you great insight into the ability and attitude of your project manager. Good project management practices dictate the creation and maintenance of a project notebook. If your project manager is unable or unwilling to do so, it's time for a replacement.

The easiest way to fix your immediate problem is to re-create the project notebook. Using the sections described in the previous chapter, find as many of the project artifacts as you can and complete the sections of the notebook. From an on-going perspective, insist the project manager keep the notebook current. You can verify the contents at each project audit.

Closing Perspective

In this chapter, we explored the questions from the previous chapter that can be used to detect the symptoms of a runaway project. We also provided corrective actions you can take to get the project back on track. All of this information can be divided into two major categories. First is the management process. If you have any hope of getting your runaway project back on track, you must employ a strong project management discipline. These project management methods, techniques, and supporting infrastructure are essential to creating your recovery plan. Compromising here may provide temporary relief, but you will soon find yourself back in trouble, maybe even to a greater degree.

The second category is people. You must have people with the appropriate competencies, skills, experience and attitude for the respective role(s) they play on the project. You can deploy the best processes and the greatest recovery plan ever devised, but if you do not have the people to execute and deliver, all you have are wonderful theoretical processes and plans. This is no time to compromise on staff and hope people can rise to the occasion. You will not get a third chance to get this project done.

## CHAPTER 6

Risk Management

Since you don't know what you don't know, it is virtually impossible to remove all possible risks from a project. This is not intended to be a defeatist attitude in anyway. Our objective in recognizing this reality is not only to work harder to mitigate known risks, but also to build a risk management strategy that can deal with unforeseen events.

A risk management strategy also involves balancing the costs of defining and building risk mitigation strategies and contingency plans with the benefits of avoiding a specific risk—when evaluated against probability of occurrence and impact to the project.

Risks can overwhelm a project for several reasons, including the following:

- Risks were inadequately identified.
- Mitigation strategies were not correctly defined.
- Mitigation strategies were not correctly implemented.
- Actual project status was not reported correctly.
- Responsibilities were unclear.

Invoking a project rescue intervention implies that at least one of the project risks has occurred. This chapter presents a methodology and framework for reworking the original project risk assessment so that it will be more effective during the rescue process. The next chapter examines specific risk factors and how to deal with them.

Basic Process

Chapter 3 described the risk management process as one of several management threads that started at the beginning of the project and continued to its very end—including post-launch support. Table 6.1 identifies some key objectives and questions that the risk management process addresses.

Objectives/Questions	Why It's Important
How does the organization want to deal with risk going forward?	Determines the strategy for dealing with risks on the project. Establishes the acceptable tradeoffs for dealing with risks. Also identifies the level of risk that worries the project sponsors.
What needs to be done to avoid the risk from occurring?	Identifies how to avoid risks on the project (i.e. mitigation).
What happens when a risk occurs?	Identifies how to deal with risks that are realized (i.e. contingency).

Table 6.1   Risk Management Objectives

The risk management thread consists of the six phases shown in Figure 6.1 that are intended to define a strategy, identify the risks to the project, and document how to proceed with each risk.

A brief introduction to each phase in the risk management process is given here and then described in more detail in the subsections that follow:

- **Risk management strategy**   The risk management strategy identifies the criteria used to identify, evaluate, and mitigate risks. It also identifies the project sponsor's approach for dealing with risks.

- **Risk discovery**   A process used to build a catalog of risks facing the project in the future. During a project rescue, this involves reviewing the original list and enhancing it.

- **Risk evaluation and details**   A process that involves inspecting each risk and providing additional details including probability of occurrence and impact to the project.

- **Risk mitigation**   Defines how to avoid each risk or at least reduce its impact. The strategy phase identifies the criteria used to select the risks for this analysis.

- **Risk reporting**   Ongoing process to review the status of each risk in the assessment list and to produce a scorecard or dashboard for management reporting.

- **Risk review**   Inspect the entire list of project risks to determine if specific items should be removed or new ones should be inserted into the risk assessment list. In the latter case, the other phases of the risk management process are re-invoked to provide relevant details.

The risk management phases are split across the project rescue framework as shown in Table 6.2. Notice that risk management is not completed in the planning phase of the project. It has to stay in front of the project team and the project manager throughout the project. Risk management does not end.

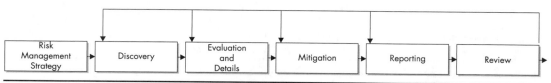

Figure 6.1   Risk management phases

	Risk Management Strategy	Risk Discovery	Risk Evaluation and Details	Risk Mitigation	Risk Reporting	Risk Review
1.0 Assessment	X	X	X			
2.0 Intervention Planning		X	X	X	X	X
3.0 Intervention Execution		X	X	X	X	X
4.0 Post-Intervention Review					X	X

Table 6.2   Cross-Reference of Risk Management Phases to Project Life Cycle Phases

Risk Management Strategy

A risk management strategy should have been adopted at the start of the project, but the fact that a project rescue intervention is needed suggests that one or more risks were not effectively mitigated. The 1.0 Assessment phase of the project rescue intervention program provides an opportunity to review the original strategy, potentially determine the deficiencies, and to introduce revisions that could be more effective.

Table 6.3 shows some of the questions that need to be answered and why these are relevant for revising the risk management strategy. This strategy ensures that the team is ready to react positively when risks do begin to emerge.

Question	Point of Relevance
What trouble did the project run into?	This is easier to answer than *why* the project got into trouble. The answer is factual. Make sure the new risk management strategy compensates for these facts.
How much flexibility will the executive sponsors support?	Be clear on what can be moved or revised so that the proper tradeoff can be argued for every identified risk.
Is there any movement in the delivery date?	Supports tradeoffs in mitigating risk (for example, more time for testing or review).
What is the organization's tolerance toward risk?	If the organization wants all the risks to be minimized, is it prepared to invest appropriately? If not, what flexibility will it show in the results? You cannot guarantee both.
What is the acceptable budget error tolerance?	If going over budget is a risk factor for the project, what is the acceptable range?

Table 6.3   Questions to Drive the Risk Management Strategy

Risk Discovery

The primary objective in this phase is to build a comprehensive set of risks that are relevant to the project. A wide variety of resources are required as input to this phase. Roles and responsibilities during this process will be discussed later in this chapter, but consider that the person driving these activities needs to be accountable, motivated, and empowered. The best quarterback is the project or rescue manager.

The original list of risks identified for the project is a good place to start this phase. Expect to spend anywhere from an average of one to three days to complete the following activities that will allow the original risk assessment list to be reviewed and augmented:

1. Locate and interview the original risk manager if there was one (asking, for example, the risk manager's opinion on what went wrong).
2. Review and understand the original risk assessment documents.
3. Interview business owners and project sponsors on the level of risk they find unacceptable.
4. Add to the risk assessment based on personal experience.
5. Solicit one-on-one input from the project team members to modify the risk.

Give the option of facilitated sessions. This helps identify risks that may go undetected in a one-on-one environment. Also, we strongly encourage organizing a mixed team of IT and business participants.

6. Solicit one-on-one input from members of the extended project team
7. Manager needs to distribute the list of risks to the core project team and the project sponsors through e-mail, hardcopy, or intranet.
8. Incorporate feedback into the risk assessment list.
9. Finalize the risk assessment list so that each risk is categorized, named, and briefly described.

Past project experiences and industry best practices based on project classification can also provide input into this. Figure 6.2 shows a final format that could be used to capture, categorize, and illustrate potential risk information at the end of this phase.

Risk Category: name 1		
No.	Name	Short Description
No.	Name	Short Description
No.	Name	Short Description

Risk Category: name 2		
No.	Name	Short Description
No.	Name	Short Description
No.	Name	Short Description

Risk Category: name 3		
No.	Name	Short Description
No.	Name	Short Description
No.	Name	Short Description

Figure 6.2   Risk assessment list template

Risk Evaluation and Details

This phase squeezes more information into what is known or assumed about each risk in the assessment list. You want to further identify the risks that are above an acceptable level based on our discussions with the project sponsors.

As a starting point, each risk needs to be augmented with the information in the list that follows. Notice that predefined descriptors are used to qualify the information about the risk. Any consistent legend will do, but we prefer a mnemonic format that provides information at a glance. An alternative numeric scale can be more precise in describing a risk, but it is not always clear what it means (for example, is 1 or 10 good) at a glance:

- **Risk impact**   Use descriptors such as Catastrophic, High, Medium, Low, Annoying.

- **Risk probability**   Use descriptors such as Very High, High, Medium, Low, Very Low.

- **Impact details**   Determine who is impacted by the risk and what will be the financial or business impact if the risk is realized. This information is important for getting buy-in from the project owners and sponsors to invest in mitigation strategies.

The risk should be compared to every outstanding task in the project plan to determine the true impact, cost, and mitigation strategies. Too often, the impact is deduced by dead-reckoning as opposed to factual diligence. A good place to look is in the estimating model of the project plan. We like using the "most likely case," "best case," and "worst case" weighted average method. If you look at the tasks that have a greater standard deviation (that is, a greater unknown,) you probably have a high impact risk associated with it.

Figure 6.3 extends the earlier template with these additional fields of information. This is only one example of a workable format. There are many others that are equally effective in describing this information. The actual format of this deliverable is less important than the knowledge it contains and how accessible it is to the team. This list can be sorted by impact and probability or probability and impact to focus on the critical or largest risks.

Risk Mitigation

The project manager, business owners, and the project sponsor should be clear on the level of risk requiring a mitigation strategy based on risk impact and risk probability. This should be documented, perhaps even on the risk assessment report, to ensure a common understanding of priorities.

Two additional pieces of information need to be added to every risk that meets the criteria established by the project sponsors and team. The first is a mitigation strategy to avoid occurrence of the risk, or to reduce its impact so that the results remain within an acceptable margin. The second piece of information involves accepting that some risks may be realized, regardless of the efforts expended to avoid them, and to also define a contingency strategy that deals with the aftermath of a risk if it occurs.

Risk Category: name 1					
No.	Name	Short Description	Impact	Probability	Impact Details

Risk Category: name 2					
No.	Name	Short Description	Impact	Probability	Impact Details

Risk Category: name 3					
No.	Name	Short Description	Impact	Probability	Impact Details

Figure 6.3 Detailed risk assessment list template

This phase completes the risk assessment by adding the following two additional pieces of information for each risk:

- **Mitigation strategy**   As detailed a strategy description as possible to inhibit occurrence of a risk
- **Contingency if a risk is realized**   A detailed description of the strategy to employ if a risk is realized

The second piece of information (Contingency if a risk is realized) is often not included on projects because its sounds defeatist. It assumes that a risk may not be avoided despite the best efforts of the project team. Experience from the trenches suggests that this bravado is better forgotten. It is prudent to plan a contingency if the unthinkable happens. Figure 6.4 shows a completed version of the template. Notice the summary of the minimum acceptable impact and probability criteria that has been prenegotiated with the project sponsors.

Risk Category: name 1							
No.	Name	Short Description	Impact	Probability	Impact Details	Mitigation Strategy	Contingency

Risk Category: name 2							
No.	Name	Short Description	Impact	Probability	Impact Details	Mitigation Strategy	Contingency

Risk Category: name 3							
No.	Name	Short Description	Impact	Probability	Impact Details	Mitigation Strategy	Contingency

Mimimum Acceptable Impact and Probability

Figure 6.4   Complete risk assessment list template

This list should be shared with the extended project team and needs to be reviewed at regular status meetings.

Risk Reporting

The risk reporting phase is repeated throughout the project life cycle. It is a critical phase and one that is not well done on many projects. The activities and results of this phase directly impact how the project resources respond to risks in an ongoing fashion. This section looks at the critical elements of this phase.

Reporting Objectives

Building the risk management strategy and the risk assessment list is only the first important step in building a sound process. The next step is to have an effective reporting mechanism that satisfies the following objectives:

- A description of how to avoid a risk or stop it from occurring. The project team is the key audience for this information.

- Clarity concerning the potential risks and the costs/benefits of dealing with them. The key audience for this information includes the business owners and the project sponsors.

- An accurate picture of each risk in the assessment list. This information should be shared with anyone who can provide more details and facts about the risks in the list. It also needs to be shared with the extended project team.

Reporting Process

The reporting process for risk management needs to provide information but also result in immediate action if problems are detected. The project manager needs to walk through the risk assessment list and verbally summarize the status of each risk during status meetings. The risk report must also be available to anyone from a central intranet or information store.

By itself, this approach is still limited. It forces the project team to interpret what the project manager really meant through voice tone, word choices, and the intensity of the conversation.

Some preliminary analysis and summarization is helpful in getting action from the project team. The risk assessment needs to stay in front of everyone involved in the project on an ongoing basis in a format that is easier to interpret than a long list. A summary report, dashboard, or scorecard is helpful in summarizing the status of the current risks, and in ensuring that everyone involved in the project knows which risks require immediate attention.

Reporting Format

Remember that the main objective of risk management is to get the right people doing the right things to ensure that risks do not occur. This requires a crisp, clean, straightforward reporting format that summarizes information at an appropriate level to raise alarm and concerns in a timely manner. Format and content are everything in achieving this. A dashboard or scorecard that abides by the following provisions is useful for summarizing the relevant risk information:

- Is the information easy to read and understand?

- Do I need to look in too many places to get an accurate picture of the current risk status?

- Is the information organized so that risk trends can easily be spotted or identified?

- Do the colors tell me what to worry about at a glance? Use basic colors such as red, yellow, and green to convey information. Tones within the colors can be used to indicate severity. Ideally, highlight the risk descriptions in their appropriate colors if you have access to a color printer.

- Ensure that the simple format can be cross-referenced to more detailed information about each risk. Anyone requiring more details should be able to find them in the actual risk assessment report or the status report.

- Keep information relevant, to the point, and to a minimum. Every reported risk on the dashboard should be important enough to demand executive-level attention on a frequent basis.

While the purpose of the risk reporting process is chiefly to identify risks that require attention from the project team, there are some additional political considerations. Providing a dashboard that shows a number of risks in red status will cause alarm that could be considered as finger pointing by some.

It's important to talk with team members and remain sensitive to individual needs and frailties. Perhaps a three-part dashboard that shows the risks that are not currently considered a problem (color green), those that may become a problem (color yellow), and those that require immediate attention (color red) would be useful and less embarrassing.

Figure 6.5 shows a one-page dashboard that contains a list of risks that are in red or yellow status. These can, of course, be spread over several pages if more space is required. This simplified format allows the project manager to focus everyone's attention on what is urgent and immediate. There is no misunderstanding that a risk was reported as a problem.

This reporting format is effective for the following reasons:

- Only risks requiring attention are listed. The other risks can be reviewed in the assessment list for those interested in them.

- Executive attention gets riveted on the red status items. Executives also see areas of future concern (for example, yellow status items) and can begin to lend their support so that these items do not turn into a crisis.

- Relevant and related information is grouped together.

- Some risks can be grouped under a green status on a second page so that high risk items are still up front, but the team can get recognition for things that are going well.

Risk Assessment – Risks that require immediate attention						
	No.	Name	Short Description	Impact	Probability	Impact Details
Status RED						

Notes:

Risk Assessment – Caution with the following risks						
	No.	Name	Short Description	Impact	Probability	Impact Details
Status YELLOW						

Notes:

Contact for further information

Figure 6.5   Sample risk assessment reporting dashboard

Risk Review

The final phase of the process is to continually review and update the risk assessment list. This process will never be complete and requires ongoing revisions and rethinking. You need to continually assess whether risks are still relevant, properly catalogued, or if new ones have emerged. Priorities and mitigation strategies also change over time and need to be reflected in this list through the following actions:

- Adjusting priority
- Removing risk items
- Adding risk items
- Adjusting mitigation strategy
- Adjusting contingency
- Collecting feedback from those impacted by a risk

Rules for Managing Risk

The effort required to manage risk has a direct impact on the resources, and the time, required for delivering project results. Figure 6.6 shows the relative impact of two different risk management strategies. The activity at the top involves dividing the project duration into small segments and conducting a risk review at the end of each one. Decreasing the duration between checkpoints increases the opportunities to successfully deal with a risk and prevent it from becoming a crisis.

The second activity example shows how wishful thinking is used, perhaps erroneously, to reduce the number of risk evaluation checkpoints. This could be more efficient, but only if things go as planned. Any problems may become full-blown crises before they are identified.

Figure 6.7 shows another common example of project planning that is used on projects perhaps because of ignorance, wishful thinking, or as a response to some other pressures. The project plan, consisting of many activities, pretty much assumes that the activities all end and start at the same time. This view looks silly but is an accurate representation of what happens on many projects. Extensive debates, changing project priorities, and complex requirements create this situation whether the project team and sponsors realize it or not.

Figure 6.8 shows an approach that attempts to account for some of dependencies between the different activities. What tends to get missed in the real world is that a delay in an activity will mean some delay in its dependent activities. Project managers need to use the risk management process to enforce this understanding.

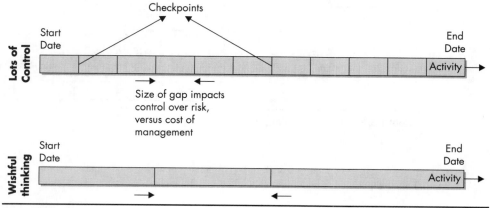

Figure 6.6 Risk management tradeoffs

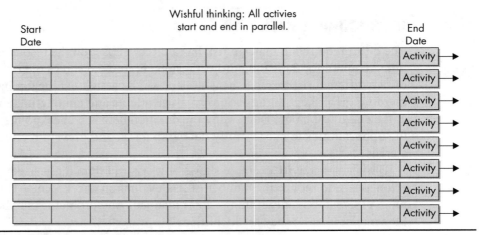

Figure 6.7   Wishful thinking

Figure 6.9 shows that we did not understand or represent all the dependencies correctly and the actual plan needed to be changed. The effectiveness of the risk review process would allow us to maintain control over the project end date, while shifting resources and priorities to match the ongoing learning on the project.

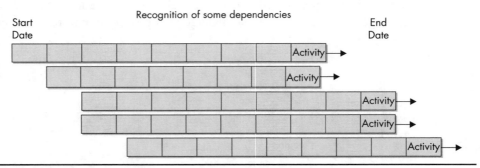

Figure 6.8   Informed planning

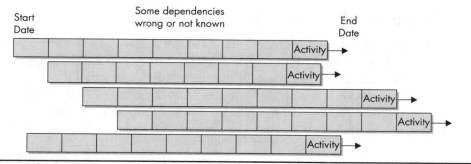

Figure 6.9   Actual experience

With these dependencies in mind, here are some key considerations for effectively managing risk on a project:

- **Early warning systems**   Identify some way to flag a risk before it happens.
- **Recovery triggers**   Identify what happens after a risk occurs.
- **Resist assumptions**   Avoid relying on unproven ideas whenever possible. If an assumption needs to be made, first try to limit its sphere of influence in the planning activities. Also, build a strategy that triggers a recovery process in case the assumption proves to be incorrect.
- **Test risk recovery programs**   Ensure that any recovery triggers that are established are tested before they are needed.
- **Review risk status regularly**   As discussed previously, risk management is ongoing and continuous.
- **Communicate risk**   Share the risk status and the risk assessment with everyone on the extended team. Keeping this private or secret to avoid worrying anyone usually works against the success of the project. Communicating risk in a simple, understandable format makes it a shared responsibility.
- **Don't go it alone**   The project manager is the ultimate quarterback, but risk management is a shared responsibility. The more people know about the risks in advance, the better they will contribute to their mitigation or recovery.
- **Don't let risk management become its own risk**   The process must remain streamlined and workable. Invest your resources in the risks that really matter.

Risk Management Responsibilities

Who is ultimately responsible for mitigating risk on a project? The short answer is that it's a shared responsibility, but there must still be a single point of accountability. The resource positioned to stay on top of day-to-day events at a macro level is the project manager or, in the event of an intervention, the project rescue manager. The following is a description of the major roles and responsibilities in the risk management process:

- The project (rescue) manager is ultimately accountable for the process.
- The project team does the work to avoid the risks.
- The project team does the work to mitigate the risks.
- The project team will implement the contingency plans.
- The business owners provide the investment to avoid the risks or to recover from them.
- The project sponsors agree to tradeoffs.

Techniques for Identifying Risks

The success of the risk management process depends on the completeness and thoroughness of the assessment that is done to produce the list of risks. Some techniques to help you extract useful information from other sources and people are shown in the subsections that follow.

Project Classification

Classifying projects by specific attributes helps to identify possible risks. A macro attribute is the project's industry grouping. This can determine the most critical parts of a project that a manager needs to validate. For example, an Aeronautics IT project will require more rigorous testing than a reporting initiative that can be released in stages. Project classification will be discussed further in Chapter 7, but consider that the details for each of the following project attributes have a direct impact on the type of risk exposure that exists as well as the mitigation strategies:

- Project duration
- Phase duration
- Team size
- Team location (co-located or dispersed)

- Team experience
- Budget
- Business complexity

Past Experiences

Past experiences should be drawn through your local resource network. This includes your own experiences, as well as those of the other project managers, the team members, and the business users. These experiences can be captured by reviewing past project post mortems and conducting interviews with people involved. Project managers should be analyzing and recording their experiences on projects over time to build an understanding of how their abilities react to different risk factors. Build up a personal network that contains colleagues in multiple industries and disciplines and interview them as well.

Industry Best Practices

Most industries have an extensive collection of experiences distilled down to best practice that you can draw on. The cost of this information varies widely, from being free to bartering (for example, an opportunity to sell you something in exchange for a white paper), nominal charge, or subscription-based. Also consider getting information from industry groups and think tanks (for example, Gartner Group, Forrester Research).

Unforeseen Risks

This chapter started with an adage: "You don't know what you don't know." The information offered in this chapter will help you to expand your understanding, but at some point, you will have exhausted your sources of information. Some risks may have been missed, or are too expensive to try and mitigate, or of such low probability that they were placed outside consideration (although the impact should similarly have been of a low variety).

The project needs to be shielded from unforeseen risks by incorporating a multipronged strategy that consists of the following:

- **Deliverables focus**   Know with clarity what needs to be produced at each stage of the project life cycle.
- **Generic contingency funds**   Bank some extra time and money to deal with new events (say 10 percent of the budgets).
- **Slack time**   Include slack time after key activities so that there is room for them to slip without affecting other activities.

Risk Management Tools

Tools can support the risk management process, but they can also be a crutch that distracts from dealing with the real issues. This is especially the case if selecting or purchasing the tool takes time away from making progress on the project deliverables. This definitely does not mean that you should not leverage risk management tools, just keep their value in perspective. Any tool selection processes can too easily get locked into a quagmire and you cannot afford this time during a project rescue.

Here are some features that risk management tools should have, followed by some of the types of tools you might want to deploy to mitigate risk on a project:

- Multiple user access
- Distributed access
- Security
- Web ability
- Relatively inexpense

Estimation Tools

Estimation tools are used to project the costs and timeframes for a project given what you know about it in the planning stages. Projects are typically segmented into project dimensions such as: the experience of the project team, the skills of the project team, level of politics on the project, whether implementation is involved, experience with the tools used on the project, and use of outside resources. Good estimation tools use this information to generate a project plan, resources at the task level, and overall costs. This usually provides a good start, but still requires customization from the project manager.

These tools can serve several benefits during a project rescue. Some surveys have reported that estimation tools have an accuracy of plus or minus 25 percent more than half the time. This is consistent with our observations as well. Not knowing which projects are going to be the exceptions means that you cannot completely rely on these tools to eliminate risk. However, these tools are useful for overall estimation. They will also help you to identify the areas that are likely to be exceptions and which will require additional analysis to get more accuracy.

Simulation Tools

By using specific data points and constraints and modeling outcomes, simulation tools are very helpful in establishing a risk assessment. These are excellent for examining what-if conditions. The tools do tend to be on the expensive side and limited in what they are able to predict. Some industries are also better represented than others. Simulation tools in the aeronautics field, for example, are more plentiful and useful than ones for payment systems.

Analytical and Decision Support Tools

Any tools that can extract or summarize key information about risks or the conditions that create them are useful to the risk management process. Data warehouses, data marts, and business intelligence can provide the raw information for decision support tools to support the project manager. However, if these have not already been implemented, it is doubtful that there will be an opportunity to do so during a time-constrained project rescue. These are separate projects in themselves and may be recommended during the project post mortem review.

Visual Tools

Any tools that present data in a visual format, with colors and shapes, are more likely to draw attention and be persuasive in a discussion than flat information. Preformatted dashboards and scorecards are useful here.

Closing Perspective

Risk management is rarely going to proceed according to plan and so tradeoffs will need to be made to preserve the most critical outcomes of the project. A project rescue essentially focuses the project sponsors on key results, while remaining flexible in attaining these, so that the end result is never an unmitigated disaster. Several levers are available to the project manager to moderate results:

- **Organizational support**   How much is the organization willing to support the project initiative, especially when things begin to go wrong? Will the organization change procedures, provide more resources?

- **Budget**   Money remaining in the budget is a cherished resource that can be spent on resources to mitigate or recover from a risk.

- **Deadlines**   The flexibility to adjust project deadlines provides another management tool for reducing risks. For example, the rescue manager may decide that it is prudent to spend more time testing some functions or completing a proof of concept to validate assumptions before committing to more intensive development. This can safe a lot of time in the long-term, but it could mean missing an interim deadline.

The risk management process involves visualizing risks and dealing with them within the time and resources available so that they do not derail the project. Effective risk management techniques require human intuition and interpretation and a process framework to be successful.

A project in need of rescue has already been affected by some potential risks. The rescue process requires a reevaluation of the original risk assessment and an improvement so that the same risks do not recur.

## CHAPTER 7

Assessment Questionnaire

The detection questionnaire, designed in Chapter 4, detects symptoms that trigger the launch of a project rescue intervention to salvage a project that is experiencing an endless cycle of decline. The assessment questionnaire developed in this chapter helps the project manager to dig deeper to better understand the root causes of project failure. This information is then used to develop a rescue plan in the next rescue phase.

Building the Assessment Questionnaire

This chapter provides a road map to building a questionnaire that will help uncover the specific sources of the problems that a project is experiencing. Figure 7.1 shows an approach to building a questionnaire to support the assessment phase. The figure shows that there are several sources to help formulate the questions a rescue manager can use to get clarity and precision around the true status of the project, including what has gone wrong, and what those closest to the project believe can be done to save it. The questionnaire also brings the rescue manager in front of different members of the project team to ask the questions and get an opportunity to interact with them. This allows an opportunity to start building trust, confidence, and an understanding of their mutual perspectives on the state of the troubled project.

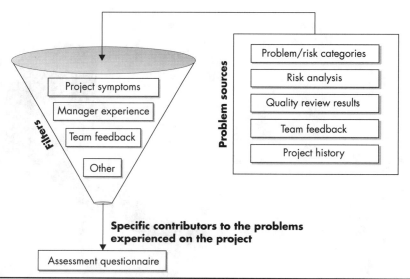

Figure 7.1 Building the assessment questionnaire

Several decades of initiatives designed to improve business efficiency through information technology related projects, business strategies, process management, and related initiatives have allowed us to gain an understanding of the common contributors to problems. There is a strong likelihood that some information from this list will be pertinent to the initiative you are trying to rescue. This generic body of knowledge, however, will be ever expanding and capturing every potential problem is impossible, or would take up enormous amounts of information. We will continue to augment this list on the publisher's web site, from which you can download a current copy.

Other sources of information, such as the risk assessment exercise and the quality assurance review, can also be used to enhance this list. Information gained from opening dialogues with different members of the project team on what they felt went wrong and what could be done better can be added to this information. The rescue manager's past experiences should not be overlooked either, including knowledge of the team's abilities, the organization's culture, and anything else that is pertinent to salvaging the project.

The resulting list of potential problem areas is quite large and needs to be trimmed down—quickly, efficiently, and accurately. Several filters are also defined in Figure 7.1 to help you identify, and then prioritize, the areas that require your focused attention.

The first filter uses the project symptoms that triggered the rescue effort to help pinpoint the areas of focus for the questionnaire with even a higher degree of accuracy. Additional filters can also be used to further refine these results. This process could include relying on personal experiences to add items to the list that were not picked up in any of the source contributors, but that still require further investigation.

The output of this process includes a set of areas for the rescue manager to focus attention and to ask additional questions to gain a thorough understanding of the project status.

Common Problem Sources

Chapter 1 introduced a set of problem or risk categories that were applicable for all business projects, as shown in Figure 7.2. Each of these categories can have an equally powerful impact on the project so they are not listed in order of priority.

This section drills deeper into each of these categories by examining the common problems encountered on projects, key considerations or mitigation strategies, and some basic questions that the rescue manager can ask. The

Figure 7.2   Common problem/risk categories

publisher's web site will continue to be updated with categories and problem areas to coincide with evolving industry best practices.

Project Team

The project team will make or break the project. The project team can be separated into several key segments or groups that have their own challenges. The core project team refers to the resources that are dedicated to the project full-time and possibly a few that have part-time involvement, but who are directly responsible for the results. The business stakeholders are affected by the outcome of the project and are needed to provide resources to supply business requirements and for accepting the final result. The business sponsors have funded the project or are empowered by those funding the project to make decisions on their behalf.

Common Problems

Table 7.1 identifies some of the common problems that are encountered within the project team category, key considerations, and some suggested questions that can be included in an assessment questionnaire.

Problem Description	Considerations	Suggested Questions
Lack of skills	Identify the specific skills that are required for the position and when they are required. Try and use just in time training approaches to ensure that all the resources have the relevant skills they need in order for the project to succeed. You might also want to use mentoring or coaching techniques to ease resources into their roles.	Is a lack of skills causing the project to fail? Will this be a problem in the future? How are skill requirements being determined? By whom? By project resource, what specific skills are required and when? What is the most effective and cost effective method for training the resources?
Morale problems	The impact of poor morale is more destructive to a project's success than many other commonly occurring problems. Most projects require the best capabilities of the resources to succeed, which is just not possible if the morale is poor. You need to strike a balance between bringing the morale up so that resources will do what it takes to get the project back on track, without getting burned out. Listen to the core members of the project team to find out the reasons for the morale problems. Deal with the top reasons for the morale problems. Explain that you are implementing change to improve the morale. Some morale issues cannot be dealt with because doing so would cause the project to remain off track. For example, some team members may not want to work on the weekends to meet a deadline. This request just cannot be met if the project is too succeed. Explain this reasoning to the project team.	Are resources sharing information? Are team members working cooperatively? Are resources working overtime, without asking for something in return? Is there a program to reward hard work without going through a lot of bureaucracy? Are team members aware that they are valued and their work is appreciated? Are team members submitting a lot of complaints?
Multiple responsibilities on different projects	Resources that work on different projects can get overly fragmented and their value begins to decrease on each initiative. Core practitioners should be dedicated to the project. If they cannot be, at least try to build a schedule that commits specific days to the project.	How many of the resources are involved in more than one project at the same time? Are the key resources dedicated to this project only?

Table 7.1   Project Team-Related Problems

Problem Description	Considerations	Suggested Questions
Lack of communication	Team members can be so focused on what they are doing that they may not receive or share information that is vital to others on the project. The project rescue approach uses a project management toolkit and regular status meetings to ensure a proper level of communication.	How is information communicated between team members? Are there different e-mail lists and phone lists for different groups on the team? Is there a place where documentation can be shared electronically?
Destructive politics	Office politics are inescapable on any initiative that has more than two people. Your goal is to eliminate politics that are destructive to the project—for example, when resources are playing games that are keeping the project from making progress. An example of this could be denying previous statements that were spoken but not written down. The rescue manager and the executive sponsors need to clearly show team members that destructive politics will not be tolerated on the project. Ensure that the formal performance review processes do not reward political players.	How is individual performance measured? Is the project team working together? Are there unresolved conflicts? Who works best with whom?
Lack of direction	Resources require a clear mandate to be effective. Mandate is defined by the project scope and the business requirements. Leverage a deliverables-based focus and a detailed project plan. The project rescue manager must be clear about the direction the project is taking and provide leadership in getting there.	Where is the detailed project charter? Has the executive sponsor signed off—for example, accepted the contents of the project charter?

Table 7.1   Project Team-Related Problems *(continued)*

Requirements

Building business requirements is a long arduous activity that involves many different resources, so it is not surprising that this category has many potential pitfalls. There is no question that strong business requirements are the essential statement of what a project is trying to achieve.

There are many levels of business requirements, starting with what is essentially a statement of project objectives, and then progressing to more levels of details. These relationships are often unclear on projects as different members of the team have different interpretations of what is adequate. Business requirements usually begin with a statement of "what" needs to be achieved. The "why" is supplied by the business case. Details need to be provided to the "what" so that the project team can explain the "how."

Common Problems

A direct lack of user involvement almost guarantees that there will be problems with the business requirements. Table 7.2 identifies some of the common problems within the requirements category, key considerations, and some suggested questions that can be included in your assessment questionnaire.

Problem Description	Considerations	Suggested Questions
Lack of clarity	A common trick that just about everyone in the information technology industry uses to mask a lack of understanding is to express themselves in vague terms. This is probably unconsciously done, but is highly wasteful. Business requirements that cannot be clearly explained cannot be satisfied.	What are the key objectives of the project? How will we know when we succeed? Who will tell us that we have succeeded?
Lack of agreement	Different stakeholders may have different requirements for the same function. The business sponsor or owner must make the final decisions to ensure that there is agreement on the business requirements.	Who are the major stakeholders that can provide business requirements? Have there been any arguments or disagreements among the major stakeholders or business owners?
Lack of prioritization	Projects get into trouble when too many requirements have to be met in the same timeframe. Deliver on the requirements that provide the best return. Deliver on the low hanging fruit first.	What is the single most important requirement for the project? Can we group the business requirements into critical, major, minor, and nice-to-have categories?
Contradictory	Maintaining a requirements document allows contradictory requests to be flagged. The executive sponsor must be prepared to resolve contradictory business requirements (for example, a report cannot be red and green at the same time).	Are there any requirements that appear contradictory?

Table 7.2   Requirements-Related Problems

Problem Description	Considerations	Suggested Questions
Ambiguous	Similar to a lack of clarity, ambiguous business requirements can have several different interpretations. Use precise English to describe business requirements. Use words that have one meaning—for example, "18 buttons" instead of "15–18 buttons" or "lots of buttons."	Which requirements are ambiguous or unclear?
Too high level	A statement of business objectives is very often confused with detailed business requirements. Ensure that the business requirements are described in enough detail for the team members to perform their jobs.	Is there enough detail in the business requirements for an analyst to write a technical specification?
Vague/ Incomplete	Examine the requirements to ensure that there are no missing items. The rescue manager or a designate must understand the details involving different permutations and combinations. For example, if a shipping method is described in detail, it would be useful to point out that a similar level of detail is required for the other shipping methods within the scope of the project.	What has been done to ensure that the requirements are complete?
Incorrect/ Inaccurate	The requirements are documented, but their implications have not been fully fleshed out and could be wrong.	What has been done to determine the accuracy of the requirements? What is the quality assurance process for the business requirements? How do we know that we are being given reasonable requests?

Table 7.2   Requirements-Related Problems *(continued)*

Planning

Thorough planning is the single most important process or tool for a rescue manager to use as it provides an opportunity to structure the resources and timeframes to identify weaknesses up front. During a rescue intervention, a project plan that can show what needs to be done, almost on an hourly or a daily basis, becomes the single most important deliverable coming out of the planning phase.

When planning tasks that are less than three hours in duration, consider using a checklist to track results. It becomes very cumbersome to maintain a project plan at this level, and attempting to do so may consume valuable management time that can be used more effectively elsewhere.

Common Problems

Table 7.3 identifies some of the common problems within the planning category, key considerations, and some suggested questions that can be included in your assessment questionnaire.

Problem Description	Considerations	Suggested Questions
Insufficient details	The plan needs to include enough information to articulate timeframe, resources, and measurement. It's as important to identify where there are gaps in understanding so that you can plan and budget around them.	How much planning was done? Did the planning activities miss anything? How well do we know what the project needs to accomplish and how to accomplish it? Where is the project plan?
Missing items	The planning may appear complete, but you do not know what you do not know. Build slack time into the plan to accommodate items that were not considered.	How do we know that the planning is complete?
No justification	Planning is not an exact science and can rely on assumptions that have no basis in reality.	What logic or justification was used to build the project plan during the planning exercise?
Insufficient resourcing details	The planning exercise may not capture enough details to support the resourcing efforts.	Do we know when the resources need to start on the project? What needs to be done to bring new resources onto the team? What tools do new resources require?
No early warning systems	Do you need to wait until the plan is unachievable before knowing there is a problem? It's important to include flags in the new project plan to point out when it is going off track early enough to make effective adjustments.	What made the project team call for a project rescue? How will I as the rescue manager know when something is starting to go wrong in the future? Who do I communicate this to?

Table 7.3   Planning-Related Problems

Problem Description	Considerations	Suggested Questions
Lack of a good Work Breakdown Structure WBS)	The Work Breakdown Structure is useful for showing the big project picture and can be useful for showing how consistent the project manager's thinking really is. Ad hoc WBS's often leave out many important deliverables and their related tasks—for example, test case planning, development, test script development, and building the test environment.	Is the Project WBS a standard template or was it developed ad hoc? Is the WBS based on deliverables or tasks?
Unjustified estimating techniques	With so many different variables affecting planning, some reusable estimating rules need to be established.	How was it done? Was a standard method used or was it ad hoc? Can the estimates be reviewed by a third party or are the estimating assumptions buried in the head of the chief architect?

Table 7.3   Planning-Related Problems *(continued)*

Technology

Not all business projects have a technology component, but for the ones that do, this can be another black hole. Technology, by its sheer complexity, can pose many problems for a rescue manager. Fortunately there are some techniques for reducing risk in this area, as we discuss in this section.

Common Problems

Table 7.4 identifies some of the common problems within the technology category, some key considerations, and some suggested questions that can be included in your assessment questionnaire.

Expectations

Managing the expectations of the expanded project team is vital for the success of a project. A difference in expectations needs to be identified early and corrected; otherwise, the longer the project goes on, the more difficult it becomes to close the gap. A large expectations gap means that the project cannot succeed according to the metrics established by different members of the project team.

Problem Description	Considerations	Suggested Questions
Impossibilities	Some technology combinations cannot do what the business wants them to do. Another organization that uses the technology in a similar way provides strong comfort in the direction of the technology. A proof of concept, early in the project, to validate the technology under the unique constraints of the project, offers confirmation of the direction with minimal up front costs.	What criteria were used to select the technology architecture? How do we know that the technology architecture is the correct one to use? Which other companies use this architecture? Can we afford this technology? Is there something we can reuse?
Incompatibilities	Incompatibilities can exist between different types of products. Product version incompatibility is a common problem. Need to have confirmation that a certain technology architecture is incompatible before accepting that direction.	How do we know that the different tools can work together? What versions of the products are being integrated? How do we know that they can work together?
New technology	Examine the proven record of the new technology that is being considered for the project. Determine the training needs of the resources that will be using the technology. Evaluate the organization's ability to accommodate new technology. How successful have they been? How well do they learn from their mistakes?	Why is new technology required to meet the business objectives? How can the learning curve be reduced?
Incorrect usage	Use the right tools for the right job. Is the technology being used for the right purpose—for example, why use a high-powered desktop for simple testing?	How do we know that we are using the right tools for the job?
Limitations	Understand the limitations of the technology, perhaps through the proof of concept, the reference sites, or by "interrogating" the supplier. Include activities in the project plan to deal with the limitations. You may need to define a contingency in the event that a limitation in the technology cannot be circumvented.	What are the thresholds of the different parts of the technology architecture? How can we expand the limits? What happens if a limit cannot be removed?

Table 7.4   Technology-Related Problems

Common Problems

Table 7.5 identifies some of the common problems within the expectations category, key considerations, and some suggested questions that can be included in your assessment questionnaire.

Problem Description	Considerations	Suggested Questions
Too high	High expectations will be met with strong emotions—exuberance or reluctance in the short term. Because high expectations are difficult to meet, chances are great that the project cannot succeed.	How do I know that the project is successful? Who is going to accept/reject the project results? What are their expectations? Have the expectations been written down and approved?
Unrealistic	These are worse than high expectations. Whereas high expectations may be met some of the time, unrealistic expectations can never be met. Unrealistic expectations will begin to cause destructive or avoidance behavior among team members who may not want to give up. Rescue managers need to identify unrealistic expectations before committing to the rescue plan. These expectations must become more realistic before the project can be salvaged.	What makes us think that we can meet the expectations of this project? What are the business drivers behind these expectations? Who is asking for these?
Improperly managed	The project manager and the executive sponsors need to manage each others' expectations throughout the project. Everyone on the project team should be responsible for communicating the right expectations and an accurate status so that expectations can be correctly managed at all times.	How are problems or changes accommodated in the project plan? When are the stakeholders and sponsors told about changes in deliverables? Have expectation changes been communicated in the past? What happened?
Unknown	When expectations have not been established at all, there is a strong likelihood that the requirements for the business case for the project are suspect.	Which expectations have not been clarified?
Too complicated	Expectations that require multiple deliverables can be difficult to attain completely. Look for ways to prioritize the deliverables. Distinguish between key project expectations for the business versus the nice-to-have ones.	How do I know that the project is successful?

Table 7.5   Expectations-Related Problems

Priorities

Most organizations have multiple priorities, with any particular project being one of many things that need to be done. Higher priority initiatives tend to receive more resources, attention and scrutiny, all of which can help to remove obstacles and problems before they derail the project.

Common Problems

Table 7.6 identifies some of the common problems within the priorities category, key considerations, and some suggested questions that can be included in your assessment questionnaire.

Timelines

Timelines can be absolute or relative. When absolute, a certain deliverable or event must become available by a specific point in time. When relative, a specified duration of time is required to produce an outcome.

There are many approaches to building timelines, with extensive debates about which approaches are best. In fact, no single approach guarantees an absolutely right answer. The best you can hope for is a reasonable approximation. In a rescue exercise, you must also learn to plan defensively—for example, include

Problem Description	Considerations	Suggested Questions
Lack of resources	There may not be enough resources to meet all the business requirements. Prioritizing the business requirements allows a better utilization of the business in terms of return on investment. Noncritical items can be moved off the critical path.	How do we know that we have the right resources? How do we know that we have the right number of resources?
Physical resource conflicts	Physical resources, such as computers and desks, may be allocated to other initiatives. The executive sponsor may be called on to deal with these conflicts.	What is the process for getting new resources? What do we need to complete this project?
Project team resource conflicts	The same people may be required on different projects at the same time. Planned resources may not be hired in a timely fashion.	Are any other projects targeting a similar completion date?

Table 7.6   Priorities-Related Problems

extensive checkpoints to flag changes to a proposed timeline and to take corrective action when necessary.

Here are some of the common approaches for building timelines:

- Timelines are given to you.

- Build the timeline from a fixed endpoint.

- Use the durations for individual tasks to establish the overall timelines.

The most common method for building a time line is the Critical Path Method (CPM). However, CPM uses only a single estimated duration estimate. A bit more realistic is the PERT method using three duration estimates: best case, most probable and worst case. The critical path is found the same way in both methods; a forward pass and backward pass through task dependencies. Those tasks with 0 float are on the critical path. The PERT method will allow more intelligent push back the user when the critical path is longer then the user desired project duration.

Common Problems

Table 7.7 identifies some of the common problems within the timelines category, key considerations, and some suggested questions that can be included in your assessment questionnaire.

Problem Description	Considerations	Suggested Questions
Too tight	Tight timelines may look good on paper, or make an attractive catch-phrase in terms of defining an intense corporate culture, but things do happen on projects and tight timeframes remove the flexibility to bring things back on track. Always keep a pool of slack time that can be leveraged at different times in the project. Tight timeframes can be met, but the rescue manager must keep the project team apprised of any events that could have a negative impact. Expectations management is key when a tight timeframe is unavoidable.	What is the project deadline? How was the deadline established? Who needs to approve a different deadline? Can we complete portions of the project before the project deadline and release only those?

Table 7.7   Timeline-Related Problems

Problem Description	Considerations	Suggested Questions
Unrealistic	Some timelines just cannot be met. The rescue manager is positioned to reveal an unrealistic timeline before committing to a rescue effort. Unrealistic timelines can be addressed by reducing scope or increasing certain resources.	What makes us think the project deadline can be met?
Overly optimistic	Overly optimistic timelines assume a certain series of events that usually do not match reality. Executive management pressure can sometimes convince a project team to accept an overly optimistic timeline.	Is there enough time to reasonably do what we're being asked to do?
No opportunity to correct	Perhaps the biggest flaw in a proposed timeline is a lack of opportunity to correct a bad situation. Include early warning flags to identify problems.	What can we do if the project begins to go off track again?

Table 7.7   Timeline-Related Problems *(continued)*

Budgets

The problems experienced by budgets closely parallel the problems with timelines. Determining a budget for a project is an inexact science, to say the least. Identifying all the elements to be included in the budget—for example, employees, benefits, consultants, development tools, testing tools, production tools, software licenses, maintenance costs, facilities, telecommunications charges, miscellaneous costs, office supplies, and so on—can require a lot of time, which itself cuts into a rigid deadline. This list is far from complete.

What makes the situation even more challenging is that some costs will be based on decisions or findings that are not available until much later in the project cycle. For example, slow application performance may require more memory cards to resolve. But how many? This will not be known until the system testing.

Common Problems

Table 7.8 identifies some of the common problems within the budgets category, key considerations, and some suggested questions that can be included in your assessment questionnaire.

Problem Description	Considerations	Suggested Questions
Lack of allocation	A budget may have been provided to the project, but it may not have been allocated. This can cause delays in the project.	Who is providing the budget? When is it going to be available? Have there been any problems paying the bills in a timely and accurate fashion in the past?
Unrealistic	A budget may have been assigned to the project without any justification or basis in reality.	How was the budget determined? What items are included in the project budget?
Cut during the project	Other events may have caused executive management to trim or even cut the budget during the project. Executive management may argue that the original budget had too much contingency built into it, thus putting the problem back on the project manager's shoulders. Reduced budget should trigger a change control process that will likewise result in a smaller set of deliverables. The rescue manager must react to a reduced budget; otherwise tacit agreement will be viewed by executive management as a signal that the original budget may have been too high.	Was the project budget ever cut after it started? Who accepted the budget cut? Were any reasons given? What was changed in the project to reflect the reduced budget?
Insufficient	The budget may be running out due to earlier problems in the project. There just may not be enough money in the budget to complete the project.	What if we need a larger budget?
Missing items	The original budget may have missed key items. Testing activities reveal items that were not budgeted for.	What is included in the budget?
New events	Despite best planning efforts, new events do arise that can affect the budget. Consider providing budget ranges for uncertain items.	What happens if we didn't budget for an important item? Are there any discretionary funds available to the project?

Table 7.8   Budget-Related Problems

Project Governance

The importance of project governance is underestimated on most projects. This involves tracing the executive relationships to the top of the organization. Is there a clear path for all decisions to be made? How effective are the escalation procedures?

Common Problems

Table 7.9 identifies some of the common problems within the project governance category, key considerations, and some suggested questions that can be included in your assessment questionnaire.

Vendors

Vendors have become important resources on all engagements. They provide tools, information, or people. Managing vendors offers its own set of challenges and rewards. Vendors have their own cultures, their own metrics, and their own interests. Plus, you have little direct control over their resources. You need to keep your options open when dealing with vendors.

Problem Description	Considerations	Suggested Questions
Lacking	A project manager needs the support of an executive governance committee to succeed.	Who owns this project? Who owns the different pieces of the project? How often are they available?
Ineffective	A governance group needs to be involved in key decisions on the project. A process for incorporating the governance group in a timely and effective manner needs to be implemented by the rescue manager.	Does the governance group provide any meaningful guidance to the project? How accessible are the executives?
Different priorities	A governance group may have different priorities than the project team. This is a disaster waiting to happen. The rescue manager needs to ensure that this is not the case, and needs to bridge this gap if it is.	What are the priorities of the governance group?
No clear involvement	A rescue manager can set regular meetings and agenda with the governance group. The governance group does not actually have to make changes to the project if things are proceeding well.	How often does the governance group meet? What do they discuss? Who's in the governance group? How do they receive accurate project status?
Overly active	The governance group should also not be overly activist on a project as this may result in significant impact to the schedule and morale.	Does the governance group micro-manage the project?

Table 7.9   Project Governance-Related Problems

Common Problems

Table 7.10 identifies some of the common problems within the vendors category, key considerations, and some suggested questions that can be included in your assessment questionnaire.

Problem Description	Considerations	Suggested Questions
Too small	Small vendors may not be able to scale to the requirements of your project.	How can we be sure that the vendor can scale to satisfy our needs?
Poor customer service	Check references to understand how well the vendor is known to serve customers. Internal references are the best. Include a penalty clause in the contract for poor service. Sign a service level agreement with the vendor.	Who else have you done work for? Are they willing to speak with us?
Unable to deliver on time	Include a nondelivery penalty clause in the contract. Recognize that nondelivery may be unacceptable to your project regardless of the penalties that a vendor can be called on to pay. You need the work done accurately.	What happens if you miss deadlines?
Go out of business	Small vendors can provide many benefits, but ensure that they are going to survive long enough to help you.	What is your debt load? How long have you been in business? How can you convince me that you're going to be around long enough to help us?
Different corporate culture	Cultural similarities are important in establishing a working relationship between vendor employees and your own project team. Select a vendor based on cultural similarity.	How will your team work with ours? What happens if we're too demanding? What happens if we need people to stay into the night or work on the weekends? How are your people being measured?
Flawed vendor Statement of Work (SOW)	The SOW needs to be clear, concise, and fair to both parties. The SOW needs to be managed by the rescue manager.	Has your lawyer or legal representative examined the SOW? How reasonable and fair is it to each of you? Will it stand in the way of making actual progress?

Figure 7.10   Vendor-Related Problems

User Training

Change management and user training are used to ensure that the people running with whatever is being built have the skills and the processes to perform their jobs after the project is completed.

Common Problems

Table 7.11 identifies some of the common problems within the user training category, key considerations, and some suggested questions that can be included in your assessment questionnaire.

Problem Description	Considerations	Suggested Questions
Untimely	User training that is provided too early in a project will be forgotten. User training provided too late in the process may result in negative perceptions about what the project is trying to achieve.	Who needs to be trained? When do they need to be trained?
Too high level	High level training needs to be augmented with separate, very detailed training courses. Training that has a half day overview, along with several multiday courses on different topics can be considered.	Who's on the list to be trained? What do the users need to understand about the project scope and objectives, in order to perform their own jobs effectively? What do they need to understand in order to do their jobs?
Inappropriate audience	Everyone in the organization does not require the same type of training. Create separate training courses to support different roles in the organization.	Which departments need the training? Are there groups that do not require the training?
Not enough	Do not assume that one or two courses is going to be enough.	How deep do we need to go in the training? For whom?
No refreshers	One-time training may not be enough. Give employees access to training materials so that they can retake courses according to their own needs. Training materials should be offered over an intranet for easy access.	How can employees retake the training at some later date?
Missing something	This involves incomplete training courses that do not provide sufficient information on what the project is trying to achieve. Provide access to Help desks, coaches, and mentors to deal with these situations.	What happens if the training has not answered my questions?

Figure 7.11   User Training-Related Problems

Methodology/Framework

Methodologies and frameworks capture the experiences of the authors or authoring organization in successfully delivering certain types of projects. No single methodology or framework will ever be foolproof on all types of projects. They cannot account for every contingency. Use of an incorrect methodology can waste a lot of project resources while imparting a false sense of comfort.

Methodologies, on the whole, tend to be more complete and prescriptive than their framework counterparts.

Common Problems

Table 7.12 identifies some of the common problems within the methodology/framework category, key considerations, and some suggested questions that can be included in your assessment questionnaire.

Problem Description	Considerations	Suggested Questions
Inappropriate for project	This could be because the methodology is poorly constructed. The methodology could be better suited for another type of project.	What is the methodology designed for? Who uses it?
Incorrectly applied	A lack of understanding by the project team may mean that a methodology is not implemented correctly.	Who implemented the methodology in the organization? How do we know when to use it?
Not enough test points	The methodology may not have enough analysis or test points to allow the project team members to know that they are proceeding on track.	What makes us think we are using the methodology correctly?
Missing phases	The methodology may miss key phases relevant to your project, either through omission or because it is intended for another type of project.	Are there any types of projects that the methodology is not suited for?
Too cumbersome	The methodology may be too unwieldy.	How flexible is the methodology? Are there steps that I can miss? What do people on the team think about the methodology?

Table 7.12   Methodology/Framework–Related Problems

Filters

You can certainly focus on all the problem categories and assemble the questions into a questionnaire—however, this takes a lot of time and energy, both of which are going to be in short supply during a project rescue. There are several filters that you can use to reduce the list of categories that require your attention because every project is not going to experience a problem in each of these categories. Similarly, projects may also be experiencing problems in categories that are not included in this list or that were not considered common enough at the time of writing.

The project symptoms that were identified in Chapter 4 are a first filter in identifying the areas of greatest pain. Trace the symptoms back to the categories to identify the core problem. However, there may be some underlying problems that have not yet manifested as symptoms, but which may creep out during the project rescue. Be careful not to discount the other categories too early in the assessment phase.

Feedback from other members of the team can also be used to determine which categories and problems to include or exclude in your questionnaire. Similarly, the original project manager and your own experiences need to be reflected in the questions that are selected from the preceding list and new questions that are formulated.

Project classification, which will be discussed when a rescue plan is being built later in this book, can also act as another filter. Certain project attributes result in a strong predisposition toward certain problems. By organizing the attributes into a couple of categories that can define projects, you can begin to shorten the list of potential problems into the most likely causes, and then focus your attention to get the most pertinent details. Some reasonable categories to consider include project length, project costs, and industry type.

Closing Perspective

Given the significant project experiences the information technology industry has collected over many decades, we are able to identify some of the common sources of problems that contribute to project failure.

This chapter discussed some of the categories that commonly contribute to project problems and identified the types of questions that a rescue manager needs to include on a questionnaire to deconstruct the project status and understand what has really gone wrong.

Another problem seems to be trying to automate a flawed business process. Most enterprises have processes that are flawed because of years of minor corrections and failure to keep up with business changes. When automation is added, it becomes an automated flawed process. Making a flawed process run faster makes no sense. This is often recognized by the users and results in changes orders to the original requirements. Instead of assuming that the current process should be automated, perhaps they may need to be reengineered first, then automated.

## PART III

Planning the Intervention

CHAPTER 8
Establishing a Management Control Office

In the previous chapters we discussed how to ascertain the causes of your runaway project. In this chapter we discuss the critical initial steps to restart the project and avoid the traps and pitfalls that got the project into trouble in the first place. This chapter focuses on how to create or enhance a central project management office to serve as a primary support center for the restarted project.

The project management control office we discuss should not be confused with an organizational PMO, also known as a Project Management or Program Management Office. The organizational PMOs have varying degrees of complexity and thus varying degrees of success. We discuss the setup and operation of a project management office charged with assisting the project manager in rescuing the runaway project. Figure 8.1 shows a simple view of the organization of a typical project that is being restarted. There may be more levels and more technical teams on your project, but the overall structure should hold true. You will notice there are really two organizations involved with the project: the project steering committee and the project management office. Both play an extremely important role in the successful turnaround of the runaway project.

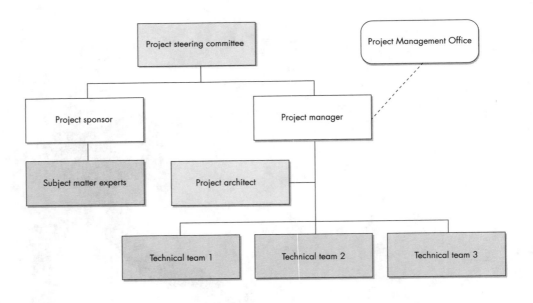

Figure 8.1   Project rescue organization

The Project Steering Committee

Before we discuss the project office, we need to step back and look at the role of the primary group that provides direction to the extended project team—the project steering committee. It's now time for this group of senior executives to share their wisdom and knowledge, exert their influence and authority and apply good business sense to guide the project. In the beginning of the project restart, the steering committee should meet at least biweekly until they are assured the project is back on track.

Politics…Politics…Politics: Who Belongs on the Steering Committee?

Recruiting the right people to serve on the project steering committee may itself be a significant challenge. Depending on your project's visibility, reputation and depth of trouble, you may find people rushing to step up to right the ship, or more likely, you will find people running away as fast as possible to avoid being associated with the "dog with fleas." This is the time to exhaust all of your options to obtain the right people. Whether you need to sell or tell, do what you must to get the right team. The following executives should be part of your steering committee:

- **Project executive sponsor**   May be the committee chair.
- **Project sponsor**   Works with the project manager to provide information on project progress
- **Technical organization leader**   Whether CIO, Vice President of Engineering, Head of the Department of Works, or some other organization, this person's participation is crucial. This executive controls the technical resources and should be part of the decision making process when there is a need to commit more technical staff to the project. This person can also help provide executive support to the project manager.
- **Project manager**   If not the committee chair, this person is the main source of information on project progress.
- **Project officer**   As leader of the quality assurance function, this executive will be functioning as the project management coach and mentor. This person provides an unbiased opinion of the project's status and overall risk.

- **Finance and accounting executive**   This executive helps with the acquisition of additional capital when needed. This person provides financial controls and guidelines to be used by the restarted project and monitors adherence to them.

- **External service provider executive**   If you are utilizing an external service provider, especially if you are outsourcing some pieces or the entire project, this executive plays a role similar to the technical organization leader from an external perspective.

Do the Right Things

Once you successfully pull the team together (congratulations!) you have to establish guiding principles for that team to operate effectively. As you can see from the preceding roster, there will be many agendas. Most likely, these agendas will conflict if left unmanaged. You will need to codify those guiding principles and keep them prominently displayed at all project steering committee meetings. Your guiding principles should reflect the culture of your company, but a few transcend all companies:

- **We're doing this project because ...**   This open ended question should be kept foremost in the minds of the project team members when trying to decide if they are doing the right things. The answers are found in the project goals and objectives right out of the project charter.

- **To do this project well we need to ...**   This is another question used to guide the actions of the project team members. Look to the project charter and the critical success factors for its answers.

- **Be prepared**   There will be a lot of information to be read and understood. Committee members must commit to doing their "homework" and come to committee meetings prepared and ready for action.

- **Stay engaged**   This assignment will be hard work, especially if the runaway project is severely astray. "Committee" starts with "commit." Each member must be prepared to provide the necessary attention over a long period of time. The project did not just go off track in a day. It took a long time to get where you are and it will take a long time to get the project back on the right track.

If you cannot get the right people to give you the necessary commitments, you should reconsider whether this project is truly needed. A lack of executive sponsorship is a sure symptom of a project that will die.

The Project Management Office

Now that we've discussed the major leadership organization of a restarted runaway project, we should turn our attention to the primary support organization—the project management office, also known as the project office. In Figure 8.1, notice the "dotted line" relationship between the project manager and the project management office. This line symbolizes the two-way relationship between the two parties. The project manager does not report to the project management office or project officer in a traditional hierarchical manner. Rather, the project manager and the project management office have a symbiotic relationship whereby each is providing the other with information and experiences that enable the other to do a better job. Most people recognize the benefits a project manager receives from the project management office. We delve into these benefits in the remainder of this chapter. However, you must not forget that the project manager provides the values for metrics (for example, actual time and money spent on activities and tasks) that feed the project management office and enable that organization to provide fact-based methods, standards, coaching and reporting.

A typical project management office for runaway projects is depicted in Figure 8.2. The key to an effective project management office is simplicity. You are already dealing with the enormous complexities of a runaway project. Now is not the time to add more complexity. Be careful and aware of the temptation to have a person play multiple roles in this organization. You may believe that will simplify the situation, but in fact it will stretch the team member and add more pressure to an already pressure-packed situation. Let the amount of work lead you to the number of staff members you need in the office.

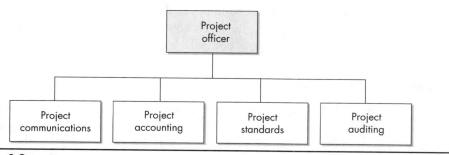

Figure 8.2   Runaway project management office

Project Officer

The project officer tends to be the most senior project manager in your organization. This person represents that magical mix of deep experience with the ability and desire to share it. This person is well versed in the four major functions of the project management office. The main goal of the project officer is to create an atmosphere of support while instituting a project management culture. This must be done in a supportive mode because almost everyone associated with the project is psychologically down and oversensitive to criticism. The project officer works to enable the project manager to be a champion and leader of the new effort to bring the project to successful completion. The project manager should feel comfortable turning to the project officer for advice and counsel when things are going well ("How do I keep it going?") or not so well ("How do I get things back under control?"). In turn, the project officer must be comfortable working behind the scenes and getting satisfaction through the success of the project manager. If there is a power struggle or other incompatibility between the project officer and the project manager, the project team will be attuned to the struggle, take sides and limp along as a divided team. Ultimately, the project officer should have project rescue experience and be able to relate that experience to the situation at hand to help guide the project manager and the rest of the senior project management team.

Often you may be tempted to move this person into the role of project manager (if you had decided to make a project manager change). This may or may not be a good decision. You need to weigh this decision against the importance of supporting the entire portfolio of projects currently underway. Some people delude themselves by thinking they can put the project officer in place as project manager "until the project is back on track". Even if this strategy does work initially—and it seldom does—making another leadership change adds more time and cost to the project and impedes the good momentum that has taken place to get the project back on track. Of course there is no single option. Pick the one that is the best fit in your company and of course—*keep it simple.*

Project Communications

We've discussed the various reasons projects go awry—from project management problems to technical failures. Clearly at the heart of all project failure is communication failure. Proper communication is critical to the success of any project, and the restart of a runaway project is no exception. Clear and concise information about the project, each member's role(s) and responsibilities, the interactions of this project with other ongoing activities and initiatives, and the way project information is distributed throughout the management chain can have a direct impact on the project. Thus, it is paramount to establish and maintain the proper lines of communication throughout the lifecycle of any given project.

Project Communication Plan

The project management office must assist the project manager in establishing and following a project communication plan. Because of the visibility of the runaway project, there will be plenty of misinformation floating around. Without properly communicating the facts, the misinformation grows and is eventually accepted as truth, greatly increasing the effort needed to set the record straight. The purpose of the communication plan is to describe the mechanisms that will be used to facilitate communications on the project. Formal communications (status reports, status meetings, and so on) should be covered. In addition, the plan should contain sample templates for the proper dissemination of project information. This plan should be read and understood by all members of the extended project team. Additionally, the Project steering committee and project team members will benefit from the information in this document. This document also serves as a roadmap for users to find deliverable documentation.

Table 8.1 contains a summary of formal project communication vehicles. The reports may be in electronic format pushed to the intended audience via e-mail or placed in an electronic repository that must be pulled by the recipient. However, a paper copy should be kept in the project notebook. Likewise, project meetings may be face to face or by teleconference or videoconference. This should be identified in the communication plan. Note that you should require separate status reporting by third-party vendors. Ideally, their accomplishments and plans for the next period should be traceable back to the contract and or the Vendor Statement of Work. This is where scope management and solid change control begin. You don't want vendors working on tasks that are not in plan—they'll charge you for it.

Item	Frequency	Prepared By	Delivered to
Individual status reports	Weekly	Project team members	Project manager
Vendor status report	Weekly	Project vendors	Project manager
Weekly status report	Weekly	Project manager	Project sponsor, Project team, Project management office
Monthly status report	Monthly	Project manager, project sponsor	Project steering committee, Project team, Project management office
Weekly status meeting	Weekly	Project manager	Project sponsor, Project team members
Monthly status meeting	Monthly	Project manager	Project steering committee

Table 8.1   Project Meetings and Reports

The project office communications person can assist the project manager in producing these documents. Note the key word here is "assist." The project manager cannot delegate this activity to the project management office and should not be allowed to do so.

Status Reporting

Notice in Table 8.1 that the primary building block of project communications is the status report. Whether it's of the individual, weekly project or monthly project variety, this tool is essential when trying to convey the true status of a project. Yet this cornerstone of project communications is often misunderstood by its preparer and is the root cause of project misinformation. The project office communications person should help the project manager assure the status reports are factual, complete and understandable.

Figure 8.3 shows an example of the content of a good status report. The first section, or report heading, states the project identifiers, including the planned and estimated budget and schedule. Just below the report heading is the overall project status. Using the familiar green-yellow-red symbolism, any reader can immediately see the overall project status. Your project management office should help determine when a project goes into a yellow or red state. These conditions should be based upon degrees of overall variance to the baseline plan. Whether the metric is in percentages or absolute amounts, the variance scale should be published and understood by all. Following the overall green-yellow-red status is the project snapshot in time—taken from the project plan. This section points to the next deliverable in the project charter.

The next area is one that requires great attention. Major Accomplishments for the current reporting period should be limited to task starts and task completions only. Here, people try to disguise limited progress by using terms such as "I feel" or "I believe" or "I continued to work on" among others. These terms point to a glaring conclusion: Very little, if anything, is being accomplished. By looking at actual starts and completions and comparing them to the planned starts and completions from the previous status report, you will quickly ascertain whether progress is being made or not. The next section, Plans For Next Period, goes hand-in-hand with its immediate predecessor. Again, this section should be limited to task starts and completions. Because good project management practice limits tasks to 80 hours of effort or less, every task in progress should be listed as a start or completion in one of these two sections.

The next section deals with issue management. All issues that are open or those that have been closed in the current reporting period should be listed here. This section is truly for information purposes only. Issue management is important enough to rate its own regular meetings where issues can be discussed and resolved. Finally, the Change Log should always be included. The changes

Project Name

Weekly Project Status Report

Project Manager:		Status Period:	3/16/2002 – 3/25/2002
Baseline Start Date:	1/2/2002	Actual Start Date:	1/2/2002
Baseline Completion Date:	12/31/2002	Planned Completion Date:	12/31/2002
Budget at Completion (BAC):	$7,900,000	Estimate at Completion (EAC):	$7,900,000
Executive Sponsor:			
Project Sponsor:			

Overall Status:

☒	Green – On track; No problems foreseen	☐	Yellow – Potential issues exist; Corrective action being planned	☐	Red - Slipping on cost, sched, and / or performance; Corrective action now required

Current Snapshot (list current phase, next deliverable & date):

Phase: Elaboration
Next Deliverable: Project Steering Committee Meeting
Deliverable Due Date: 3/28/02

Major Accomplishments:

Plans for Next Period:

Current Issues:

Change Log:

Figure 8.3   Project status report

should be prioritized with the open change requests listed first and the disposed change requests listed last.

If done correctly, the status report can serve as the agenda and main information document for its respective status meeting.

Project Accounting

With all projects, especially large projects, numerical data proliferates. So much that trying to make sense of it, or trying to balance the data becomes a huge management effort. The building block of all of this data is the actual number of hours worked on each task. That seems pretty simple, but that simplicity is deceiving. These hours are usually captured multiple times by multiple systems. From a project management standpoint, you are trying to capture the hours in your project management tool of choice. You need this in order to ascertain variances, relevel the project plan and provide reference points for your estimating repository. But other organizations want this information also and not necessarily in the same form or level of detail. Project team members may be entering these hours onto a timesheet and into a corporate time-keeping system. If they are external service providers, they may also be capturing time for their own company's time-keeping system and for their billing system as well! Some people have been able to automate some of this data collection but many have not. With so many differing points of data entry, discrepancies can occur. This situation gets worse when time reporting is due before the end of the work week and then the actual hours change between the time the data is entered and the end of the week.

Besides the labor collection, there are verification and balancing activities for other project assets such as hardware, software, office supplies, office space and any other item for which you have been invoiced that a project manager may have to approve. These items are very important when determining the total cost of a project. Likewise, untimely payment for goods or services can have a negative effect on the project schedule. These items do not manage themselves! Managing the project is tough enough without having to untangle this accounting nightmare. This is an excellent opportunity for the project management office to assist the project manager in real-time everyday activity.

The project office accounting person does not have to be an experienced project manager, although it is an excellent position for project managers in training. Obviously, this person must have excellent analysis skills and a great attention to detail. As with other project office positions, this person and the project manager can be mutually beneficial to each other. While the project manager can teach the would-be project manager the practical ins and outs of project management, the project office accounting person can provide much needed relief of important administrative functions. Specifically, the project office accounting person can:

- **Verify actual hours recorded in the project management tool**   As mentioned previously, this function is critical to reconciling the various timekeeping mechanisms and deriving the labor cost of the project.
- **Reconcile invoices and purchase orders**   Usually the project manager is the first line of approval on purchase orders for labor, hardware, software,

and other project-related items. Matching and reconciling invoices to purchase orders can be time consuming, especially when discrepancies arise. The project manager can be more efficient by having the issues resolved and ready for approval when the time comes for authorization.

- **Track project budget performance** In a project rescue situation, the project manager is constantly asked for this information. Besides providing it formally on the weekly and monthly status reports, ad hoc requests appear to come non-stop. Having another person focus on the entire budget performance decreases the chance of the "surprise" items that were really known at the onset of the project but received inadequate attention when compared to other project issues.

You may find other meaningful tasks the project office accounting person can perform to help the project manager. As in the preceding examples, these tasks should be of assistance but this person should not have direct accountability. That is reserved for the project manager.

Project Standards

In project rescue situations, great attention is given to *how fast* the project is going to be completed but not to *how* the project is going to be completed. In a mad dash to cross the finish line, project quality suffers. In what may be the most difficult situation, especially when budgets and schedules have been drastically exceeded, the project management office, the project manager and the system architect must take a united stand on doing the job well. The project office standards person can play a significant role in quality assurance from a project deliverable perspective in both the content of a deliverable as well as the method by which the deliverable was produced.

The best person to fill this role of the project office standards person is someone with extensive experience in the methods employed by the technical team. Senior level architects and engineers that possess excellent communication skills can provide very valuable assistance to the project manager and especially to the system architect. As the number of teams within the project grows, more and more pressure is put upon the system architect. The project office standards person can assist the project architect in the following ways:

- **Conduct peer review sessions** No matter what phase of the runaway project is being executed, the most effective quality strategy is to conduct extensive peer reviews. These sessions, also known as walkthroughs or informal reviews, allow small teams to remove defects early, when the cost of the defect is still low. The more reviews your teams conduct, the more they will be able to remove defects before they get implemented. Unfortunately, the more sessions that are conducted, the higher the demand on the project architect's time. Having an experienced substitute will allow for more sessions and lead to higher quality.

- **Review deliverables**   Project deliverables must meet a standard of quality and consistency according to the process or methodology employed by the technical team. Because the project office standards person has intimate knowledge of these standards, the deliverables can be prescreened before the final review by the project architect enabling a faster, higher quality review.

- **Mentor team members**   Some team members may be stretching their personal knowledge and experience on the technical methods they are trying to employ. Similar to the deliverable review activity described previously, the project office standards person possesses an intimate knowledge of the technical method and can assist the project architect in helping the less experienced team members work through the methods while on the job.

As with the other project management office positions, the standards person should be an assistant, but the responsibility of assuring the technical team adheres to quality and process standards still belongs to the project architect.

Project Auditing

The final position in the project management office is the one that is most helpful to the project steering committee. The project audits are designed to give the project management team an unbiased snapshot of the project's progress to date and a forecast of where the project is headed. We discussed the audit function and the types of audits in Chapter 4; now let's take a look at the person who conducts the project audits.

Because of the heightened sensitivity associated with a runaway project, the project office auditor must not only be an experienced project manager but that person must also be very tactful in portraying the project's status. Everyone knows that the first couple of audits will be abysmal. Without watering down the project audit, the project office auditor must concentrate on the efforts the team is making to recover the project. Of course, the project office auditor's primary job is to let the project management team understand where the project is headed. Falsely glowing reports are not acceptable either. But it is important to focus on project improvements and determine over the course of two or three audits whether these improvements are being sustained. Some areas of improvement to look for are listed in Table 8.2.

Of course there are other areas where you can look for immediate and sustained improvements. If no improvements are found, the situation must be addressed immediately. Otherwise you will be starting your project rescue efforts from the beginning again—if you are given the opportunity to do so.

Smaller organizations have the project officer double as the project auditor. Larger organizations separate the roles, which frees up the project officer to mentor the mentors. Remember the goal of the project management office is to create a supportive project management culture. If you can achieve that, you will greatly increase your chances of a successful project rescue.

Improvement Area	Questions to Ask
Quality programs	Is the project team conducting peer reviews? Is there a documented test strategy and test plan? Are the subject matter experts involved with the quality efforts?
Project work effort	Is the project team capturing actual hours for each task? Is the project manager reviewing the actual hours and applying them to future task estimates?
Risk management	Is the project team conducting regularly scheduled risk management sessions? Is the extended project team involved with the risk management and mitigation strategies?
Issue management	Is the project team conducting regularly scheduled issue management sessions? Are issues getting escalated in a timely manner—before they cause changes to the project plan?
Change management	Are the project manager and the project sponsor engaged in active change management? Is there budget and scheduled time for change investigation?
Project communications	Are weekly status meetings held weekly and do they use the weekly status report as the agenda? Are monthly status meetings held monthly and do they use the monthly status report as the agenda? Is the project status accurately portrayed in the weekly and monthly status meetings?

Table 8.2   Project Rescue Improvement Areas

Closing Perspective

This chapter looked at the two organizations charged respectively with leading and supporting the project rescue team. At this tumultuous time, the project steering committee must step up and provide the leadership necessary to give the project team confidence and the path to successfully rescue the runaway project. Often project steering committee members will have conflicting agendas. They must be able to put aside all differences and work toward the common goal. This group must perform at peak levels or the rescue attempt will fail miserably.

The bulk of the chapter described the support functions of a project rescue management office. This group's primary function is to provide "how to" guidance to the project manager, project architect and technical team. Another immediate form of assistance is to perform some administrative support functions in the project communications and financial areas. The primary goal of the project management office is to provide a supportive project management culture using very simple techniques. In other words, project management office personnel need to perform the activities that will allow the project manager to manage and the system architect to architect.

Effective performance by these two groups will help assure the project team will not fall into the same traps that got the project askew in the first place.

## CHAPTER 9

Defining the Project Rescue Approach

The preceding chapter focused on how to create or enhance a central project management office that can serve as a primary communication hub and enabler of the new project approach. This chapter looks at how the project rescue manager can build a new approach that will be supported by the extended project team.

Several factors will be working against the project at this point. Time is going to be in short supply, the project team is likely to be exhausted and perplexed, and the environment will be filled with strong, negative emotions. In fact, we'll examine how to turn these negative factors into healthy contributors to a rescue approach.

Objectives of the New Project Approach

There are obvious reasons why projects fail, such as a complex business case or lack of adequate funding. However, there are less understood, insidious reasons as well. There are factors that appear to be so obvious that raising them is embarrassing. Things slip by because everyone assumes that they are being done correctly.

A simple example of this is having an executive sponsor who also wants to be the business owner/user. Problems arise when the executive sponsor refuses to play the role of the business user by providing business requirements, but instead just criticizes everything that is placed in front of him or her. This is a prime recipe for project failure that will go unnoticed or at least unarticulated on many projects.

Nothing should be taken for granted when designing a project rescue. It's not just the difficult or complicated things that derail a project—such as complex functionality or technology that is too new to be reliable. Obvious or subtle activities can be just as culpable—and are even more painful because they could have more easily been mitigated.

In this phase, the rescue manager needs to be very open-minded and thorough in building a plan for moving the project forward. While it's still important to think outside the box, it is necessary to think inside it as well to capture all the possible exposures that face the project. Figure 9.1 shows some of the types of questions that should be asked, and how these are different from the assessment phase. The key objectives of these activities are as follows:

- Gain an understanding from the executive sponsor about the new scope, acceptance criteria, and deliverables. This should be included in the Statement of Work (SOW).

- Gain acceptance from the executive sponsor and other stakeholders about the new scope, acceptance criteria, and deliverables. This should be included in the Statement of Work (SOW).

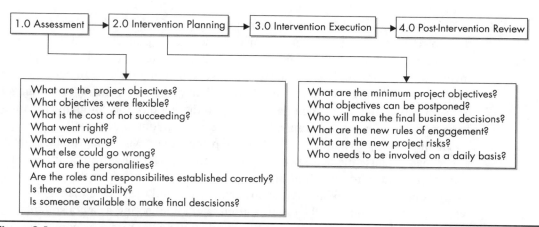

Figure 9.1 Questions to consider while building an approach

- Articulate what went wrong before the project rescue was invoked without allocating blame, to reduce the likelihood of repetition.

- Articulate the pros and cons of what is going to be done to salvage the project.

- Identify future critical decision points. This should be included in the Statement of Work (SOW).

- Capture the sense of urgency that exists in the organization and put it into constructive action.

What You Can Leverage

A project rescue involves leveraging all the emotions, history, best practices, intuition, and compromises that are available in a highly charged and stressed environment to salvage what is possible and turn the project around as much as possible. Lots of actions, both obvious and subtle, can be used to accomplish this.

There is a lot of optimism at the start of a project, and a lot of strong opinions about the way things should be done. Differences can exist at any level of the extended project team. It is not unusual to have a strong difference of opinion between a sponsor or stakeholder who is driving toward a specific conclusion and the project manager, who is driven to complete the project on time and on budget—or vice versa.

A lot of nice to haves, what ifs, ideologies, personal vendettas, strong opinions, and philosophies that are pretty much impossible to address empirically come into play at the start of a project—when everything appears to be going well. These differences of opinion can sometimes put enough pressure on the system to bring the project to the verge of failure—hence the need for a project rescue.

More often than not, the project rescue initiative takes place when everyone involved in the project has a lot to win or lose depending on the project outcome. This creates room for some new thinking and an opening for the rescue manager to use. Positive messages include focusing on the good of the company, learning from past experiences, building a stronger team, and looking forward.

The interesting dynamic here is that the project team wants the rescue manager to succeed because the team benefits in the process. But they ultimately may not want to give away too much of the recognition and accolades for the recovery. Many consultants speak about this circumstance—and the rescue manager, whether inside or outside the organization, is in effect acting as a consultant and needs to be prepared to let go of the project once the rescue is complete.

What's Healthy

While the environment driving a project rescue is highly charged and stressful, there are several inherent characteristics that can be healthy to the future of the project. The focus of the project rescue intervention is to leverage whatever is available in this area.

For example, a common enemy or objective—for example, getting the project done—can unify the different players on the team like nothing that came before. Fear of failure can be turned into a driving force to turn the project around.

The rescue manager, with clear support from the executive sponsor, should make it clear that the past will not be used to punish the team in the future. Energy that might be spent on self-protection can now be channeled into efforts that more directly impact the project. The team can be given another chance to prove itself.

This doesn't mean abandoning accountability or responsibility. A project review must recognize the mistakes that were made in the past. New metrics for the project team that give it a chance to look forward is healthier and more productive than explaining the intricacies of past failures.

You also need to leverage lessons learned from past experiences. The root cause analysis that serves as input to the lessons learned on the failed project can serve as strong reminders why the new approach must be embraced and not merely paid lip service.

What's Unhealthy

Fear of failure can and will lead to negative emotions. The project rescue manager needs to be attentive to signs of the following in the project culture.

With support from the executive sponsor, the rescue manager must ensure that the following do not lead to negative actions:

- Negative emotions
- Allocation of blame
- Desperation
- Team politics consuming energy
- Time spent trying to escape blame
- An "I told you so" attitude on the part of team members
- Desire for the project to fail
- Reemergence of the problems that led to the project rescue.

Building a New Approach to the Project

The research and interactions thus far in the project should give the rescue manager an understanding of how to proceed. But there are still major challenges that need to be resolved, including the following:

- Making it clear to the entire team that there is no magic wand to fix all the problems, but that the initiative is not doomed to failure either
- Incorporating details into the new approach
- Generating enthusiasm and motivation in the extended project team
- Taking control so that future decisions are made more quickly
- Building an approach that can be adjusted from time to time

Building a new approach should never be done in a vacuum; otherwise it will be wrong or will be rejected by members of the extended project team. Figure 9.2 shows a process that has worked well on different sized projects. The process begins with a definition of a new approach by the project rescue manager based on the findings and conclusions of the Assessment Phase.

There are two basic processing directions. Process Loop 1 involves working directly with the executive sponsors, stakeholders, and project team members to share the approach that the rescue manager defines and then incorporate his or her feedback. This requires several iterations to get right. Going into these discussions with a predefined approach, with the stipulation that you are prepared

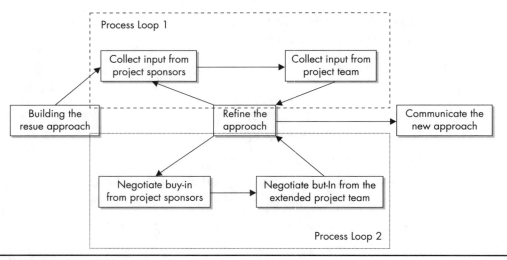

Figure 9.2   Processes for building a new rescue approach

to make any changes that make sense, provides a better start than sitting down with team members and beginning from scratch.

Process Loop 2 is used to negotiate buy-in from the contributors to the approach, and the extended project team. The key people that are going to ensure that the new approach is followed should already be aligned with the approach because of their involvement with Process Loop 1. However, it may be necessary to show them how the individual contributions of the other stakeholders should fit together.

Getting buy-in from the extended project team in some cases may require some additional changes to the approach. This may require further discussions with the stakeholders. In most cases, if the extended project team has already been interviewed in the Assessment Phase, their buy-in may be implicit or relatively easy to obtain.

The final step shown in Figure 9.2, after the extended project team has offered support for the new approach, is to communicate the approach in its final version. This will be discussed in more detail in the next chapter when we examine considerations for the new project plan.

Key Elements of the New Approach

Rescuing a troubled project requires leadership. This starts with recognition of a problem, continues with a request for dramatic help—which can be deflating to everyone involved in the project—and continues with doing whatever it takes to salvage what is available to be saved while maximizing value to the business.

Leadership is perhaps the single most important contributor when rolling out a new project approach. The rescue manager needs to demonstrate a strong commitment and a belief that the project is going to get better. The rescue manager needs to make this a number one priority for as many people in the organization as possible. The stakeholders that have the most to lose from a failed project need to see this commitment in order to lend their support.

By this point of the project rescue, many pillars are in place to support the salvage operation. The following list summarizes some of the key areas that the project rescue manager should have investigated by now or that will require additional investigation during this phase in order to draw usable conclusions:

- **Transparency**   An open and honest dialogue with the project team and sponsors about what went wrong in the project, what can be salvaged in the future, and what is needed to make the salvage a successful operation should now occur.

- **Accountability**   Every major decision or deliverable on a project requires signoff from a decision maker. Accountability, coupled with action, are needed to move a project forward. Problems in this area are not always discernable because assumptions are often made about a stakeholder's involvement that may not be true. This is an opportunity to document owners, accountabilities, timelines, and other expectations from every stakeholder *before* committing to another deadline.

- **Level playing field**   As discussed before, recriminations and "what ifs" that do not push the project forward need to be avoided; otherwise you may not get the truth, the energy, and the dedication required to execute a difficult salvage operation. The project rescue should be started with a new set of metrics that allow the team to worry more about the future rather than explaining the past.

- **Acceptable business requirements**   Because you need to clearly identify future decision points to determine if the rescue is working, also document the absolute minimum that will be acceptable to the business, as well as priorities, in case there is room to do more.

- **Flexibility**   This requires identification of the project variables that can be changed in the future. A general mood needs to be extended by the entire team to be more flexible in attaining some sort of project success. For example, is more budget available, can some timelines be extended, can resources be brought in from other project initiatives in the organization that are deemed to be less of a priority than the rescue initiative? This measure compares the amount of work that was planned with what was actually accomplished.

- **Tracking**   Document how project progress will be tracked going forward—for example, through a project plan, issues log, and updated budget. Just about everyone agrees that tracking is important, but there may still be complaints about efficiency, and about the time spent on what appear to be administrative tasks. Consider using three quantitative metrics to help with tracking the project. Earned Value (EV) is a measurement of planned work compared to actual work completed. If EV is accepted by the senior team, then the complaints about efficiency and the time spent doing it will be moot—without the effort, the project manager cannot report progress in the agreed metric. The cost performance index (CPI) and the schedule performance index (SPI) are also good tracking indicators. CPI is a measure of budgeted planned costs versus the actual costs. SPI is a measure of work performed versus work planned/scheduled. Both the CPI and the SPI are pretty easy to understand and do not allow much room for verbal dancing with respect to the project status.

- **Deliverables**   A list of key deliverables that require further rework before the project rescue can proceed, and what needs to be built by the end of the project.

- **Early warning systems**   Identification of how symptoms can be trapped and problems solved before reaching another cliff on the project.

- **Specific training**   Identification of specific skills that were lacking in the initiative. A training approach that identifies specifically who needs the training, how the training will be conducted, the timing, and the source of revenue.

- **Poor processes**   Identification of the processes that were identified as being problematic, unnecessary, or contributors to the problems faced by the project (for example, the time it takes to get equipment ordered).

Project Rescue Rules

Project rescues can be rife with conflict for several reasons: People may not understand what is being done; people may not agree with what's being done;

and people may believe a different direction is better for the project or for themselves. The following is a set of project rules that will resolve these concerns. They should be posted on your intranet and appended to the initial status reports so that the project rescue rules are known to everyone:

- **Leadership**   A project rescue requires someone to define a workable vision that others can understand, buy into, and move forward with. This demands that someone, usually the project rescue manager, leads the effort through the problems and solutions.

- **Be clear**   Clarity is lacking on many projects, but it is the best way to reduce risks. This includes clarity of business requirements, design, acceptance, and responsibilities. This is *not* about the format, structure, or grammar of the information, although this helps, but rather the unambiguous statement of what is really required.

- **Communicate**   Build a culture that inspires the team to communicate often and completely to one another. Such communication should include expectations, decision points, and meeting points, for the purpose of sharing information, maintaining buy-in, and reducing surprises. The area of communication is very important. It might even make sense to bring all the members of the rescue team together in the same geography to improve informal communication and team bonding.

- **Listen**   Listen to what other members of the team are saying and what they have learned from being in the trenches. Strong leadership coupled with the knowledge gained from listening to experiences are a powerful combination.

- **Always streamline**   The rescue manager and the project team should continually think of ways to reach their end goal with less effort and without introducing new risks. Continue to remove all non–value-added processes/tasks to get rid of wasted effort.

- **Single decision points**   Identify the deadlines by which specific decisions need to be made throughout the project life cycle and by whom. The Roles and Responsibilities section of the Statement of Work (SOW) is the best place to unequivocally identify the team members that have both the responsibility and authority to make decisions.

- **Find problems early**   Go into every project assuming that you are going to hit a wall at some point during the life cycle. This usually occurs when the complexities of the project become clear to the project team. The sooner you reach this point, the more time you have to resolve the problems.

- **Test early and test often**   Start reviewing and testing deliverables as soon as they are built. Keep testing them throughout the development cycle and avoid those common, nasty last-minute testing surprises that plague too many projects.

- **Trust and verify**   Believe what people are telling you, but always verify with other sources.

- **Ask every question**   Don't be afraid to ask any question that could help the project succeed. Nothing should be considered too stupid to ask.

- **Share what you've learned**   Do not withhold information that is gathered from the rest of the project team. Be truthful and be known to be truthful.

- **Work as a team**   Create a sense of one project team that is invested in winning or failing together. The project outcome is a shared responsibility.

- **Be ready for compromises**   The project rescue manager should also beready to make tradeoffs to get the project back on track.

- **Be smart about efficiency**   Be careful that a search for efficiency does not derail the project. For example, some people ask why status meetings are being conducted if things appear to be going well. The answer is that maybe the status meeting will identify what is *not* going well.

Project Classification

Project classification is a particularly powerful technique for forecasting the problems a project is likely to encounter. Certain project attributes result in a predisposition toward specific problems. By organizing the attributes into a couple of categories that can define projects, you can begin to shorten the list of potential problems into the most likely causes, and then focus your attention on getting the most pertinent details.

The cost of dealing (measured in time, costs, people, or some combination of these) with any of these attributes increases with their absolute value. Uncertainty also goes up the further out you go. As shown in Figure 9.3, this is one reason why "mega" type projects, which have a high value in most of these attributes, require extensive project management or they are likely to fail.

Being in the top quadrant is not a bad thing. A long project duration is not a bad thing either. Both situations just require special handling. The following list describes some of the commonly used dimensions, which are then explained in more detail in the sections that follow. Most of these do not have simple "yes" or

Attribute Values
Project duration
Cost/budget
Complexity
Degree of clarity & depth
Degree of unproven technology
Degree of user involvement
User training requirements
Resource sharing

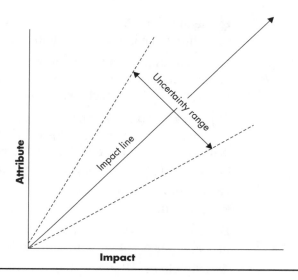

Figure 9.3 Project classification

"no" answers and, in fact, will fall somewhere on a continuum, requiring the rescue manager to gauge just how extensive the impact will truly be.

- **Project duration** The length of the project initiative expressed in some units of time. This refers to the elapsed time from start to finish. This can be confused with project work effort, which is a measure of the actual time devoted to the project, and may be shorter than the elapsed time. The project work estimate can be expressed as the total estimated hours of labor budgeted for the project.

- **Cost/budget** As discussed previously, this is a combination of human resources, infrastructure, environment, tools, and software costs. Human resources are usually a large or the largest component in this equation. The cost of human resources can be calculated as estimated labor in hours multiplied by the dollar cost per hour. The sum of the labor budget plus material costs is the project budget at completion (BAC). The BAC is the sum of all budgets allocated to a project and is synonymous with the term Performance Measurement Baseline (PMB).

- **Complexity** Refers to the level of difficulty of the project expressed in terms of the business users, technology requirements, and processes.

- **Degree of clarity and depth** Refers to the unambiguous interpretation of the project objectives, and whether additional work or assumptions need to be made to let the technical team do its work.

- **Implementation required** Refers to whether a project initiative requires a solution to be implemented into a production environment.

- **Degree of unproven technology** Refers to previous successful implementations of the technology architecture being used on the project. Integrating different technology components is always an intense effort.

- **Type of industry** The precision and complexity of the business requirements can vary by industry. This is also true of the amount of testing that is required and the willingness to be flexible in the types of variances that are acceptable to the executive sponsors.

- **Degree of business impact** Refers to the magnitude of changes that the solution will pose for the business conducted by the organization.

- **Degree of user involvement** Refers to the level of involvement in defining the requirements of the application by the people who are going to be using it.

- **Type of client** Refers to the level of maturity of the client in terms of understanding their own requirements and project management processes.

- **User training requirements** The level of new information, skills, and tools the business users require to do their jobs at the completion of the project.

- **Previous experience** Whether the people involved in the project have prior experience on similar types of projects.

- **Resource sharing** This refers to whether resources from the project will be shared between other groups in the organization.

- **Team personalities** Describes the collective personalities of the project team, as a combination or rollup of the individual ones.

The following subsections examine what the different values for these project attributes mean. By classifying a project into each of these attributes, a project rescue manager can pull together a new project strategy.

Project Duration

Project duration can be described on a scale (for example, one month, two months, and so on) or with adjectives (short, medium, long, mega). Small projects keep the team off balance as team members try to do many things in a very short period of time. This trend reverses itself as the duration moves to the mega description.

Larger projects tend to inspire overanalysis, overengineering, and a general delay in making the difficult decisions. Because the timeline is large, accountability for results is not immediate so a lot of mistakes continue to compound in the background without being noticed until it is too late to do anything about them.

Short projects are best handled by experienced project teams that can hit the ground running. Larger projects should be broken into medium-sized projects with measurable milestones that provide an early warning system if they are missed. The key approach regarding project duration is to build a project with incremental, measurable steps.

Cost/Budget

Project cost or budget can be expressed in a couple of different ways—we will use a financial measure as a common approach. This can be on a continuum as an absolute number. The budget is x or the budget is in the range of x to y, or the budget is x with a tolerance of plus or minus z. Cost can also be described in relative terms, such as low, medium, large, or mega.

The dollar values associated with each of these descriptions can have different values in different environments. A low budget for a project with NASA could be in the tens of millions of dollars, whereas a high-budget project for a non-profit or a startup organization might be $200,000. With the prevalence of offshore development, the absolute definition of these terms is also beginning to change. A $1,000,000 U.S. budget expressed in Indian rupees can become quite large and may qualify as a mega project.

The definition of these terms enjoys a higher degree of clarity within the same organization or industry. You can talk of a low-budget project or a high-budget project within a Fortune 100 banking environment and they have a clear relative distinction.

Project cost and project duration have similar key considerations and impacts on projects. Low budgets will force the project team to make artificial decisions to save money, while higher budgets tend to invite overspending without any contribution to the final objectives and a general lack of accountability. Higher budgets can help to hide problems until it's too late.

Even though budgets can be assigned in a vacuum, the rescue manager or project manager should break the total budget down into the detailed components to get a realistic understanding of what is available, when, and if there are some showstoppers right out of the gate.

In terms of people costs, remember to factor in travel costs, any relevant currency exchanges, and future raises/promotions. In terms of equipment costs, consider leasing as a way to reduce upfront capital costs.

Complexity

Project complexity is more difficult to break down than the two previous project dimensions. A project can be straightforward, average, complex, or very complex. But what does this really mean? Some organizations define complex projects in terms of the number of functional departments that are affected, the number of pages in the business requirements, and the extensiveness of the business rules. None of these measures is precise enough to have a consistent definition.

The commonality in describing project complexity is around the number of different pieces that need to come together to get a solution. Straightforward projects have very few moving pieces, affect maybe one or two departments, and have a small set of business requirements. Complexity grows as any of these measures grow.

Several "proof of concept" subprojects should be leveraged to validate the direction of the project by focusing on the complex pieces and proving that they are being handled correctly.

Degree of Clarity and Depth

A lack of either of either clarity or depth is usually a sign that the extended project team (including the business users) do not have a good understanding of the project requirements or intended solution. In fact, the greater the push you receive when trying to achieve clarity and depth, the more likely it is that these details have not been finalized.

It is impossible to complete a project without clarity and depth. For example, the objective "Let's redesign the web site" is clear, but it has no depth. Too many project managers are given this level of depth and expected to successfully deliver a project without the accompanying time or business knowledge required to do this successfully.

Clarity and depth can best be achieved at the start of an initiative—either the start of the project itself or at the beginning of the rescue intervention. It gets harder to ask for these later in the project cycle because the stakeholders who have not provided either up front will assume that the details are already available and will be less likely to accept responsibility because it is easier to blame the project team. These facts may simply not be known.

Implementation Required

The answer to the question of whether implementation is required as a part of the project is a straightforward "yes" or "no," which belies the otherwise large impact that implementation has on the project's level of complexity. It refers to the need to launch some sort of application into the real world after building, integrating, or customizing it.

The aforementioned proof of concepts, which highlights technology problems early in the project life cycle and provides more time for correction, should be leveraged when implementation is a requirement.

Degree of Unproven Technology

The answer to the question of whether unproven technology is being used on the project is "yes" or "no." An answer of "yes" must be accompanied by more information to determine the level of impact this will have on the project timelines, budget, or people. Implementation requirements are exacerbated with the use of unproven technology as part of the solution. This has become a significant problem with the continuing growth of new technologies and the release of new versions of existing technologies. Offshore development is adding further strain. Integration issues can exist at any point that the technologies touch.

Early integration test beds should be used to validate the selected technology in parallel with the development activities. The testing can be performed with a minimum set of business functions, as the purpose of these activities is primarily to prove connectivity between the technology components.

Type of Industry

Common industry groupings include the following: financial (includes banking, insurance, and security as subgroupings), retail, manufacturing (with automobile, hi-tech, aerospace, and pharmaceuticals being subgroupings), entertainment, healthcare, government, and energy.

Industries tend to exhibit their own cultures that impact how a project can be executed. Financial systems, obviously, have a strong emphasis on number crunching and balancing. Long test cycles are expected.

An entertainment-based solution, on the other hand, receives a premium for creativity. It is not complex per se, but an enormous amount of effort will be spent on details of appearance and content. Entertainment solutions will also likely be tied to some marketing campaigns so time of delivery will also be a key metric. Launching a movie site after a movie is in the theatres is not valuable.

Degree of Business Impact

Business impact can be expressed in terms of low, medium, and high with distinctions made in a number of ways. Distinguishing between low, medium, and high may involve counting the number of business functions affected, the percentage of revenue being touched, percentage of the client affected, or the number of employees being affected. Our preference is to rely on the following descriptions:

- **Low impact**   No impact on the major businesses of the organization.

- **Medium impact**   Impacts about 20 percent of the businesses of the organization.
- **High impact**   Any project with an impact on more than 20 percent of the businesses of the organization.

Projects that have higher impacts on the business require a higher degree of user involvement, written user signoff before launch, and a detailed contingency plan. The contingency plan needs to be tested so that it is ready to be invoked if the new solution is launched but fails in the production environment.

Degree of User Involvement

This can also be expressed in terms of low, medium, and high. Low user involvement is problematic. You can almost guarantee that anything you bring to a user is going to be changed the first time the user sees it, and maybe even a few times after this meeting. It is necessary to keep users involved throughout the project life cycle. This ideally means including users as core members of the project team. If this is not possible, they need to be included at checkpoints throughout the life cycle and their involvement needs to be guaranteed.

If users keep changing their minds early in the project, it is highly likely that their acceptance would be much more difficult to acquire if their involvement was delayed to later phases in the project. Withholding the solution to avoid getting bogged down in early debate does not appear to be a successful mitigation strategy.

With the continuing growth of offshore development, it is becoming more difficult to have the close proximity required between users and the development team for this sort of collaboration. More extensive documentation and conference calls can be used to bridge this gap. Collaboration tools are also emerging that can be used, but discipline and process will need to be mandated by the rescue manager for them to be useful.

Type of Client

Clients can be internal or external to an organization, depending on how a project manager defines them. Anyone who requires services can be considered a client. They can be described as newcomers, experienced, or highly sophisticated. Each of these client types offers a different set of opportunities and challenges.

Newcomers require support, but they may be highly skeptical of the way the rescue is unfolding. They will require more extensive explanations and demonstrations before they fully buy in to what is happening.

Experienced clients have gone through similar projects before and so may understand the project rescue direction. They may be able to provide better assistance to the rescue manager if they have not been jaded by past events. Sophisticated clients may already know exactly what they need and may just be looking for someone to implement the revised solution.

User Training Requirements

User training can be described in terms of duration, depth, content, and frequency. Values can be expressed as low, medium, and high. Team resources are often required to support or conduct user training, at least in the early phases after launch.

Users who are not properly trained will end up causing a great deal of noise and confusion that could otherwise derail a successful launch. This training should be conducted early in the lifecycle of the project rescue. This is more likely to win the enthusiasm and support of the user community as they learn more about the project. The caveat is not to avoid conducting the training so far in advance that the information and new skills are all but forgotten by system launch time.

Previous Experience

Nothing is better than past experience. Described in terms of yes, no, and some, previous experience by team members can be leveraged to build a better approach, and can also be counted on to deliver as per an aggressive project plan.

Resource Sharing

Sharing any non-trivial resources between projects in the organization creates an overhead on top of the project duties. Sharing resources requires a serious consideration that key resources cannot be counted on to be available when the project needs them.

Dedicated usage of key resources may be considered a prerequisite to any successful project launch. Fewer responsibilities or distractions will improve the productivity of key resources on the project. Testers, business users, architects, and project managers are often split between projects.

Team Personalities

While individual personalities can vary, teams generally end up taking on a specific mega-personality. The project rescue manager needs to use his or her leadership to turn a team into a motivated, assertive, focused unit. Other types of team personalities can exist that need to be changed:

- **Jaded**   This team has been crushed by past failure and is pessimistic about any chances at renewal. They will be like anchors to any new approach and will need to be coaxed and prodded to believe in something else.

- **Angry**   Instead of pessimism, this team has become angry and resentful at their lack of success. They will openly argue with each other, fight regularly, and offer lots of criticism to their teammates.

- **Political**   This team is trying to find blame and the members are trying to position themselves to be untarnished by the lack of project success. This team will be very difficult to deal with, as the members will try to use the project rescue to their personal advantage and may try to subtly derail it.

- **Anxious**   Members of this team are anxious about their careers, feel bad for the company, and are nervous about future prospects. They are likely open to some new ideas if the person offering them is also taking responsibility and is confident of success.

Closing Perspective

This chapter focused on building a new approach to the project (for example, a project rescue approach). The information collected in the past activities and the nature of the project are the basis for the first draft of this approach. To be successful, the rescue manager needs to involve as many people as possible in improving this approach.

In some rare cases, the activities defined in this chapter may force the inevitable conclusion that the project cannot be rescued. This needs to be communicated immediately to the project sponsors so that they can look for another opinion.

In most cases, a project rescue is possible with certain provisions. These provisions must be clearly defined, communicated, and supported by the project team and the executive sponsors to move forward.

## CHAPTER 10

Building a New Project or Rescue Plan

A relevant, revised project plan is an essential tool for a successful rescue intervention. This chapter assumes that the reader already has some knowledge of the basic techniques for project planning and building project plans. The original project probably had a project plan, albeit one that did not address all the potential pitfalls. Instead, this chapter focuses on the additional or special techniques and information that are required to turn a good project plan into a stronger one—one that is relevant for rescuing the project. The key concept of "relevance" is examined in more detail in the sections that follow.

Guiding Principles for Building a Project Rescue Plan

The culture of an organization is often reflected in the project plans produced by its managers. Are deadlines realistic? Do people really know what is going on? How introspective is the organization? How involved are senior managers? Is senior management willing to invest freely in an initiative when there is a strong upside? Are deadlines usually missed without accountabilities or penalties? Does senior management trust their managers? What checks and balances are required? Answers to these and other questions are reflected in the way the activities and tasks are defined, who is involved, and how they are validated.

Even corporate policies such as the payment of supplies makes a difference to how a project plan is structured. Late payments to vendors could result in a lack of commitment on their part, making it difficult to count on their cooperation during tight timeframes.

The lessons learned during the assessment and earlier planning stages need to be included in the plan that will control the rescue initiative and need to satisfy the following objectives:

- **Inspiration**   Prove diagrammatically and mathematically that a successful turnaround is possible for the project.

- **Directions**   Show what needs to be done to facilitate a successful turnaround, by whom, and when.

- **Tracking**   Track the milestone dates and deliverables that are important for reaching the project targets. What are the important goalposts?

- **Maintainable**   The structure of the project or rescue plan needs to accommodate modifications on-the-fly and allow a rapid turnaround for incorporating new tasks or activities.

- **Story**   In some ways this is the most important objective. The plan should reveal the logic and flow of how the project is going to be rescued and the philosophy that is being followed. Does the plan tell a story?

A project plan that does not satisfy these collective objectives is likely to be rejected out of hand, and is unlikely to succeed even if it succeeds in getting the support of the project team. Table 10.1 examines why each of these objectives is crucial for a successful outcome and provides the key instructions for achieving them.

Objective	Justification	Instructions
Inspiration	This will be the first physical proof to the combined project team that the project can be saved. Inspiration will focus and energize them, temporarily removing their collective resignation. They will find the strength to try again.	Without getting bogged down in details, lay out all the major deliverables so that people can see the project coming to a successful end. The story element is very important. The team needs to see that a positive end is in sight.
Directions	When the team begins to believe that the project can be salvaged, team members need to understand how to get to the destination. Time is going to be short, so the team will need to know what to do and when to do it.	Use deliverables and milestone events to identify major goalposts. Can you identify champions for each major grouping of activities? Who does what and when?
Tracking	Continually measure progress against the rescue plan and be prepared to make corrections to bring it back in line. The systemic reasons why the project originally went off track may not be adequately suppressed yet.	Tracking results versus the plan is only the first step for the project rescue manager. The results need to be communicated to the project team with an immediate inclusion of corrective action to ensure that another round of project rescue is not needed. Be aggressive in tracking the plan.
Maintainable	Significant complexity needs to be captured in the project plan, but you still need to be able to make changes in a brisk fashion as changes are identified on an ongoing basis.	You need to leverage a physical format for the plan and an electronic tool that can be updated within an hour or two—in time for the next status meeting.
Story	Because you can almost guarantee that further changes to the rescue plan will be required, the plan needs to relate the story of how the project is being rescued. This will show the big picture to the entire team. The story always makes the plan more readable.	Show how the different phases and activities flow into one another in the overall plan. What principles are being followed? Is there enough time to do the activities? Is there a logical grouping (for example, hiring a resource, training the resource, using the resource)? Are the internal policies of the organization incorporated in the plan (for example, equipment requisitions being produced prior to purchase and usage by the team)? A Work Breakdown Structure (WBS) is a good tool for this.

Table 10.1   Rescue Plan Objectives

Common Elements and Features of a Rescue Plan

Building a project plan is a combination of art and science. So many different techniques, variables, and permutations are available for the exercise that no two project plans can be identical. Building a project plan is not like building a car, a chair, or a widget, although there have been many attempts to industrialize the nature of business and technology projects in the past few decades. While some success has been achieved, we are very far away from building a factory floor–like process that cranks out project plans based on a tested and accurate blueprint.

Even Enterprise Resource Management (ERP) solutions, which are arguably the most factory-like of the technology solutions that have been developed, require a significant amount of customization in most organizations. In fact, even ERP training programs often need to be modified to suit the specific requirements of a team of business users. Isn't training just training? Even at this level, the solution is not a "cookie cutter" or repeatable factory floor approach.

So what does this all mean for projects in general? There will always be differences at some level of the project (for example, vacation schedules will vary, decision makers will have different personalities, and team expectations may have gone up in terms of compensation expectations).

Project plans will always be affected by an inherent measure of uncertainty. It's your job as a project or rescue manager to build them in such a way to meld best practices with flexibility to produce a predictable result.

While project plans are unlikely to be identical across projects, there are still some significant commonalities. The following elements must be incorporated into every project plan:

- **Timeline**   This includes the standard start and end dates for the project. This needs to be extended with a clear statement of any remaining contingencies that are still available to the team if other problems arise before reaching the end date. Clarity around this is important for building an honest rescue plan that will survive the inevitable ups and downs of uncertainty through the dedication of the project team.

- **Milestones**   Milestone events are prerequisites for another unit of work that leads to the completion of the project. Identify every significant milestone event that leads to the ultimate end goal of the initiative and mark it clearly on the project plan. Missing one of these is a giant red flag that requires an immediate corrective response. Again, be honest about including any contingencies that are still available if something does not go according to plan.

- **Deliverables**   Identify the name of a deliverable, when it needs to be completed, and who needs to sign off on it. Try and allocate ownership of each deliverable to a single resource. This reduces training requirements and administrative overhead, while building a sense of strong accountability.

- **Resources**   Start by identifying the roles and responsibilities and get very specific about the individuals who will be involved. Also indicate when these resources are needed, how they are brought onto the project, their level of involvement, the milestone dates, and the deliverables they own.

- **Activities and tasks**   Start and end dates for every activity, subactivity, or task. Keep the process more general by identifying duration for the unit of work. This will make it easier to shift the items around in the schedule. Anything that is critical should be tied or linked to a milestone. Also, try to allocate a group of related items to the same resource(s).

- **Budget**   This could be derived information based on resources and their timelines on the project. However, we recommend exercising caution when trying to maintain a budget and a timeline in the same toolset because it can become a logistical nightmare. It is more efficient to track budgets at a higher level—for example, many units of work—rather than trying to use every low-level item (for example, hours) to generate a total number. Information at this level is uncertain and difficult to maintain.

- **Dependencies**   Use a milestone to identify every major dependency in the project plan. Every linked activity or task should then end in a clearly identified milestone. This makes it much easier to move milestones around the plan along with all their associated activities.

- **Contingency**   Being open, honest, and accurate about the contingency that is available in any of the remaining deadline dates will improve your ability to react to future obstacles. Show the contingency directly in the project plan using named activities, or consider positioning the milestones to visually reveal the slack time that is available in the life cycle.

- **Objectives**   Explicitly reading through the project plan with clearly stated deliverables, roles, responsibilities, and timelines should make the project objectives clear to the reader. This is not intended to replace the project charter but may be a good indication of how well the plan tells a story that can adapt to future uncertainty.

Common Problems

Project planning is difficult because of all the different variables and unknowns that go into the process, how they integrate together, and ultimately how they relate to a moving target. There are just so many problems that it's little wonder that surveys continue to show that three-quarters of all projects fail in one of the important measurements of on-time, on-budget, or meeting all the functional requirements.

While some problems can be mitigated, the real challenge facing project managers is that some uncertainties cannot be resolved during the planning phase. Some answers are not available, things change, and more accurate information ultimately becomes available. Uncertainty is an undeniable part of project planning and cannot be wished away, mandated away, or yelled away.

Consider the following specific issues that can impact the accuracy of a project plan and judge how realistic it would be to overcome all future uncertainty in the collective answers—while the clock is quickly ticking during the project rescue:

- **People issues**   Will the appropriate resource be found and hired according to an established timeline? Will the resource suffer through a personal problem that could impact their work on the project? Will the resource find a significantly better paying career opportunity? What if the resource is not as competent or knowledgeable as he or she appears?

- **Timeline issues**   How do we accurately estimate the length of each task? Previous benchmarks are not exactly the same as the project in question. As commonly stated with financial results, past performance may not necessarily be indicative of future performance. How will all the little uncertainties in individual tasks add up in the final result?

- **Vendor issues**   Will the vendor's resources buy into your tight timeline? How can you guarantee this? Is the vendor able to put your interests above their self-interest? For how long? Under what conditions? How do your different vendors work with each other?

- **Detail issues**   Is too much detail being included in the project plan? Do you have enough information to go that deep? How can you confirm the accuracy of the underlying assumptions? How much work will be required to fix the details when more accurate information becomes available?

- **Prioritization issues**   How do you know that other priorities will not impact your project in terms of the availability of resources in the future? How do you stop legislative issues from hurting your dependencies? What happens if a key executive changes and has a different set of priorities, but still expects the same results?

- **Policy or process issues**   What happens when a developer wants a $5,000 development computer, while the CFO is not willing to sign off on it because of a $2,000 machine that could be used in the evenings? Which executive processes are making it difficult to get things done in the trenches? What if this de-motivates key resources, perhaps even causing them to leave the project? What if the resources are just de-motivated and working inefficiently? How will you even know, and what can you do about this?

- **Ignorance issues**   "You don't know what you don't know." This is perhaps the biggest cause of project failure. It is also a big contributor to most arguments. Everyone is proposing an answer, and it generally takes a lot of time to empirically prove the correct direction. Known risks have a chance of being mitigated. It's the stuff that you don't know about that can't be assessed in advance.

- **Distance issues**   How do you get employees in different time zones to get involved in the project, while supporting their local customs and way of life. This is becoming even more important with the growing popularity of offshore development. How is information shared? Does it take a day just to pose a question in Asia, get an answer in North America, and then a response in Europe?

Not all of these will be a problem on every project. But there will always be some uncertainty about which ones to mitigate and by how much. Trying to defend against all of them would be cost prohibitive or impractical given real-world deadlines.

Figure 10.1 shows a process for building a project rescue plan. These activities offer another level of categorization for the list of potential problems that can affect the process, as discussed in the text that follows.

Basic Assumptions

Why do we make assumptions? Some people say that you should never assume anything. They insist on doing the research to be sure. By all means do this; however, as we've examined previously in this book, the act of making assumptions cannot be entirely banished. Even accepting something that two people tell you requires you to make an assumption that they both cannot be wrong. Similarly, you may make the assumption that a business owner understands their business and can be trusted to sign off on the business requirements.

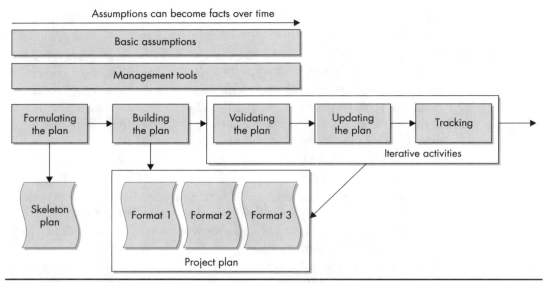

Figure 10.1   Process for building a project rescue plan

Your goal is to rely on assumptions that are as close to being facts as possible. This requires you to dig deeper before accepting what you hear, and to get other sources, including external best practices that support the assumption.

Project plans are based on assumptions at some level. Do everything you can to ensure that the assumptions being made are true. The team and especially the project sponsors need to agree with this and also need to accept that there must be a collective resolve to move ahead if an assumption proves to be invalid. This is an absolute requirement.

Formulating the Plan

This is a group of activities, generally owned by the rescue manager, to build a skeleton for the project plan. This will consist of identifying the core project team and establishing the high-level activities that will be followed. At this stage, consider the following questions:

- **Methodology**   Is the methodology being used appropriate for the project being rescued? As a validation, identify similar projects that have used the same methodology and achieved some level of success. Ensure that you are following it in the same way. Ensure that there is appropriate expertise within the team to use the methodology correctly.

- **Estimates**   This is not the right time to include details around task durations, but some knowledge of how long things take will be required. Begin with past experience and interviews with team members to lay this foundation. You will look deeper into estimates in the next set of activities, but for now there are some questions to consider. How does the current project compare to similar projects that were completed before? Should a contingency factor be put into individual estimates? What are the key factors that can impact the estimates? Is the current situation better or worse than average?

- **Core team**   Aside from the rescue manager, who else is committed to the project on a full-time basis? There may be many part-time commitments, but these do not count during a project rescue. Full-time involvement is mandatory from everyone deemed to be a key resource. Are the right skills available to the team? What can be done to make them better?

Figure 10.2 shows a type of skeleton rescue plan that can be constructed at this point. This is in the form of a Gantt chart, although this is not the only format that

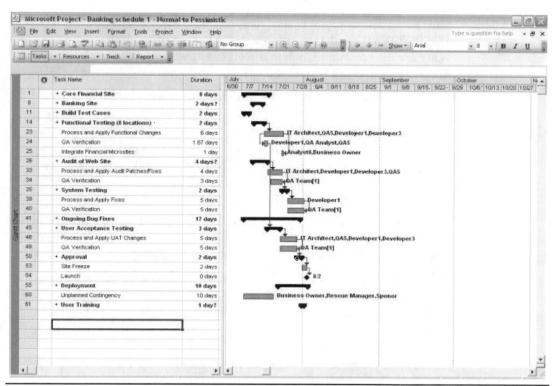

Figure 10.2   Rescue plan skeleton

could be used. We recommend about three different formats for a rescue plan, which are discussed later in this chapter. At this point, you have a sense of timeline, major activities, and an idea of the resources that will be needed during the rescue.

Building the Plan

We're going to examine a number of different approaches for building the rescue plan later in this chapter, but consider some of the potential problems and tradeoffs that you will need to address in the process:

- **Level of detail**   What is the right level of detail? Too little detail, and the plan is little more than guidelines. Too much detail and the plan may not get finished in time. It might become too much work to maintain. It might be impossible to understand. Should you identify activities that are a week in duration? A day? An hour? A few hours? Is time even the right measurement? There are many real world examples in which months and months were spent building detailed project plans only to be thrown out because they were too cumbersome to maintain.

- **Skill sets**   How do you ensure that the resources will have the correct level of skills? What are the specific skills? What are the complementary skills? What are the compromises and offsets? Where is the training going to come from? At what cost? How frequently?

- **Estimates**   Let's get back to the difficulty of working with estimates. How do you rely on an inexact science for something as important as a rescue plan? Try and work with ranges. Try and maintain some level of contingency across the project. Continually adjust estimates as you go forward in the rescue intervention. New information will allow the estimates to be refined with more accuracy. The contingency may be required to offset initial inaccuracies.

- **Commitments**   How can you commit resources to certain events that may be weeks or months away? What personal or professional conflicts will involve them? What happens if you miss a key commitment? Where should duplicate resources be retained to prevent a worst-case scenario?

- **Third parties**   How do you get third parties to give you their best work and dedication without getting into detailed financial negotiations and contractual obligations too early in the project? The more desperate you are, the more expensive they may become. Counting on their professionalism and long-term relationship prospects will be worth highlighting to the third parties.

Validating the Plan

Walk through the rescue plan to collect further input and information from the extended team members. Be clear about the assumptions that are being made to accommodate the plan and what needs to be done to make them accurate. Use the techniques and procedures discussed in earlier chapters to facilitate this information capture.

Updating the Plan

Contradictions may be collected during the validation activities from different stakeholders and team members. The rescue manager will need to resolve these and build a revised plan that will again need to be validated. Contradictions that cannot be resolved will need to be tabled and dealt with when new information becomes available. The contingency that is available to the project team will be necessary to accommodate this.

Tracking

Tracking is also a problematic activity. How do you know that the tracking information you are receiving is accurate? Team members have their own perspectives, often aligning with an extreme viewpoint that is either too optimistic or pessimistic. Neither of these approaches is particularly helpful within the tight tolerances of a project rescue. You need to look around and find your own way of identifying accurate information. This may require you to offset information that is reported to you. If a particular team leader tends to report pessimistically, you might try and change that leader or figure out a reasonable offset to apply to the reported information going forward.

Management Tools

All the project planning is going to be done with certain tools. Are you using an appropriate project management tool? Is it too complex? Does it do some things in a very complicated manner? Are you even using the tools for the right purpose? Is an inappropriate tool being forced on you for procedural reasons? Be careful not to let this common problem destroy your chances for conducting a successful rescue operation.

Misuse of the Project Plan

Is the project plan being used for the right reasons? Is it causing too much overhead work from the project team? Is the information being assessed on the plan accurate?

Because the project plan contains a great deal of information, it lends itself to misuse in the name of efficiency. Why not use it to calculate and track the project budget because all the detailed involvement of the resources is shown step by step? Why create an extra status report when the plan can be used to show what is complete and what is not?

The answers to these questions will be obvious at the end of a project that has not succeeded. For example, to use a project plan for a detailed budget analysis will require a significant amount of extra time *when* it is being updated and maintained. This creates a bottleneck around updating the project plan, which makes tracking more difficult.

In the second example, how do you store and manipulate open and closed issues using a status report? What about simple action lists such as "Amanda will take minutes in the next workshop"? Do you really want to keep that level of excruciating detail in a project plan? The ripple impacts are insidious. The maintenance overhead becomes a nightmare, so it becomes difficult to keep the plan up-to-date. It either gets out of date or a lot of work that could be spent on active ventures is spent on administrative activities. There may be larger gaps between status meetings, or the rapid culture of a project rescue may be discouraged.

Formats

The clarity and ease-of-use advantages from using an appropriate project planning format cannot be understated. Many different formats are available for project plans, but we recommend three that are the most effective for project rescue interventions: Gantt chart, timeline slide, and tabular format. The critical project path is implicit in these formats.

Gantt Chart

Perhaps the most basic and widely used project plan format is the Gantt chart because it combines a visual flow to the project, along with the necessary details to control and track it properly. Gantt charts that show the entire project in one, two, or three pages are the objective of the rescue planning effort. If more complex details are required, consider having a "reporting Gantt chart" as the primary reporting tool and link it to separate subplans that contain further details.

Timeline Slide

An even higher level of reporting is possible through a simple timeline slide that attempts to fit high-level activities and any information truly worth mentioning onto a single page or two. This does not require a specialized project management tool like the Gantt chart does. Any software, like Microsoft Project or Visio, which can support presentation style graphics can be used to manage this format.

Figure 10.3 shows an example of this format. The advantage to this approach is that it provides a good overview of the entire process. It also offers a good tool for describing the process to other members of the extended project team. Business sponsors can focus on the important dates and not get bogged down by details. It is also very easy to incorporate changes—perhaps an hour or so to update the entire slide regardless of the changes that are required. On the flip side, the absence of details may require you to augment it with one of the other project plan formats.

It is useful to start the rescue process with this type of project plan until there is some agreement on the skeleton and then to switch to one of the other formats.

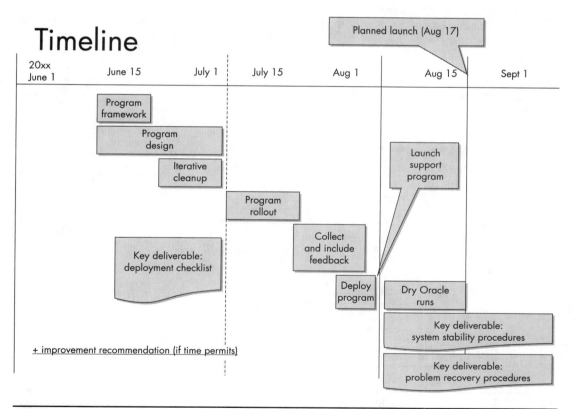

Figure 10.3   Timeline slide

Table

The table format can hold a lot of detailed information and is easier to manipulate than the other two formats. It lacks the visual impact of the Gantt, which is useful for explaining the flow and story of the project rescue. The table format, however, is well suited for discussions about the details once these are understood. This format is a good complement to one of the other two.

Using a tool such as a spreadsheet or a word processor offers the significant advantage of rapid data entry and modification. Figure 10.4 shows a project plan in table format using a spreadsheet. Notice that the logical grouping of the resources reduces the amount of typing and makes it easier to move resources between tasks. The tool, of course, offers a lot of functionality for additional analysis.

Activity	Tasks	Duration (days)	Resources	Start Date
Planning	Gather Information	15	Business Resources	1-Apr
	Interview Users		ESponsor, Manager, Business Owner 1, Business Owner 2	
	Define Business Functions			
	Build Project Charter Draft			
	Review and Update Project Charter			
	Confirm Business Case			
	Build Business Models			
Architecture	Review Product Candidates	10	Rescue Manager, Project Manager, Architect	5-May
	Review Best Practices			
	Short-List Architectural Choices			
	Build Architecture "To Be"			
	Build Pricing Options			
Business Review	Review Architecture, Pricing Options	2	Project Manager, Esponsor, Rescue Manager	17-May
	Update Deliverables	2	Rescue Manager, Architect	
	Get Business Signoff	1	Project Manager, Esponsor, Rescue Manager	17-May
Environment	Shop for Hardware	5	Project Manager, Architect	28-May
	Shop for Software			
	Place Orders			
	Implement development environment			
	Implement staging environment			
Design	Detailed Design	5	SdevArch	28-May
	Evaluate Overall Design			
	Update Overall Design			
	Content Management Suite			
	Digital Asset Management			
	Search (internal, External, addons)			
	eCommerce (new members)			
	Design Review Signoff	Milestone		3-Jun
Creative	Information Architecture	15	Business Group	3-Jun
	Storyboard			

Figure 10.4   Project plan in table format

Defining Date Commitments

How exactly do you build the duration of the project initiative and the placement of the milestone events? This can be a source of intense arguments on a project team, and the perspective can vary depending on who is involved in the negotiations.

Consider these perspectives. The business sponsor and the business owners want the solution right away (because yesterday is impossible) or no later than a specific date. The intermediate details will not be as important.

The development teams on the other hand will be reluctant to provide a final answer without understanding all the details and will want to work bottom up in producing their timeline. The ultimate deadline will be dependent on these parts. Project managers will take a view somewhere in between, recognizing the need for speed, while being sensitive to the details.

This leads to several high-level approaches for building dates into the project or rescue plan: date-driven approach, resource-driven approach, combined approach.

Date-Driven Approach

Date-driven approaches tend to be favored by business users and sponsors. This approach assumes that the delivery date of the project is the key driver and cannot be moved. The team needs to ask the question, "What needs to be done to meet this date?" This could, for example, require an increase in resources, more funding, or a reduction in functionality.

With a pre-established end date, you can begin to work backward using a methodology as a guide. As this is a project rescue, you presumably have completed most of the planning and requirements gathering. How much more time is required for the architecture and design development? Who needs to be involved? How tight can you make this timeframe?

Now move to the next set of activities and lay them out as well—at a high level. Leave three weeks to test and accept, four weeks if a lot of financial transactions are involved. You should now have a sense of how the overall plan is unfolding. If the times are too tight, you need to get the project sponsor's support in reducing the requirements or getting more resources.

The manager's expertise needs to be used to ensure that the remedy does not create additional problems on the project. Adding an unskilled developer in an offshore location is not going to help, and may be more problematic. Perhaps a higher cost local resource is a better answer?

Something will need to give to meet tight, nonmovable deadlines. We examine this in further detail when we talk about consensus building in the next part of the book.

Resource-Driven Approach

This approach is generally favored by development teams because it appears to be more reasonable from a detailed perspective. Because it takes so much time to do something well, the idea is to build the detailed activity and task list and consult with the people doing the work to determine how long the project is going to take to complete.

The project completion date is based on a bottom-up approach that is a sum of all the individual pieces. Unfortunately, this may not correspond to a date that the business requires or needs. What happens if the client is launching a product in two months with a multimillion dollar marketing campaign. This bottom-up approach is not going to be acceptable to those paying the bills.

To make the dates more acceptable, you could try and affect the very same variables that are available to the date-driven approach. This could involve adding resources in some places, while removing functionality in others. The improvement may be useful, but at some point, the plan that the current resources dictate may not be sufficient to meet the business objectives. At this point, the rescue manager needs to drive the following questions:

- What do we need to do to satisfy the prioritized business requirements?
- What other investments to we need?
- What can be taken off the table?
- What can be done after the initial delivery?

Only the answers and support for these questions will determine what will ultimately be delivered.

Combined Approach

The combined approach is perhaps the most reasonable. Begin by placing the major goalposts in place and then use a bottom-up approach to fill in the details. Attention can be focused in the areas that are not fitting together properly.

Closing Perspective

The project plan is the most important tool for a project rescue. Done properly, it can encapsulate many of the elements that need to be communicated to the project team and the project sponsors. This chapter did not try to teach you how to build a project plan. Project managers have developed their own styles for doing this. The focus was rather on the type of project plan that needs to be built to facilitate a successful project rescue. This incorporates elements of standard project planning, but there is a much stronger focus on efficiency, clarity, and maintainability. The essential questions for the rescue manager to answer with the rescue plan are as follows:

- What can we do with what we have?
- What do we need to do to meet our objectives?
- What compromises do we need to make?
- Who needs to make the compromises?
- Do we have the executive support to make these compromises?

Execute the Intervention

## CHAPTER 11

Managing the Intervention

Y ou might hope that if all the work in the earlier phases was done properly, as shown in Figure 11.1, that the execution phase would be painless, but this is rarely the case. The rescue manager needs to stay on top of everything in the rescue plan and be prepared to go deep into areas that look like they're getting into trouble. You might, for example, have to wake up an unresponsive employee in the middle of the night in a different time zone to make sure that a computer has been set up for a new employee. This is a simple example. In many cases, the involvement will probably call for a lot more creativity, business knowledge, and persuasion abilities.

The Essential Process

How much time has passed since the project break point was reached? It all depends on the nature and size of the project. In most cases, however, it should not be more than one to three weeks in duration. Anything more than this will begin to lose the attention and faith of the extended project team. Too little time and the answers and solutions may lack sufficient accuracy and wisdom to be effective. If you cannot find the answers to rescue the project in this timeframe, you will need to restructure the objectives of the initiative to further break it into smaller phases.

The project team, and specifically the manager charged with rescuing the project, will need to change focus from investigation mode to a tactical, hands-on one. The Execution phase requires a different set of skills and focus from the project rescue manager. This new involvement can be summarized as "Lead-Track-Resolve."

Leadership is needed to implement the rescue plan and ensure that the extended team remains committed and focused on the results. Frequent tracking activities are necessary to capture the truth about what is really happening. Resolution will be required to deal with the additional problems that will arise in this phase.

"Lead-Track-Resolve" is illustrated in the center of Figure 11.2, with some of the factors that could potentially damage the momentum of the project once again shown around the perimeter of the circle. These factors are particularly nefarious because they cannot be mandated away by the executive sponsor. These wildcard problems

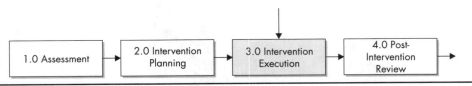

Figure 11.1   The Execution phase

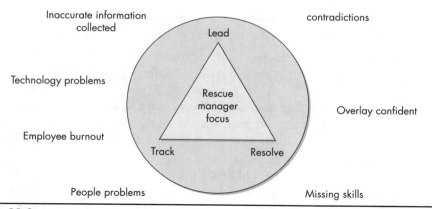

Figure 11.2   Project rescue manager's role

could or could not materialize, so mitigation strategies have to be reasonably flexible. This is the reason for building contingency into the project rescue plan.

Identifying these issues before they become big problems through extensive and proactive tracking provides an opportunity for resolution with minimal use of contingency built into the project plan. It is a good idea to preserve as much of this contingency as possible for as long as possible. Leadership abilities are required to offset the negative emotions that will arise when yet more problems appear and the team confidence starts to waver.

The following list identifies some problems that can plague a project at this stage of the rescue life cycle:

- **Inaccurate information collected**   Despite reasonable efforts to validate the information that was collected in the assessment and planning phase, some facts could just be plain wrong and will need to be readdressed.

- **Overconfidence**   Overconfidence needs to be actively managed to avoid a false sense of security. Overconfidence is as bad as a lack of confidence. Overconfidence can lead to shortcuts and assumptions that prove to be false. It can also create conflict within the team by rubbing some team members the wrong way.

- **Missing skills**   Someone can look great on paper and do well in interviews, and may be the best you can find, but there may still be some missing skills.

- **Contradictions**   Some of the basic objectives, requirements, and metrics may be in conflict as deeper analysis is done in this phase.

- **Technology problems**   Certain conditions may never have been identified and tested and materialize only after a lot of work has already been expended.
- **Employee burnout**   The project team may be working so hard and intensely that some members begin to burn out and lose productivity.

Mitigation strategies should be in place to deal with each of these problems, or at least reduce their impact. A contingency or workaround should be planned for each of these and other similar problems that may still materialize despite your best efforts.

There is another set of problems that could arise in this phase; however, these problems can be addressed by the executive sponsor. Some examples of these include the following: process problems, change of direction, new business requirements, loss of buy-in, and funding cuts. These can and must be dealt with by the executive sponsor and business users. New requirements cannot be accepted in the current release. Funding cuts cannot be accepted by the project team unless time is set aside to assess which functionality can be removed from the scope of the project. Accepting these types of changes is the same as starting another project and needs to be treated as such.

Getting Started

The final buy-in from the executive sponsor will usually be given based on the personal commitment of the rescue manager. Regardless of how the situation arose, the executive sponsor now wants to hear something like "I guarantee that this project will succeed." The sponsor will also want to continue hearing this message from the rescue manager throughout the intervention.

A lot of pressure is on the rescue manager, who instead needs to replace the sponsor's perspective, with something similar to the following words: "We have assessed the situation and now have a plan we can implement. But we do not know what we do not know and anything new will be brought to the steering committee for immediate resolution."

The first message, which may be gratifying to hear, may nonetheless have been the source of problems in the first place. There's nothing wrong with wanting the job to get done; however, the wish leaves a lot of details out of the equation. The phrasing of the guarantee seems to say, "Go away and get the job done." However, there will still be many questions to ask and decisions to make. Guarantees at this time could prove to be embarrassing and really are meaningless. They only serve to postpone the difficult conversations.

The guarantee must be a partnership in which the project rescue manager and the executive sponsor(s) agree to make the project a success, and then work collaboratively toward the positive outcome. Without this commitment to make important give-and-take decisions together, the project rescue manager is going to encounter significant obstacles getting the difficult things done. The executive sponsor needs to unequivocally demonstrate support for the rescue manager in front of the rest of the organization.

The second message, as stated by the rescue manager, tends to take a more conservative approach that will make the listener uncomfortable. The executive sponsor will be happy that qualified words such as "very," "may," and "should" are not being used. However, there will be discomfort around the use of the words "what we don't know," which leaves uncertainty in the equation. But let's look at this in more detail to see if there truly is more uncertainty.

Artificially guaranteeing a result is more destructive to a project than recognizing that stuff happens and it must be dealt with. The fear of being wrong, the embarrassment of being wrong, and the fear of owning up to a problem are strong contributors to project failure. You definitely do not want to go this way again. By owning up to this uncertainty and embracing it, the rescue manager can provide no stronger impetus to making sure that tough decisions are not avoided. In fact, the total commitment of the rescue manager to the salvage effort is really the stabilizing factor for the executive sponsor. The manager needs to provide this confidence unequivocally to the sponsor.

In a significant project that was being watched by Wall Street analysts, a rescue manager built an aggressive plan to salvage a project that involved six different geographical locations. The project had been going on for about a year with three major deadlines missed, and the project was beginning to experience very strong negative emotions. This project is discussed in Chapter 19 as a case study, but it's introduced here to highlight how the well-regarded executive sponsor began to subtly demonstrate his support to the rescue manager from the beginning of the initiative, without offending other senior members of the team.

After the Assessment and Intervention planning phases were complete, regularly scheduled weekly status meetings were instituted that brought the management team together. The rescue manager and the executive sponsor bonded, but not over the deliverables from the first two phases, but rather over their shared commitment to turn the project around. At the very first status meeting, the executive sponsor sat beside the rescue manager, said nothing, and let the rescue manager walk through the salvage plan with the other technical managers and business stakeholders—who had clearly been involved in the two rescue phases.

Everyone in the room naturally looked at the executive sponsor—the focus of true authority—and saw the rescue manager in the same line of sight. It was clear that the salvage operation was going ahead. Past conflicts, misunderstandings, and arguments were no longer important to the executive sponsor, who was essentially empowering the rescue manager with his authority to turn things around. People could either be part of the solution, or they could go do something else.

The two most important enablers of change on a doomed project are the executive sponsor and the rescue manager—the executive sponsor because he or she has the authority to make things happen and the rescue manager because he or she is the catalyst for change. The symbolism of the bonding between the sponsor and the rescue manager will demonstrate to the rest of the team that project rescue is the most important focus of their attention going forward.

Checklist for Getting Started

An early checklist for the rescue manager to follow is shown in Table 11.1. Recall the three primary activities in this phase for the project rescue manager: Lead-Track-Resolve.

Checklist Item	Description	Proceed With
Communicate to the team	Be clear about why things are being done, what is being done, and how it is going to help the organization.	A memo should be sent out by the executive sponsor to all the team members laying out the new direction of the project.
Demonstrate your seriousness	This is more than showing commitment. The team and the project sponsors need to see right away that all the assessment and planning that was done is going to be seriously applied, and that past difficulties are not going to stop future success.	Tackle the difficult decisions first, the ones that may have been avoided in the original project. Lack of visible progress in these areas will cause discomfort for the team and make them question future success.
Get an early win	Success brings confidence. You need to find something that can be completed in a short period of time that provides value to the organization.	Look for something measurable and nontrivial that has been a thorn in the past. This could be correcting a procedural problem, making a difficult decision, or completing a key function.
Kickoff meeting	Bring the extended project team together for a few hours and walk through the details of the rescue.	The invitation should be sent out under the names of the executive sponsor and members of the management group.
Execute regular touch-points	Get the team in the habit of regular touch-points where important information will be shared and disseminated.	Call all the leads every day, if only to see that things are going well. Request walkthroughs of what they are working on.

Table 11.1   Early Win Checklist

Checklist Item	Description	Proceed With
Organize information	The rest of the project team may not yet understand all the work that has been done in the rescue to date.	Capture all the issues, plans, direction in the basic rescue management toolkit (discussed in the next section).
Issue collection and resolution	Let everyone know that every issue or concern raised is going to be dealt with, so they should freely raise these.	Maintain this information as part of the rescue management toolkit.
Team communication	There should be open, honest, free flowing of information.	Meet daily or several times a day to build momentum in this phase.
Regular walkthroughs	Hearing that something is done is not the same as actually seeing the details.	Get the team into the habit of showing the details of what they are working on and learning from the feedback they receive. On the flip side, ensure that reviewers are not inhibiting creativity and hard work by focusing on criticism instead of constructive suggestions.

Table 11.1   Early Win Checklist *(continued)*

Basic Rescue Management Toolkit

Certain facts, objectives, and information must be immediately available to the rescue manager at all times. Just as importantly, it must also be clear to the entire extended project team that this is the case—otherwise team members will lose faith in the turnaround prospects. These specific tools are shown in Figure 11.3 and discussed in the material that follows This section also provides recommendations on how long it is likely to take to update the deliverables for the next session.

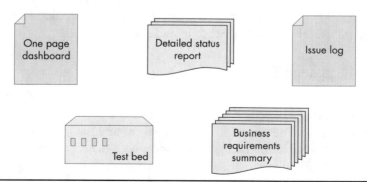

Figure 11.3   Rescue management toolkit

The management process during a project rescue is operating at an intense and rapid pace. This requires the rescue manager to keep the toolkit up-to-date at all times and to present it to different combinations of the project team on a daily basis. There will be times when some of these specific tools will need to be updated and shared several times a day to keep the forward momentum. This is in addition to their electronic availability over an intranet or Web site. Availability is simply not enough, because these tools will not generate the necessary personal attention to detail unless there are physical walkthroughs by the rescue manager with individual team members.

Dashboard

It might appear that everyone on the extended project team is involved in the details. This just is not the case for some of the key members, especially the business stakeholders and sponsors. They may be emotionally involved and heavily invested in the project. They may be thinking about it all the time, worried about it constantly, but this is not the same as understanding the intricate details. This group needs a simple way to understand status and whether they need to take an action.

Furthermore, even the team members who are heavily involved in the details of the project can benefit from a visual tool that highlights the important things they need to know, what danger the project is in, and when an action needs to be taken.

This should take about 30 to 60 minutes to update in every cycle. Much more time than this implies that the best structure has not been selected for the dashboard.

The dashboard and the detailed status reports must show progress relative to the project plan. Without contrasting them to a time-phased project plan, the report does not tell how close you are to the finish line. Earned Value Management (EVM), Cost Performance Index (CPI) and Scheduled Performance Index (SPI) are useful measurements to include here.

Detailed Status Report

As mentioned previously, the detailed status report needs to identify all the work that has been done in the reporting period and the work to be done in the next reporting period. It should also capture the essence of conversations and decisions that are being made throughout the day. These types of decisions are often forgotten, misinterpreted, or contradictory. Knowing that they are being recorded keeps everyone in the project on their toes.

Status reports get a substantial amount of bad press—some believe that they waste time that could be spent doing actual work. Do not give in to this propaganda. It certainly takes work to keep detailed status reports, but they are always useful and relevant on projects—especially ones that are complex enough to require a project rescue.

A good detailed status report can take one to two hours to update in every cycle. You may not want to update it for every meeting. The important thing is to have a schedule and stick to it. During tense times on the project, this could be done every day or every other day, depending on how much new information needs to be shared.

Project Rescue Plan

The project rescue plan should be used for tracking progress and should be appended to the status report to support the regular walkthrough sessions. Whatever management tool you have selected should allow you to move the percent complete forward at the task level. This gives the rescue manager a good reason to call every deliverable or task owner every day, or several times a day, to get an accurate update for this figure.

A lack of progress requires the rescue manager to investigate further and to bring the task back on track. In a project rescue, time is not available to allow the task to be corrected at the mercy of the team members. A late task for a second reporting period requires emergency action.

Special attention needs to be paid to the dates applicable to completion of milestones or deliverables. These are the major warning flags that should terrify the rescue manager and require deep intervention if they are passed.

The rescue manager needs to make it clear to everyone on the project team that there is going to be an extraordinary emphasis on hands-on involvement during this period. You are going to be in everyone's face to ask the really difficult questions to bring and keep the project on track. No offense or misunderstanding is intended in the degree of micro-management that they will be subjected to when the planned dates are in jeopardy.

It takes about 30 to 60 minutes to update the project rescue plan for each reporting period.

Issue Log

The issue log should also be appended to the project plan. It should be used to record every single item that is raised by anyone on the project team so that nothing is forgotten. Each item then needs to go through a process that allocates next steps—which may or may not impact the project plan. Changes need to go through an approval and change management process that absolutely must involve the executive sponsor who may decide to put all of these on hold until the existing rescue initiative is completed.

At first, a lot of issues will be identified when the process starts. This tends to taper off as time goes by. Note that the issue log is not the same as the bug log that is produced during the testing processes, and which is discussed later in the chapter.

It should take 15 to 30 minutes to update the issue log for each reporting period. Rescue managers who are collating issues from other team members should also try and solicit them through e-mail to reduce misunderstandings and repetition.

Test Bed

A test bed is probably one of the most important tools in a project rescue and the ultimate fact checker. Team members can sometimes present their personal preferences and their wishful thinking about progress as facts. Because most team members want to see progress, they are likely to give the benefit of the doubt and see more progress than there actually is. The test bed becomes the reality check.

A process needs to be defined to integrate everything that is being reported as completed into the test bed and to run some routine tests while construction is still being done. The extra effort to integrate deliverables as they are being built and test them at a high level in the test bed is a mandatory value-added investment.

This is the only confirmation that a project rescue manager can have confidence in. It also sets a standard of quality and delivery so that the project team knows that it needs to deliver today, right now, and to receive feedback, rather than having a false sense of security and the crutch of waiting until a later phase.

The test bed does not replace the other testing phases. Test results should be documented on an ongoing basis, but they do not replace the results of the normal unit, functional, and acceptance testing.

A bug list, similar to the issue log, but one that can remain online for the most part, needs to be maintained for the results of the testing. It also needs to be examined one-on-one with the leaders of the group owning the bugs that are being reported. There are some open source products, or low cost products, available over the Internet to maintain bug and issues lists.

A test bed that can be quickly refreshed is an invaluable tool. During a project rescue, anything that can reduce delays, waiting time, and other changes should be instituted immediately.

Business Requirements Summary

Given the continuing discussions with different stakeholders, and ongoing compromises that will need to be made to keep the project on track, it is a good idea to maintain a clean set of business requirements and keep them readily accessible. When changes are made, updated versions of this document should be sent directly to the stakeholders, as opposed to being posted on a board somewhere that they may not visit anyway.

The format of the business requirements document should be kept simple. English constructs are fine. Things such as changes to the budget can also be tracked in this document.

Once built, this document requires a relatively modest amount of time to maintain. It needs to be changed only when the business requirements are renegotiated. For budgeting purposes, assume about 90 minutes a week or 18 minutes a day.

One way to implement a requirements management process is through the use of a requirements traceability matrix that shows each requirement as a row. Some information to include as attributes in the matrix are date-entered, requesting party, schedule release phase, and ultimately the physical implementation module. The matrix is supported by the source documents that can be hyperlinked to the appropriate requirement tag.

Taken Together

The recommended time to maintain the project rescue management toolkit for regular meetings is in the range of 105 minutes (just under two hours) to 210 minutes (just over three hours). This is a substantial amount of time, but certainly doable. It also does not include the modest time to maintain the business requirements document.

Coupled with about one to two hours to walk through the tools with the appropriate team members, this time commitment is still manageable. The average workdays during project rescues, which are significantly longer than this sum, still leave the rescue manager with enough cycles to accommodate a lot of other work.

Management Skills to Deal with Insidious Problems

The rescue manager will be called on to play a significant number of roles during the execution phase. He or she may even need to play many roles in the same day—or even in the same meeting. There's a lot of pressure, a lot at stake, and virtually no margin for error. The rescue manager needs to be comfortable with his or her level of skills in the areas discussed in this section, or complement these with the skills of strong second-in-commands.

Many problems that projects face are highly localized. They may be highly destructive, but with the right help, they can be overcome. For example, if a database is not being built because of a lack of skills, the answer may be to hire a database specialist for a week to come in and mentor the team. The same can be said of many other business or technology processes. The problems are severe and real, but tools are available to focus and correct. People are aware of the problems and with the appropriate prioritization and management support, they can address them.

The more insidious problems that lead to project disasters are often the ones that go undetected. Insidious problems remain hidden below the surface and may only be nagging feelings in the minds of project team members.

For example, perhaps the stakeholder does not really know what he needs, but he is along for the ride until he is needed to sign off on a deliverable and refuses. Consider the possibility that the team is working very hard and cannot see that they are not moving toward a stationary target. Perhaps resentments are piling up and forcing the team culture to sour, until the buildup means that the extended team can no longer function together.

The latter insidious problems need strong management to bring them to the surface before they become severe, discourage the problems from manifesting themselves, and also to create a positive atmosphere that is no longer a catalyst for the problems to multiply. The key skills the rescue manager requires to enable this to happen are discussed in the sections that follow.

Persuasion

The strongest skill or trait required of the rescue manager is the ability to persuade everyone on the project team to remain focused, committed, and in control. This will require dealing with individual problems, personal problems, and professional jealousies. We look at this in more detail in Chapter 17.

Because the rescue manager can be a facilitator from another group or from another firm, there may even be the perception that this person doesn't know what we do. The key is that the rescue manager knows about salvaging projects and should be used as a catalyst to make things happen. The rescue manager is ultimately going to return responsibility back to the project manager when the salvage operation is successful, so the faster things turn around, the faster they can return to a better normal.

This is a powerful persuasion technique. Without an axe to grind or any history to prove, the rescue manager can persuade the different, sometimes opposing parties, to look past differences and focus on common objectives.

Negotiation

While persuasion is the art of getting someone to do what you want them to, negotiation in the context of a project rescue is slightly different. It involves having the ability to make reasonable tradeoffs so that the executive sponsor comes out looking good, the technical team is motivated to complete the mission, and the business users get a useful solution that benefits the bottom line. Negotiation skills are about giving everyone what they need so that they will be constructive participants in the initiative.

Decision Making

Not every decision is going to be optimal, but the rescue manager is going to be looked at as the person to push the envelope and make things happen. This requires the skills to compare several solutions, create an audit trail, and make a defensible decision. This is further proof to the extended project team that everyone is serious about doing what it takes to get the project done.

Prioritizing

If you consider that you don't know what you don't know, along with the fact that resources have limitations, you need to play it safe by prioritizing the project goals up front and focusing on what can be reasonably delivered. This allows the project team to focus their energy on delivering the most important items, and moving down the requirements list as resources and time allow.

New items will need to be evaluated objectively, not in embarrassment or defensiveness that they were missed, and priorities may change. The ability to prioritize, persuade, and perhaps negotiate will then come into play to convince the executive sponsor, business users, and the delivery team to, yet again, adjust the direction of the initiative. In most cases, the prioritization will involve convincing this same group of people to keep the status quo until the rescue plan is completed.

Organizational Skills

With so many different things happening at once, the rescue manager is going to need to be highly organized. The messy desk, unkempt office, or corrupted disk drive is not going to convince a highly energized and nervous project team to entrust the future of their project if all the deliverables and justification for the deliverables are a mess. You need to have organized electronic and paper files that can be located within minutes of a request. A common problem here is version control or maintaining control over changes to any of the documents.

Here is a real-life example that emphasizes these points. A project team for a major manufacturer had missed several project deadlines in the past. The one coming up was critical to the business and another missed deadline would go over very badly. The entire project team committed to staying up overnight until the release was signed off and working in the Production environment by the following morning. Some problems were detected in one of the acceptance tests at 1:30 a.m. A meeting run by the project manager examined the bug list and divided responsibilities among five different teams of developers. The teams immediately went to work.

One of the executives who decided to lend moral support to the team by staying up with them asked the project manager where each individual group was going to save their changes and how they would be tested. A look of awareness crossed the project manager's face with the realization that all the groups could be working in different technical environments. This would make a merge of their changed code bases very difficult, if not impossible, with the tools that were available. Things were stopped, and the team reconvened. They agreed to a process and went back to work. The release was delivered in time to satisfy the users, who as it turned out were skeptical about the team's ability to deliver, but were ecstatic to be proven wrong.

Many problems were encountered and resolved that night. Many required substantial hard, technical, or business skills. But the lack of organization in one element, such as change control, which appears so obvious that many professionals would just nod their head and say it was obvious, was the difference between keeping a major client happy or ready to look for another vendor.

Cheerleading

Let's remember that the project team is probably very tired by this point in the project rescue. They are going to need substantial encouragement to keep their passion alive and their minds focused. This encouragement should not be false, but should rather be based on true events.

The rescue manager needs to keep the team pumped through several approaches. They should be told when they are doing a good job. Reassurance should be provided when doubts set in. It's important to consider how new problems are successfully dealt with to keep confidence high.

The rescue manager also needs to ensure that all the tools that are needed are readily available, comfort is being provided, and that the extraordinary efforts of the project team are being recognized and supported.

Problem Solving

Apart from tracking progress, the rescue manager is going to need to go deep into some areas of the project when a problem or problems are identified. Other members of the project team are going to be intensely busy in their own activities.

The rescue manager needs to take the initiative and gather more facts and information and possibly reach a conclusion before turning it over to someone to fix. Obviously, a problem solving rescue manager can save the time of other team members and use their time more efficiently. The ability to multitask is mandatory as problems materialize in clusters. The rescue manager also needs to have the ability to complete the many tasks that are started.

Honesty and Integrity

Honesty and integrity take a long time to build, but can be destroyed in seconds. It is vital that all the members of the project team feel that management, and especially the rescue manager, is being totally up front and honest about progress and the rewards. The project rescue, which is going to require enormous effort from everyone involved, cannot succeed without this. We are going to talk more about honesty and integrity in Chapter 17, but the important message is to walk the walk and talk the talk.

Flexibility

By now it should be a given that it is impossible to capture every aspect of a project 100 percent accurately before it starts. The difference between good and excellent management is the ability to deliver while real world impacts are hitting the project.

Some managers accept too much and trying too hard to please. Other managers simply refuse to budge from their usual way of doing things. Neither of these approaches is particularly helpful. The rescue manager needs to be flexible in how an end goal is reached, while maintaining consistency in the end goal.

The key to tradeoff-flexibility is having a tradeoff method that the stakeholders understand. The method consistently applied should help remove the appearance of arbitrariness. This method can be included in the change management process.

Communication

Managers should enjoy communicating to the rest of the project team. There is no such thing as too much communication during a project rescue. People should be copied on e-mails, included in meetings, and allowed to ask their questions. Trying to be efficient by limiting communication can be highly detrimental in a project rescue.

Detail-Oriented

This is also not the time to trust that things will fall into place. It is necessary to work with checklists and to work at a low level of detail because there probably will not be enough time to do another rescue.

The test bed is a good tool for automating some of the detail checking early in the rescue intervention. This should be augmented with a strong focus on the little details in the project.

Strong Lie Detector

People may sometimes tell you what they believe you want to hear, or what they themselves want you to believe, or they may even believe it themselves. The ability to pick up on subtle word choices and phrasing to identify untruths or half truths is another important characteristic. This also has to be done in a non-confrontational and nonthreatening manner.

High Energy

Because the project rescue is a dynamic period with many concurrent activities, the team needs to be highly energetic. Things have to be done *now*. They cannot be left until tomorrow. If some business clarification is needed, someone needs to make a call *now*—not send an e-mail and wait two days for a reply.

Rescue managers, by virtue of their position and role, are watched carefully by all the team members who are making up their minds to follow and believe or not. High energy exhibited in meetings, status reports, and conversations is infectious and will inspire many to try and rise to the occasion.

Closing Perspective

Launching the execution phase requires a shifting of attention by the rescue manager and the project team. The strength of the deliverables in the two earlier phases of the intervention will allow this phase to go more smoothly, but there will be new challenges to overcome. The rescue manager needs to provide the leadership to deal with these challenges by ensuring that a process is being followed so that the extended team does not panic if these new challenges materialize.

The rescue manager needs to be very nimble in this phase to ensure that the aggressive revised direction is being followed. These responsibilities were summarized as '"Lead-Track-Resolve." These activities will be required every day of the rescue to keep it on track.

## CHAPTER 12

Incremental Adjustment

The project rescue methodology required parachuting an external rescue manager, or changing the focus of an existing project manager, onto a troubled project. The first project rescue phase required a detailed assessment of the situation, including extensive team interviews and information collection and analysis. The second phase involved detailed planning around the rescue intervention.

The third project rescue phase, the execution phase, which is the focus of this part of the book, involves an even more intense set of activities. As shown in Figure 12.1, the rescue approach is likely to involve branching back to a project development methodology in order to complete the project deliverables. You will then return to the final phase of the project rescue intervention.

This chapter focuses on the key vulnerabilities that can still upset the project rescue as you follow the detailed activities of the development methodology and rescue framework.

What to Expect from a Project Rescue

This section examines the common situations that can arise during a project rescue intervention. The project team is given new opportunities that are not available outside a project rescue process. Similarly, the project team potentially may encounter additional negative factors that it must guard against or resolve. Some of these factors are obvious extensions of the problems encountered in the original project, while others are manifestations of the rescue process. Both the positive and negative aspects of the rescue process are discussed in the following sections.

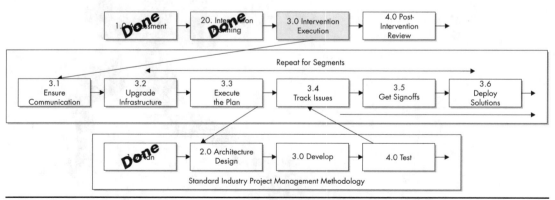

Figure 12.1   Integrating the rescue approach with a project management and development methodology

Positive Factors

The project rescue process offers a chance at renewal—another shot at success. It offers an opportunity to call a time out, to learn from previous mistakes, and to set things right. Some of the positive factors that the project team should leverage are listed here:

- **Constructive pressure**   Knowing that project failure may be around the corner, all the team members may forgo personal issues and politics to accept best practices that will move the project toward success. Keeping this constructive pressure in the forefront is an ongoing responsibility of the project rescue manager.

- **Another chance**   This is a sanctioned opportunity to clarify what the team knows and needs to know, and to ask new questions. A new approach can be built. Ask open-ended questions that encourage the sponsors to identify any other latent ideas, issues, or concerns that have not been shared before.

- **Re-energized**   Even if it's only due to adrenalin, the extended team will feel a sense of revitalization and renewal that can help it break past losing patterns. Progress will help to maintain this passion.

- **Refocused**   The new project rescue strategy offers an opportunity to get everybody focused on the same things and to field the same priorities. They can focus on the newly validated priorities.

- **Jettisoning the baggage**   Failure breeds a lot of negative emotions and factors that, in essence, create a runaway train that is hurtling toward disaster. There is a lot of momentum that resists the simple fixes. The project rescue is a forced stop with an opportunity to jettison heavy baggage by redefining the rules of engagement and offering amnesty to the sources of the previous problems before starting up at full speed again.

- **Chance for a positive contribution**   Turning to a new project direction also allows the experienced project team to define an end state that will be successfully achieved. The sponsors and stakeholders are now familiar with the challenges the project is facing, and need to focus on generating value for the company from a zero base.

Negative Factors

Time is short, pressures are high (which can have negative or positive consequences), and team confidence is lacking. While the past may have been painful, the future territory is uncertain and can be filled with both old and new problems. Key negative factors that can impact the project in the execution phase as a whole are discussed in this section. Negative factors are examined at the subphase level in subsequent sections of this chapter.

Resistance to Change

People have a tendency to resist change for any number of reasons. They may feel they have a lot to lose, they may fear a new outcome, or they simply may believe that their way is the right one and the only way.

The solution is to focus on achieving the limited change necessary to get through the project rescue. This solution must also be mandated by the executive sponsor and stands the best chance of working.

At some point, it may turn out that some people just cannot become part of the solution and the team. After a reasonable due diligence period to try and turn things around, the only recourse left open to you may be to identify the potential contributions of these people and find a replacement source, remove the related requirements from the rescue initiative, or reduce the scope as much as possible.

Hidden Motives

People on the project team may also have their own agendas that can hurt the project. This is not uncommon, but in some cases, these motives may result in bad decisions, delayed implementations, and team conflicts.

It's hard to prove a hidden agenda, and trying to do so is also disruptive to the project. Rescue managers should not be oblivious to this possibility. Dealing with it requires a tighter project schedule and more checkpoints with individuals who appear to have contradictory motives.

Inaccurate Information

It is possible that information collected during the assessment phase was inaccurate. Of course, increasing the number of data collection points and checkpoints reduces this likelihood. Increasing user involvement throughout the build process is also a powerful defense mechanism.

Using the test bed or harness, which should be established at the start of the execution phase, offers a good touch and feel environment for members of the extended team to view the implementation of the facts that were collected and analyzed.

The contingency built into the rescue plan may need to be used to respond to any inaccurate information that still gets through.

Employee Burnout

Strong passion and enthusiasm will inspire members of the extended project team to work hard and work long hours. This will produce results within the tight framework of the intervention. However, some team members may start exhibiting signs of burnout.

Some symptoms of burnout include a loss of energy, more than usual sarcasm, physical anxiety, disillusionment, and anger. Employees may begin to seem resigned to an outcome. They may stop exercising and begin overeating. Some employees may work long, late hours without producing value. This latter point will be identified by the project rescue plan.

Burnout is a complex problem that requires professional assistance. Reversing the effect, once it starts, is very difficult, if not impossible, to do in a short time. It's best to avoid creating an environment that is a breeding ground for this type of reaction.

Supporting the team members by removing activities that are not valuable to the rescue initiative can be helpful. Rewarding their efforts and showing appreciation is another approach. Being open to their concerns is also important. Team members need to be treated as professionals. They need to be reminded of the goals of the initiative and why all the effort being expended is valuable to the organization. Their trust needs to be earned and returned. Above all, listen, observe, and talk with the team members and do not let them experience feelings of burnout.

Missing Skills

It may turn out that some team members do not have all the relevant skills they need to be effective. Training is difficult during the tight timeframe of a rescue intervention, so it may be necessary to bring in experts in the topic area from elsewhere in the organization or from third parties. The executive sponsor's commitment is required to tap into resources in other departments.

It is also a useful idea to speak to several third-party vendors to see whether they have resources with the key skills that the project could require at some point. It's also useful to get done the negotiations about price, commitment, service levels, and resource availability—as a precaution. These resources could also be called on to deal with spikes in the workload.

Lack of Buy-In

Team members may verbally agree to the rescue plan but secretly withhold their full buy-in to the process. Getting this is mandatory for success. Dealing with a lack of buy-in is not as politically charged as uncovering hidden motives. It can be met head on by asking direct questions and marketing the power of the direction being followed. The plan being followed derives its authority from executive management so all team members should get on board. The message needs to be repeated to maintain the level of buy-in.

Overconfidence

Overconfidence is a significant risk factor at any point in a project life cycle. It may cause the team to accept requirements that are impossible to implement, avoid making difficult decisions, or be loose with missed deadlines.

Any project is susceptible to failure—no matter how small and straightforward the project may appear to seem. Even a tight rescue plan requires hard work and discipline to salvage the project. Overconfidence is actually not that rare. Showing overconfident team members the ongoing error log, and the original business requirements, is a good tool for bringing back a sense of perspective.

Reverting to Previous Bad Habits

As the pressure subsides, the organization and the team may begin to revert to the habits that plagued the project in the first place. Previous motives, conflicts, competition, and bloated processes could begin to return. As a successful outcome becomes more probable, team members may begin to try and position themselves favorably in the organization. They may attempt to get more power and more recognition. They might want to take more credit for the positive results of the rescue.

From a consultant's perspective, the goal of the rescue mission is to save the project and empower the project team to continue. Permanent employees of the organization share the same goal, but they cannot reasonably dissociate themselves from the internal structure and hierarchy of the organization.

With the support of the executive sponsor, use the lessons learned from the errors that originally afflicted the project to delay the onset of these reversals. The rescue manager has little influence after the rescue is completed, but can use the rescue management toolkit to keep the true status of the initiative in front of the extended team so that it is not lulled into a false sense of security too soon.

Continuous Improvement Through Incremental Adjustment

The call to action in the execution phase involves incremental adjustments to the rescue plan using the Lead-Track-Resolve guideline that was described in the last chapter. The extended project team needs to understand that additional problems and stresses can still arise and that it should not become disillusioned when they do arise. Indeed, the sooner further obstacles are encountered, the more time that is available to deal with them.

By identifying the problems early, they can be turned into tools for adjusting the project requirements and schedules in small steps to keep the final deliverables on track. This is the essence of the incremental adjustment approach in the execution phase. Building the best rescue plan is only the first step. Adjusting the plan according to what is actually being observed on the project is the second one.

Moment-to-Moment Measurement

Traditional project tracking is intended to minimize the number of interruptions experienced by project team members as they do their work. While noble in its intent, this approach relies on several assumptions that can prove to be inaccurate. Not forcing project team members to confront the true status of their initiatives contributes to delays in and of themselves. They may continue independently working on something that could be solved with someone else's help. In fact, they may even be focused on the wrong thing altogether.

There is a common statement in project management groups that says something to the effect that "nothing gets done until the last minute." Looming deadlines get people focused. A series of deadlines will keep them focused on the details. Missing the first of these deadlines is an immediate call to action.

Avoiding Previous Mistakes

Lessons from the pre-rescue portion of the project need to be analyzed and summarized. This knowledge in hindsight needs to be reviewed with the extended project team. Some of the mistakes that were made may be culturally influenced. These mistakes will be difficult to overcome. The project rescue initiative may be shielded from the negative influences of the corporate culture temporarily—with the support of the executive sponsor. But the influences will paradoxically return with mounting success.

Knowledge of past efforts is a powerful tool for dealing with these influences as they emerge. This must also be done without resorting to an "I told you so" attitude, in order to maintain a sense of business as usual and to keep personality out of the situation. Fulfilling personal objectives or seeking personal satisfaction can damage the network that has been crafted to enable the rescue.

It is also common for behaviors of the team members to begin to revert to their previous states as progress becomes visible. Some team members will be on your side during the emergency, but they may begin to want things their way as soon as they sense that disaster has been averted. The previous mistakes list is an important reminder of the dangers of retracing past missteps.

Deliverables

The project deliverables need to reflect the current state of the project. Any incremental changes or adjustments need to be reflected in the deliverables list, discussed earlier in the book and shown in Figure 12.2. While the figure shows the deliverables that created the first significant draft of the deliverables, each needs to be maintained in subsequent phases.

These documents are important for keeping all the team members in alignment and for resolving misunderstandings that can arise when lots of people are busy doing lots of different things in parallel.

Measuring Progress

How can you know how well you are doing during this phase? The tolerance for error is very low at this point, so the most accurate picture needs to be known at any given time. Progress needs to be measured in several dimensions to get a complete picture of how the project is doing and where to allocate resources if problems are identified:

- Measure activities on the project plan
- Measure progress against deliverables that need to be completed

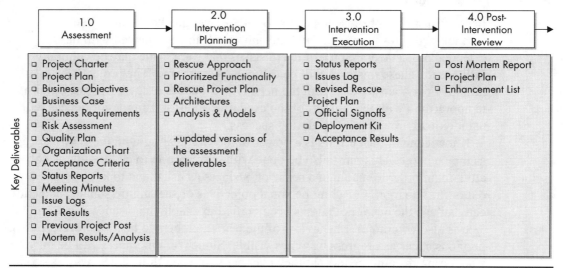

Figure 12.2   Integrating the rescue approach with a development methodology

- Measure against the milestones
- Assess the work captured in the issues log
- Ask team members how they feel the project is going

A weakness in even one dimension detracts from a statement of overall progress and should trigger additional work to catch up. These dimensions should be included in the project status report or portrayed on a dashboard as color-coded symbols. The status of the project needs to be clear so that it can be surmised at a glance.

Incorporating Feedback

The openness, flexibility, and forgiveness that went into planning the project rescue should not be discarded at this stage. While the project rescue manager accepts accountability for the results, along with the executive sponsor, it is still a team effort overall.

Identification of missing activities or even deliverables should not be met with defensiveness. By this time, there have been several opportunities to collect input from every member of the extended project team. If something was not identified during those opportunities but becomes known now, it is a collective responsibility to incorporate it into the project plan and resolve it going forward.

Feedback can be collected in a number of ways. An open-door policy should be encouraged. Team members should also be asked to raise issues at any time. They can also simply respond to the frequent status reports that are distributed and raise their concerns to the group.

Identification of a missing or inaccurate requirement may not automatically mean that it needs to be incorporated into the project plan during the current phase. There is another reason to remain objective and not take things personally. A proper analysis can only be done if everyone is skeptical about the business advantages of inclusion and are not perceived to be defensive.

Details of the Execution Phase

The execution phase is going to be the most active and potentially contentious. The first two phases of the project rescue were an opportunity for team members to express their opinions, vent their frustrations, and allow the people identified as the core rescue assessment team to do a lot of the required legwork. The execution phase is going to require some new rules and disciplines.

The previous chapter focused on the different aspects of the subphase "Ensure Communication" to inform the extended project team about what is going to be done, how they will be participating, and what is expected of them. The remaining subphases in the execution phase are described in this section.

Upgrade Infrastructure

The subphase "Upgrade infrastructure" was introduced in the last chapter and needs to be completed as early as possible in the execution phase to avoid creating any unnecessary bottlenecks. This activity includes upgrading just about any physical resource, including desks, personal computers, development infrastructure, and testing infrastructure. Infrastructure itself consists of both hardware and software components.

Infrastructure can become a bottleneck because the processes related to its selection, procurement, and installation involve several different groups in an organization, as well as external vendors, who are also affected by their own external factors and corporate cultures.

Consider this example: After a mission-critical web application was launched, one of the primary servers went down due to a physical memory problem. The production system would crash whenever a few dozen people around the world signed on—which was pretty much all the time. The replacement machine was ordered, but was caught in traffic for over a day!

Short of hiring a helicopter, there was not much anyone could do after the problem occurred. Analysis during the planning stage would have shown that there was only one, very busy, highway between the hosting facility and the stocking center. The correct answer would have been to stock a backup at the hosting center.

Infrastructure processes can be delayed in the following areas:

- **Selection process** Trying to find the absolute right fit involves evaluating every product combination in the world. This is impossible. Always work from a prioritized functionality list that has been accepted by the stakeholders.

- **Ordering process** You need to identify the person who is going to sign the purchase order once the recommendation is made. Bring them into the discussion and find out exactly what they need to know in order to feel comfortable with the process.

- **Accounts payable** Companies have different payment policies. You need to ensure that the accounting group understands the urgency of sending out the checks to ensure there are no delays in processing the infrastructure orders.

- **Vendor culture**   The vendor may want the sale but may not be able to fulfill the order, for any number of reasons. Are there other high-profile clients placing orders for the same equipment? Where will you be on the priority list? Are you asking the vendor for exceptions that only someone at the executive level in the head office can provide?

Execute the Project Rescue Plan

The basic process in this phase is governed by the activities described in the project rescue plan. The completeness of this plan should be driven by the following sources of information (which were used to construct the plan in the first place):

- **Original project plan**   This should be a deliverable from the pre-rescue duration of the project.
- **Rescue methodology**   This involves the four-phase methodology introduced in Chapter 2 and used throughout this book.
- **Development methodology**   This is a proven development methodology that describes architecture/design, development, and testing processes. It should be based on any one of a number of underlying philosophies, such as Agile Approaches, parallelization, or extreme development, that have enjoyed wide popularity in the Information Technology profession in recent years.
- **Best practices**   Knowledge from industry sources for the type of project being followed can provide additional checkpoints for the project plan. For example, what are the key risks for an offshore development team using the same technology tools?
- **Practitioner experience**   Every practitioner brings a great deal of experience with them that may not be captured in any other source. Solicit this information through walkthroughs and build their experience right into the plan.

Architecture/Design Subphase

The architecture/design subphase uses the business requirements to build a complete picture of the final solution. Here are some of the problems that could arise during this exercise:

- **Unproven solution**   The concepts may have appeared to be fine in principle, but may prove to be unworkable. You may need to involve the vendor to validate a prototype, incorporate some manual processes, or work with the stakeholders to define a workable solution.

- **Too expensive**   If the architecture/design is becoming more expensive than the budget that was allocated, consider scaling the solution back so that it can support the first year of operations and building an upgrade budget.

- **Setup**   New architecture usually requires longer implementation time than generally assumed. The systems team almost always provides the most optimistic estimate. You should drill deeper to identify the areas of uncertainty. These should then be incorporated to adjust the estimate to a more likely range.

- **Different versions**   You need to get the right software versions of the different tools installed and integrated. Simple version changes can have a significant ripple effect throughout an intricate architecture.

- **Bottlenecks**   It's difficult to get the right configurations of hardware components. Build several proof-of-concept or pilot deliverables that allow you to test various configurations.

Development Subphase

The development subphase is going to require intense sustained effort from the project team. Many activities will end up being done in parallel, as developers begin to deliver their components. These will enter the test cycles. Some components will require modifications to corrected reported errors. Other components will be moved to the next subphase. New components will continue to be placed into the test cycles. Here are some of the specific problems to watch for:

- **Distance**   Development resources are becoming more geographically distributed, especially with offshore initiatives. It is a challenge to get the different groups to work efficiently together, especially to overcome the time-zone delays. All the groups must share some core hours, even if that means requiring some resources to be at work during their normal sleeping times.

- **Standards**   This is another area that gets neglected during tight timeframes. Come into the execution phase with these already defined and use walkthroughs to help the team leverage them to their benefit. Standards will help make life easer for the team.

- **Changing requirements**   Developers should be using the technical specifications or the documented business requirements to build the solution. New requirements may emerge, but these must go through the rescue manager and the change request procedure.

Testing Subphase

The testing subphase consists of many different subtests. These include integration testing, functional testing, stress testing, regression testing, and system testing. The final step is acceptance testing, the results of which are shown to the project stakeholders for final signoff to proceed to deployment of the solution. Some of the problems you may encounter in this phase during a project rescue are as follows:

- **Going back to the old ways**   For whatever reason, users may insist on using the functional requirements from the original attempt and may try to ignore the revamped, streamlined requirements that were agreed to for the project rescue. There should be an extensive audit trail of decisions made and directions followed. A set of test scenarios or test cases, that are agreed to by the executive sponsor(s), should be maintained so that everyone involved in the project understands how the solution is going to be evaluated.

- **Lack of business resources**   The testing activities may be completed in the early-morning hours or at another time during which the business users are not available. The executive sponsor is empowered and required to make these resources available.

- **Lack of testing resources**   If there is a need to have additional hands-on resources, consider contracting with lower-cost contractors who can work with a detailed test script and are available 24/7 to be called upon when work is ready for them to test.

- **Lack of tools**   Testing can be a tedious process that can be improved with the use of automated tools. These tools tend to be on the expensive side. Some open-source tools can be used as a lower-cost alternative.

- **Dealing with the results**   There must be clarity on how to process the test results (e.g., defect identification and resolution). This includes recording the findings, prioritizing them, and fixing the ones that are urgent for launch.

Get Signoffs

You may get to the finish line and feel positive about the results of the project rescue, but three major activities still need to be completed before the project rescue can be deemed a success:

- Get official signoff to proceed to implementation or rollout of the solution.

- Successfully deploy whatever product that was being constructed
- Finish post-project cleanup

The first two activities are part of the execution phase, while the third is part of the post-intervention review phase of the project rescue.

The signoff process is different for every executive sponsor. Some mandate it to a stakeholder or users, others distribute the responsibility, and some want to be the final gate. Clarifying the process was one of the objectives of the planning phase, so there should be a consistent understanding of what needs to be done.

It would be unfortunate indeed to get this far successfully, only to miss the deadline because the final signoffs cannot be secured in a timely manner. Some problems with the signoff process can still arise for any number of reasons, as follows:

- **Looked good on paper** The designated acceptor may have thought everything looked good on paper, but may feel uncomfortable about making a commitment. Avoid this by keeping the designated acceptor, as well as the other stakeholders, apprised of the test results on an ongoing basis and listen to their concerns.

- **No one to sign off is available** The acceptance testing may be completed early in the morning and the person designated to sign off may not be available. The acceptance process should identify 24/7 coverage.

- **Fear of accountability** Get this cleared up with the executive sponsor before agreeing on the final signoff process. Also, get signature signoffs for the earlier test results to build comfort in taking this accountability.

- **Verbal approval, but not written** A verbal approval to launch should be avoided. But if it is a necessity, it needs to be followed up by an audit trail that signifies that verbal was acceptable and that it was given. This is a fuzzy area and needs further legal clarification if it is going to be pursued.

Deploy Solutions

While this book has a strong information technology theme, the suggestions can apply to any type of deliverable, be it a report, restructuring of a department, reengineering, or offshore migration. Deployment planning needs to start in parallel with the launch of the execution phase. Here are some key considerations for this subphase:

- **Lack of a contingency**   Do not even try to launch a solution unless a contingency has been defined. Any number of things can go wrong. Business interruption cannot be allowed, so another strategy needs to be tested and ready to be implemented.

- **Testing the solution in production**   After rolling the solution into production, be ready to test portions of the application in the production environment before it is available to others.

- **Availability of resources after launch**   Publish a list of all the skills that are required for the production day, for the production week, and for a few weeks after. Contact information for 24/7 support is needed. The rescue manager may need to remain engaged until this sensitive period is passed.

Closing Perspective

This chapter examined the project rescue execution phase in more detail. The focus of this chapter was to point out some of the things that can go wrong during a project rescue and to provide some mitigation strategies. This chapter also discussed ways to leverage some of the positive levers that become available in a project rescue. Activities and tasks for the subphases are described in our companion book, *High-Value IT Consulting: 12 Keys to a Thriving Practice* (McGraw-Hill/Osborne, 2003).

## CHAPTER 13

Execution Phase Questionnaire

At this stage of the project rescue, you do not want the business users to make any changes to the business requirements. At the same time, you want the technical or development team to deliver against the business specifications that have been built. Unfortunately, the project rescue may not transpire this cleanly, so you will need to make further adjustments. You may need to remind team members about the roles they need to play. Additional information may become available that needs to be captured and incorporated into the project rescue.

This chapter identifies a series of questions that the rescue manager can pose to different members of the extended project team throughout the execution phase. In addition to information gathering, these questions provide you with additional guidelines for the work that needs to be done. Furthermore, these questions establish a safety net by giving the stakeholders and business users ongoing active involvement in this phase.

Asking questions of different members of the team is also a nonthreatening technique for posing difficult scenarios. Instead of telling professionals to do a job that they may already be doing, a series of questions can be asked that does not make them feel like they are being accused of messing up. It also allows them to suggest corrective courses of action.

Asking questions, of course, may produce answers that are uncomfortable. The point of asking the questions is to solicit the information, which allows you to maintain better balance than if the same information gets presented to you by the business community. The latter puts you on the defensive and could lead to additional mistakes. The former allows you to ask for help and creates shared ownership.

Executive Sponsor Questions

Executive sponsors generally have the greatest latitude to change their minds because they are in effect the owners of the project. Even though they will be responsible to other executives in the organization, they can be flexible in what they are willing to accept and the types of workarounds they are willing to fund in the interim if the plan needs to change again. All of these questions are critical for the actual and perceived success of the project.

Here are some of the questions that the rescue manager should pose to executive sponsors during the remainder of the execution phase:

- *What do you need to see to give your acceptance to deploy whatever is being built?* This question refers to the final format and content of the deliverables that the executive sponsors need to see to give their written acceptance for launching the completed product, including the required test results.

- *How much time do you need to make a decision after these final deliverables are provided for your review?* This is an important question because some sponsors may not understand the importance of their involvement in the final days of the project or, more likely, may be getting cold feet and need to be pinned down to make binding decisions. This time provision should be part of the deliverable acceptance criteria defined in the SOW.

- *Which of the issues marked critical in the bug log can be downgraded to a more acceptable status?* Having liked the results of the rescue initiative so far, the sponsors may be more comfortable launching with some bugs in a noncritical status and letting these be fixed later on.

- *Do you have any more suggestions or comments?* This open-ended question will encourage the sponsors to identify any other latent ideas or feelings that could still prove to be useful to the initiative. They should be pressed to identify any issues or concerns that they have not shared.

- *Will you support our workaround processes? For how long?* These question are relevant only if workarounds are being identified because some of the functionality is not going to be delivered as per the original scope.

Management Questions

The management-related questions are intended to nudge all the management-level resources forward on the project rescue plan. Here are some of the questions that the rescue manager should pose to other managers and leaders during the remainder of the execution phase:

- *How can we improve the efficiency of our status meetings and communications?* Letting people be part of any decision-making process and/or provide their input always increases their buy-in. This question may also result in some valuable insight for improving the efficiency of the management process.

- *Are you comfortable with your quality assurance processes? What are they?* These questions should be posed to the deliverable owners. The answers give you a sense of the attention they are giving to the finer details of their work in progress. These may be appropriate questions to ask the business users as well.

- *What criteria are you using to evaluate deliverables?* This question should be posed to the stakeholders, team leaders, and managers. This ensures that everyone is working toward the same end goals. The answers should be recorded and shared with every person who is going to be involved in accepting the project deliverables. This may be an appropriate question to ask the business users as well.

- *How are your team members doing? Is hard work being recognized?* These are morale questions that should be posed to anyone in the project who is managing people. The intent is to ensure that all members of the team, though working very hard, are being made to feel appreciated. The intent is also to give them some small rewards along the way to thank them for their ongoing efforts.

- *Do you see any new risks and are we mitigating the existing ones effectively?* This open-ended question should be posed to everyone in the extended project team to keep them engaged, to gather new information, and to keep everyone in a nimble frame of mind. The question reinforces the possibility of making further changes to the project plan without panicking the team. This question could also be included in a formal risk management process.

- *What else can we do to improve results?* This is another open-ended question that is intended to gather any other information that has not been brought into the open. It is also intended to remind team members that they have to be part of the solution, and not just the ones who raise problems.

Stakeholder Questions

Aside from the executive sponsors, the stakeholders are the other significant users who have at least some power to accept and/or pay for deliverables. Stakeholders and the executive sponsors may also have some sort of a matrix-based relationship, where one reports to the other in some capacity.

The questions previously presented for the executive sponsors are fair game for the stakeholders as well. Here are some additional questions that the rescue manager should pose to the key stakeholders during the remainder of the execution phase:

- *Do you have any additional input on what you are seeing so far in terms of the progress we are making?* This question is an opportunity to get some relatively early feedback so that you can adjust the project direction and, more likely, resolve any misunderstandings that may exist.

- *How will you make your decision to go or not go with the products of this project?* This question helps you to confirm how the stakeholders are going to evaluate the final project deliverables. The rescue manager should confirm that this information is represented in the test plan.

- *What are the three most important results you want to achieve on the short list already identified?* Just in case additional problems arise, this question sets the stage for another round of prioritization. However, be careful not to ask this in a way that could cause alarm or misunderstanding that further cuts are going to be made. This is being asked only for information purposes at this time.

- *Will the users be ready to test or inspect the products as per our plan in the prescribed durations?* This question reminds the stakeholders to manage the user work schedules to ensure that they will be available at the time specified in the rescue plan.

- *What other information do the testers need to be successful?* This is an information-only question. It may identify something that was not previously considered and now needs to be incorporated into the process.

- *Do you have any other recommendations on how we can do things better?* This is an open-ended question to increase participation and gather information.

Business User Questions

The business users originally provided the detailed business requirements, and will be involved in the final evaluation of the products that are produced by the project efforts. The business users may actually be the ones with the most tactical power on the project, as they may be making the final recommendations to the stakeholders and the executive sponsors.

It is important to understand what the business users are thinking, how they will be testing the application, and what is going to drive them through the process. Here are some of the questions that the rescue manager should pose to business users who will be using the solution when the project is completed:

- *How will you decide if the solution is acceptable?* Every business user is going to have input into the quality of the solution. This question gathers their input, both involving them while helping the development team get more data that can be incorporated into the test plan within the scope of the SOW.

- *Has the testing team captured all your test cases?* The business requirements need to be converted into detailed test cases or scenarios with help from the business users. They need to get started early in the process so that the test cases can also be used by the development team to further validate what they are building as they are building it.

- *Does the project plan fit into your other priorities? Will you be available during the dates described in the rescue project plan?* An answer of no is a major red flag, because the product cannot be accepted without business user involvement. These answers need to go on the status report and must be escalated to the sponsor level—without pointing fingers or assigning blame.

- *Is there anything else we should be doing? Do you have any other suggestions?* This is another open-ended question that is designed to encourage participation, demonstrate flexibility, and gather additional information.

- *Do you know how to access the bug or issues list?* This question is intended to further validate that all the issues, concerns, and observations are being recorded for subsequent processing—rather than leaving people with the feeling that information is being lost.

- *Is there any other training we can provide?* This question is intended to reassure the business users that it is acceptable for them to acknowledge that they do not know everything. This question gives them an opportunity to ask for help, without embarrassment, and will hopefully avoid making them feel defensive, so that they continue to be constructive.

Technology Questions

Here are some of the questions that the rescue manager should pose to the technology architects and designers during the execution phase:

- *What technology components have not been through integration testing yet?* This question should be directed to the architects and product vendors.

- *Have you tested the limits of the technology? How?* These question should be directed to the architect and the product vendors. Insist on seeing the actual results.

- *What are the security provisions?* Direct this question to the technology architects to ensure that security provisions do not become an afterthought in the planning process. The rescue manager needs to assess whether the answers are robust enough, or whether an external team needs to be brought in temporarily to punch up the security provisions.

The security plan should be included as a deliverable within the SOW along with the functional and nonfunctional requirements for security. Accordingly, you should also be able to see it in the project plan.

- *What else needs to be done to set up a testing and production environment?* Asking this question early in the phase gives you the lead time normally required to select, order, deploy, and configure these tools.

- *Has all the technology been ordered?* This question should be directed to the financial or procurement people. The financial or procurement team may not understand the urgency of the project rescue, and this question will keep it in front of them.

- *Do we have the appropriate licenses for all the hardware and especially software that we need?* Address this question to the system administrators to ensure that there are no legal problems following launch. The money to buy these licenses may not have been included in the budget. The executive sponsors may need to lobby for more funds to build this compliance.

- *Where is the backup support going to come from if something goes wrong with the technology?* This question should result in several pieces of contact information for each support representative for 24/7 support coverage.

Development Team Questions

Here are some of the questions that the rescue manager should pose to the development team during the remainder of the execution phase:

- *What standards are being followed?* This question should be directed to the senior developers or project leaders.

- *Are you unit testing all your applications?* Anything that is not unit tested cannot be considered finished.

- *Do you have all the tools you need to maximize your effectiveness?* The answer to this question could be anything, including another computer, additional software, a cell phone, office equipment, or transportation. The intent is to provide whatever additional support that can be reasonably provided.

- *Is there anything else I can do to make your job easier?* This question should be directed to the senior developers or project leaders.

- *Are the requirements clear? Do you have any issues with what you're building?* These questions should be addressed to anyone who is implementing the business requirements, which includes the developers, testers, and administrators.

- *Can I get a quick walkthrough of what you're building?* Ask this question from time to time, both as a surprise quiz and as an opportunity to lend additional experience to the development team.

Testing Questions

A test lead or manager, who could also have a different role on the project, needs to take charge of the testing activities. This could be part of the testing phase, or any testing-related activities that are going on in parallel with the development activities. The testing phase is part of the execution phase in the rescue.

Here are some of the questions that the rescue manager should pose to the testing users and test support staff during the remainder of the execution phase:

- *Is the testing architecture set up?* This question should be addressed to the technology architect.

- *Are the test environments set up?* This question should be addressed to the system administration group to ensure that the technology has been configured so that testing can begin.

- *Have the test cases been documented?* This question should be directed to the testing resources.

- *Do you have all the testing tools you need?* This question is intended to gather information to ensure smooth testing.

- *How are bugs or issues being identified, recorded, and processed?* This question ensures that all of these are being documented and processed.

- *Have all the testing resources or users been identified?* This question should be posed to the testing manager to confirm the availability of the testing organization.

- *What types of tests are you going to do?* This question should be posed to the testing manager. The answer should be negotiated to conform to the standard development methodology testing phases, including regression, stress, integration, functional, and acceptance testing.

- *What are the test results showing?* This question is a quick way to determine the high-level quality of the application.

- *How long does an end-to-end test take?* Direct this question to the Testing Manager or Lead Tester. Determine if this is too long to schedule into the plan or too short to do a good job. Update the project rescue plan accordingly.

- *Do you have any other issues or concerns?* This open-ended question can be addressed to anyone on the testing team.

Deployment Questions

Someone needs to be the designated deployment manager from the start of the rescue initiative. Here are some of the questions that the rescue manager should ask to support the solution deployment. The questions should be directed to the deployment team, which may be a subset of the development team and some of the key stakeholders.

- *What deployment approach are you going to use? Pilot approach? Big Bang approach? Running parallel with the existing system?* While this question supposes that a decision has been made, this may not be the case. This question should be asked of several different groups within the organization.

- *What training is needed prior to deployment? Right after deployment?* Training information needs to be captured in a detailed plan that includes specific dates, specific names, and training requirements. This plan also needs to include any training equipment requirements.

- *Where is the detailed deployment plan?* This question should be directed to the deployment lead, who needs to gather all the details from the groups that will be involved in this activity.

- *Is the production architecture deployed? How did we test it?* There is usually a lot of last minute scrambling to get the production architecture online and properly configured. These questions should be asked no later than the final testing phase, to ensure there is enough time to order any last minute equipment or software that is needed, have it delivered, and implement it.

- *What is the contingency plan if the product fails during deployment?* This question should be asked of the stakeholders and the technical architects to capture what the business needs and what the technology is capable of doing. The rescue manager needs to collaborate with the different groups to ensure that the answers converge.

- *What happens if there is a problem after launch?* This is an open-ended question that is designed to capture the requirements for post-launch support, which could extend anywhere from a few days after the project ends to many years of warranty support. This can include a combination of help desk, call center, e-mail, and beeper support. Planning for this contingency is often left to the end of most projects when there is no longer enough time to do this well. It takes at least a few weeks to plan and execute the right solution.

Training Questions

A training lead should be identified in the core team to coordinate the training requirements for the business and technical sides of the extended project team. Ongoing training requirements, and refresher courses, also need to be established. Here are some of the questions that the rescue manager should ask to support the training requirements in the remaining phases of the initiative:

- *Where is the training plan?* This question should be posed to the training lead. The plan needs to incorporate the answers to the three questions described below.

- *What are the training requirements for the business users?* This question should be directed to the stakeholders. It is necessary to collect specific names, what they need to be trained on, and when they are going to be available. The stakeholders need to solicit permissions for the users to attend the training.

- *Who is responsible for training the users? Who is responsible for training the support teams?* The answers to these questions should be left to the training leader. The solution should also include how the training costs are going to be paid.

- *What training requirements are needed during the project?* This open-ended question should be posed to any of the leads, managers, and stakeholders at the start of the initiative.

Vendor and Third-Party Questions

Vendors and third parties are becoming a large component of almost every corporate project, especially those that have a technology component. Offshore service offerings have complicated the picture by adding geographical and cultural challenges.

Here are some of the questions that the rescue manager should ask vendors and other third parties before signing deals with them:

- *What metrics are used to evaluate your representatives?* You want to ensure that the vendor resources are rewarded only if your project rescue effort is successful.

- *What happens if you miss your deadline?* You need to judge whether the vendor has enough at stake to make sure that you are going to be successful.

- *How do we reach your consultants during off hours and on the weekend?* Since your project team will likely be working long, hard hours, you want to ensure that the vendor resources will also be accessible if they are needed.

- *Who in your company needs to sign off on key decisions and pricing? What is the process?* You want to be able to get the best prices, the best service, and whatever else you need to succeed. You want to involve a vendor executive who can totally bypass internal obstacles if you need extra support.

Many assumptions that are made on European and North American projects are not true in the numerous offshore high-activity hubs. Many of these hubs are experiencing dynamic job growth. Every professional is getting several new job offers each week. In this vibrant, job seekers' market, the workers are demanding. They are self-confident because they know that another job is available around the corner. Asking the right questions of the offshore vendor can help make this their problem, and not yours.

Finding a suitable offshore vendor requires good research, and ideally a reference from a trustworthy and experienced colleague. The following questions should be posed to offshore vendors that are included as part of the project rescue plan—preferably before entering into a formal relationship with them:

- *What national holidays do you observe?* People in different countries observe their own national holidays, some of which are extremely relevant and unmovable.

- *What statutory limitations apply regarding overtime and weekend work?* Many of the larger companies have become accustomed to evening and weekend work to make deadlines. Some countries actually have employment laws against this, or at least regulations. The amount of time that an offshore team can devote to making deadlines needs to validated.

- *How do we ensure that communication is not delayed?* You do not want to ask a question, wait a day for a response, and then another day for the next response. Regular conference calls or instant chat sessions need to be set up to make communication more effective.

- *Who's dedicated to our project? What human languages can they communicate in?* Try to get these answers locked down early. Offshore vendors are busy, and you want to ensure that you are getting sufficient attention.

Closing Perspective

This chapter provided a series of questions to ask different members of the extended project team to ensure that the executive phase proceeds successfully. The answers to these questions could require additional changes to the project rescue plan; however, the questioning allows smooth adjustments and transitions to continue the rescue effort.

Post-Intervention

## CHAPTER 14

Forensic Project Review and Lessons Learned

Congratulations! You've recovered your runaway project and you are being showered with praise and honor. But the question remains—was this recovery the result of a disciplined approach or dumb luck, or a combination of both? Hopefully, you have been using a form of the process described in the previous chapters that has been tailored to your company's culture and particular needs. But how can you be sure the recovery was process oriented? More important, how can you be sure your company won't fall into the same traps the next time it embarks on a significant project? In this chapter, we discuss how to conduct a deeper forensic project review and how to document lessons learned so they can be referenced in future projects.

The Forensic Project Review

Now that your project has been successfully completed, it's time to find out what really happened. To do so, you are going to use a technique that should be very familiar to you at this point in your journey. The forensic project review has components that are very similar to the project audits you have been conducting in the recovery process. This review goes deeper into the process to ascertain the root cause(s) of the initial project failure. Once the root cause or causes are identified, your company will be in a position to prevent further runaway projects by implementing new or revised methods, procedures, and policies. In the forensic project review, we look at the four key categories in which projects tend to get out of control:

- Project management
- Executive support
- Subject matter expert involvement
- Project team skill levels

Poor Project Management—The Leading Category of Bad Projects

By now, you've gotten the idea that project management of a significant project is not for an amateur. If done right, project management is a demanding discipline that can be complex and time consuming. Because project management can be so complex, there are many areas that can go awry. Table 14.1 lists the key project management questions that you need to ask and answer to do your root cause analysis.

Project Management Area	Question	Why We're Asking
Change management	Were changes to the project managed according to a formal written procedure?	This area is the number one reason in the number one category for projects going wrong. Without a formal, rigorous, change management procedure, projects will experience scope creep in small and large increments.
	Was a contingency or change management budget been established?	Without this budget, change investigation is done as a new task, is done without tracking time, or is hidden in other tasks. Each of these situations causes management problems when the budget erodes and there is no easy way to find out where the time was truly spent.
	Was there evidence that the change process is useful and effective?	Of course, having a process is only the first step. Exercising the process in an effective manner demonstrates the value of the process.
	Did the team members understand the change management procedure?	Each individual contributor of the team has the power to make or break the change management process. If they understand and enforce it, scope creep is halted and changes can be made based upon their business value.
Project charter	Was a formal project charter present?	We spent a great deal of effort explaining the value of the project charter. If one does not exist, there is no use trying to audit a project for adherence to a nonexistent entity!
	Was the project charter signed by the project executive sponsor?	You need to ensure the project executive sponsor approved the project's reason for being and the plan to complete the project.
Scope management	Were the in-scope statements well defined and quantified?	Within the project charter, the logical scope, deliverable scope, financial scope, organizational scope, and schedule should be clearly defined and approved to establish the project baseline.
	Was out-of-scope defined within the context of the in-scope statements?	It is important to be as specific as possible to avoid confusion and misunderstanding. Some projects are best defined by what they will not do.
Estimating assumptions	Was the project estimated according to a written formal procedure?	The entire project return on investment's expense side was based upon the project estimate and the management team's ability to manage to that estimate. An ad hoc, wild guesstimate produces no logical return and no way to track real progress.
	Was there evidence of a project baseline showing effort and duration?	If the team utilized an estimating method, it should have recorded the estimated effort and duration in the project management tool of choice so that the management team can manage to the inevitable variances.
	Did the project baseline change since the project inception?	If the answer is no, you are either the luckiest person on the planet or the recipient of a lie. Since the project got out of control, it was most likely the latter.

Table 14.1   Forensic Project Review Questions

Project Management Area	Question	Why We're Asking
Estimating assumptions (*continued*)	If the baseline changed, is there evidence of signed change requests authorizing the changes?	Obviously, the project scope and estimates changed. If you do not see those changes reflected in the project plan, you know the plan was not being used. If you find the changes without the supporting authorized change requests, you know the change process was not being used. Either case presents a huge but common problem for runaway projects.
Requirements management	Were the requirements formally documented?	The requirements contain the scope of your project. Each requirement should be documented and approved before subsequent work is done on it. Undocumented requirements are the conduit for scope creep.
	Were the requirements tracked within a traceability matrix?	This technique is not necessarily required in all methodologies. It does provide an excellent way for each project team member to track their work back to a project requirement. This is especially useful during the testing phase.
	Were baseline requirements separate from subsequently added requirements?	For clarity and ease in documenting an audit trail, the original requirements should be documented separately, as should each version of the project requirements along with the supporting authorized change requests.
	Were approved change requests in place to support added requirements?	You should always be able to see when a requirement was added, changed, or removed from the scope of the project via approved change requests. As previously stated, the lack of approved change requests means change was not controlled and your project got away because of a lack of scope management—the infamous scope creep.
Project status reporting	Did a formal communication plan exist?	Project communication breakdown starts with missing communication plans. These plans keep project communications flowing smoothly to the appropriate recipients instead of trying to accomplish project communications via ad hoc, incomplete, nonmatching lists.
	Did the project team members prepare weekly status reports for the project manager?	The entire status reporting process starts with each project team member's individual status report. Besides providing the basic input to the project's weekly status report, these individual status reports provide yet another audit trail when trying to determine where all the hours of effort were spent.
	Did the project manager prepare formal weekly status reports for the project sponsor?	Status reports must be produced on a weekly basis. With large project teams, too much effort and money is spent each week to be unaccounted for in status reports. A lapse here tells you the project manager was not performing one of the most important project management tasks.

Table 14.1   Forensic Project Review Questions (*continued*)

Project Management Area	Question	Why We're Asking
Project status reporting (*continued*)	Are team and project manager status reports filed in a project notebook?	The most important communication tools must be kept in the central repository of the project documents. If this is not being done, you are dealing with an amateur project manager.
Project planning tracking and control	Did a formal project plan exist?	A plan is not a plan unless it is recorded. No project plan means there wasn't any project management.
	Did the project plan reflect the deliverables in the project charter?	Each deliverable listed in the approved project charter should be easily visible in the project plan. All activities should produce a project deliverable. If an activity is not associated with a deliverable, it is probably a superfluous activity that adds cost but no value.
	Were the project deliverables evenly distributed across the project?	Beware of project plans in which all the deliverables are backloaded into the last few months of the project. You really cannot gauge true project progress until you have some approved deliverables accomplished by the team. Like a manufacturing process, the idea is to keep your work-in-process to a minimum to avoid huge cost swings due to rework.
	Were weekly estimates to completion performed?	Projects can get out of control in a hurry. By reviewing the estimate to complete all open tasks and verifying the estimates of the unopened tasks, you have a weekly handle on project-effort variances and the subsequent effects on budget and schedule.
	Did the project manager understand how to compute, track, report, and manage project variances?	These skills are basic for project managers. If this is not being done well, you can deduce the project manager was really a project administrator and was not managing the project.
Issues management	Were issues managed according to a formal written procedure?	Issues are merely items that left unresolved by a specific date will result in a project change. Active issue management is an excellent tool in the battle to keep a project under control. The issue management process should be documented and distributed to the entire project team.
	Were the issues maintained in a formal log?	Keeping the issues in a formal log produces many benefits. First and foremost, when discussing issues, the central log is the common communication vehicle and meeting agenda. Secondly, the issue log provides a good audit trail of those items that affected or may have affected the project.
	Did the project charter specify a formal escalation procedure?	Obviously, not all issues can be resolved at the ground level. A formal escalation process describing to whom and when issues are to be escalated removes the guesswork of "when should we take this to the boss?"

Table 14.1   Forensic Project Review Questions (*continued*)

Project Management Area	Question	Why We're Asking
Issues management (*continued*)	Were issues being actively managed by the project team?	Issue management is not just for the project management team. Formal issue management meetings with the project team members should be held regularly and reflected in the project plan.
Risk management	Were risks managed according to a formal written procedure?	All projects have risks. Variances in the estimates represent unknown factors or risk. Risk must be managed according to a formal risk management procedure that should be reflected in the project plan.
	Did the project charter contain an initial set of risk and mitigation strategies?	Task estimating is inherent with uncertainty. Therefore, the initial estimating effort should have a set of associated assumptions based upon the unknown factors or risks. These risks should also have respective mitigation strategies to be employed to prevent the risk from coming to fruition or to execute when the risk occurs.
	Were the risks reviewed at least monthly?	Risks and the likelihood of a risk occurring change from month to month. The entire project team should be engaged in a monthly risk management meeting to update risk levels and mitigation strategies.
Acceptance management	Did a formal, written, acceptance management procedure exist?	One of the most intriguing questions asked in any project is, "How do we know we are done?" The answer lies in the acceptance management procedure, which defines completion criteria, the process to accept a deliverable, and who has the authority to accept each deliverable.
	Were the formal deliverables accepted by the project sponsor or designee according to the acceptance management procedure?	Like other procedures and plans, acceptance procedures are only as good as the adherence to them. There should be no assumed acceptance. That tactic is a thinly veiled attempt to force acceptance of an incorrect or incomplete deliverable.
	Was a log of accepted deliverables maintained?	You should be able to go to one place to see when and by whom all deliverables were accepted, to assure the deliverables were properly accepted.
Quality assurance	Did a formal, written, quality plan exist?	Quality does not just happen. There should be a formal quality plan to measure adherence to both the project management and technical methodologies.
	Was the quality plan tightly coupled to the project charter and the project deliverables?	The quality plan should address each deliverable and the associated quality methods that will be employed to assure that the deliverable meets the accepted quality standards.
	Did the team members understand their responsibility to support the quality plan?	Each project team member is the doer of the quality plan tasks. They need to understand how to do these tasks as much as they need to understand how to do their respective technical tasks.

Table 14.1   Forensic Project Review Questions (*continued*)

Project Management Area	Question	Why We're Asking
Process compliance	Was the project managed according to a formal methodology?	This should be the primary question of all your project audits. If there is no formal methodology, you do not have a baseline against which to measure the effectiveness of your project management methods.
	Did the technical organization conduct periodic process compliance audits? If so, is there evidence of formal audit action items?	As stated earlier, you should conduct the project audits at regular intervals. There should be a set of action items designed to help get the project on the right track. These action items should not be overly burdensome; rather, they should be practical in getting the project to where it needs to be. These action items should be logged and managed like issues and risks.
	Were the action items followed up?	Beware of the action item list that is collecting dust. If the action items were not managed and worked, you are wasting your time conducting the project audits.

Table 14.1   Forensic Project Review Questions *(continued)*

As you can see, there is plenty to review when looking at how any project is managed, especially runaway projects. Consequently, there are more things that can go wrong with project management than with any other aspect of a project. It's easy to understand why a project management failure is usually at the root of the problem with runaway projects.

Management Support—Following the Leaders

People look to their leaders for direction. This holds true in most facets of life and is especially true with projects. In most cases, senior management will give vocal support for a project, and even follow up that support with financial support. But that is not enough. The senior management team must provide support of the project through action. They must vote with their calendar. The answers to the following questions will help you determine whether the senior management team truly showed support for the project.

Did a member or members of the senior management team

- Speak at the project kick-off?
- Relate how the project fits in the company's strategic direction?
- Attend the monthly project status meetings?
- Attend the project audit review meeting?

- Attend informal project social gatherings?
- Provide the appropriate key people for the project, even though they may have been involved in the daily operations of the business?
- Resolve issues in a timely manner?
- Approve deliverables in a timely manner?
- Show support even when the project schedule slipped or the budget was overrun?

In general, the senior management team should be project advocates. Its advocacy will be contagious and spread throughout the organization and across the company's value chain.

Subject Matter Expert Involvement — The Business Is in Control

Previously we described why it is important to get the right people involved. Important projects require subject matter experts who have actual knowledge and experience in the areas addressed by the project. Remember our old friends Crusty, Dusty, and Rusty? They should not have been near the project. It takes the right people to be effective subject matter experts. Here are some questions to ask to be sure you got the right ones:

- Did the management team of the affected business areas provide direction?
- Did all members of the affected business areas have peer representation?
- Did the one or two key people identified by the business area team members participate and "break away" from their day-to-day responsibilities?
- Were you able to separate the subject matter expert management and nonmanagement teams?

Having the right people assigned to the project and getting them to work on it are two different things. While conducting your forensic project review, you need to determine whether or not the assigned people actually worked on their assigned tasks, by asking these questions:

- Were the subject matter experts available when scheduled?
- Were definition or review meetings held without the assigned subject matter experts?

- Did the subject matter experts review and sign off on each noninfrastructure project deliverable before the deliverable was submitted for final approval?

Your goal is to determine whether or not the business area made the key decisions on the project with respect to business rules, scope, and function. When the technical team has to assume the decision-making role, you will definitely have a disconnect between expectation and final product.

Project Team Skill Levels—The Right People for the Job

In Chapter 4 we discussed the importance of having the right people on the technical team. By "right people," we mean team members who have experience relevant to their position on the project. The following list of questions should be asked for all project team members, especially the project manager, project sponsor, and project architect.

Has the project team member

- Been on a project of similar size and scope before?
- Performed in the same role in that previous project?
- Previously worked with this team?
- Previously worked with the business area(s)?
- Had their skills updated for the role they played on the project?
- Worked with the project's technical methodology?
- Worked with the project's management methodology?

The more "yes" answers you have for each of the questions for each of the project team members, the higher the skill level the team possesses for your project. As we stated previously, many troubled projects have compromised on the experience of the technical and subject matter expert team. Obviously, the higher the skill level of the team, the better chance for success. Finally, attitude is a major factor in project success. Teams with members who possess a positive "can-do" attitude increase the chances for success dramatically.

Lessons Learned

Once you have completed your forensic project review, you need to share the results with different project groups—the project management team, the business area team (including subject matter experts), and the technical team. You want to conduct separate meetings, because these groups have different areas of interest in the forensic project review report. Conduct the sessions in an open and honest atmosphere. Explain that the purpose of the forensic project review is to find where processes failed and how to avoid those failures in the future. Affirm that there was no desire to conduct a "witch hunt." Present the results of the review and leave time for questions.

After all the questions have been asked (and hopefully answered!), explain it's time for the respective team to contribute to the project shut-down process by participating in the lessons learned phase. Prepare an anonymous questionnaire with the following questions:

- What did you like best about the project?
- What did you dislike the most about the project?
- In what ways were your perceptions of the project affirmed?
- What surprised you the most about the project?
- Next time, what will you do in the same or similar way?
- Next time, what will you do differently?

Give each team no more than two weeks to complete the questionnaire, and then summarize the results. Review the final summary with your quality management team for adjustments to the technical methodology.

Don't forget, an important lesson learned is the actual hours it took to complete each task in the plan. This information should be fed back to the estimating repository to further refine how long it takes to work on tasks at your company. This information can then be used by subsequent project teams when they prepare their project plans.

Closing Perspective

This chapter discussed the need for conducting a deep, forensic project review on the completed project. The purpose for this review is not to persecute any individual, but rather to understand where the project management or technical development process failed. Unlike the previously discussed project audits, the forensic project review is extremely comprehensive as its singular goal is to identify the root cause(s) of the failed project. The project review concentrated on four areas: project management, executive support, subject matter expert involvement, and project team skill levels. The majority of the review is in the project management area since that area is the most complex. The other three areas are just as important, just not as complex.

After discussing the forensic project review, we looked at the lessons learned process. You can conduct all the reviews you like, but if no one is able to apply what was learned to everyday practice, you are wasting your time. All quality cycles are continuous loops of feedback and adjustment. Improve your chances of not having another runaway project by conducting these important project shut-down processes.

## CHAPTER 15

Realigning with Industry Best Practices

We have generally been aligned with industry project management best practices and principles throughout the project rescue intervention. However, there are some aspects of the rescue intervention that require an intense and streamlined approach to move troubled projects forward. Project rescue interventions always focus on the project areas that generally result in troubled or failed projects.

There is a cost to the rescue approach. By following the "essential" path—which is one step above the critical path—we control an uncertain environment to produce a set of positive results. We also expect extraordinary effort from the extended project team, high priority within an organization, and a level of intensity (e.g., several checkpoints a day) that are just not sustainable over the long term.

After a project rescue is successfully completed as per the revised objectives at the start of the salvage process, a realignment with industry best practices is required. As shown in Figure 15.1, the rescue methodology is completed, and the project team begins to transition back to the standard corporate management and development methodology. The rescue organization begins to transition out of the process at this time as well.

Best Practices

A corporate standard may not be defined for the management and development methodology, or the rescue process may show that the one already in place is not capable enough to support the demands of the project. The lessons learned from the intervention can be used by the executive sponsor to drive the selection of another methodology.

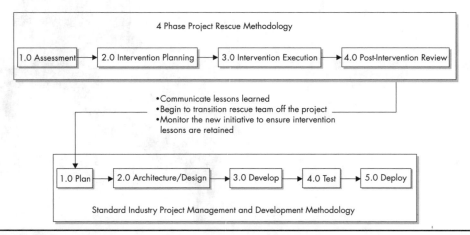

Figure 15.1   Returning to the standard corporate methodology

There are many sources of best practices that can be used to establish the corporate methodology. Some of these (e.g., flavors of Agile methodologies) are available for free on the Web. Others can be purchased with a project management tool. Most of the larger consulting organizations also have proprietary methodologies that they can offer to client organizations in return for a consulting engagement or an upfront fee.

Several groups or standards, such as the International Organization for Standardization (ISO), Control Objectives Information Technology (COBIT), Capability Maturity Model for Software (CMM), and the Project Management Institute (PMI) *A Guide to the Project Management Body of Knowledge*, each offer a separate "body of knowledge" that can serve as a template for your project methodology best practices.

No single source is thorough enough to cover all the needs of most organizations. To build a rigorous project development methodology or project management methodology, it will be necessary to thread different pieces of knowledge from these sources based on your organization's specific needs.

For example, the PMI's *A Guide to the Project Management Body of Knowledge* offers a generic project management approach that can be used to either drive the selection of a third-party methodology or form the basis of a new corporate standard. The PMI approach consists of a combination of project management knowledge areas and project management processes. In particular, risk, quality, communication, controls, and change control are well covered. These can be adopted within the high-level phases shown in Figure 15.2.

Figure 15.2 also shows the generic horizontal linkages between the different phases of a standard project management and development methodology. These linkages are important for ensuring the integrity of the collective processes and the accuracy of the deliverables that are produced.

Figure 15.3 shows a more detailed view of a generic project management and development methodology. The deliverables shown in the figure are the minimum number that are required for most projects to be delivered on time and budget. Missing even a few of these is quite risky. By the time problems are identified, a substantial salvage operation may be required to undo the damage. The deliverables are shown in the phase that typically creates them. They are modified in subsequent phases of the life cycle.

Development Approach

The development approach can be based on a variety of techniques. The commonly used ones are still some variant of the 1990s' Iterative Development, Rapid Application Development (RAD) approach or the waterfall approach, which were discussed earlier in this book.

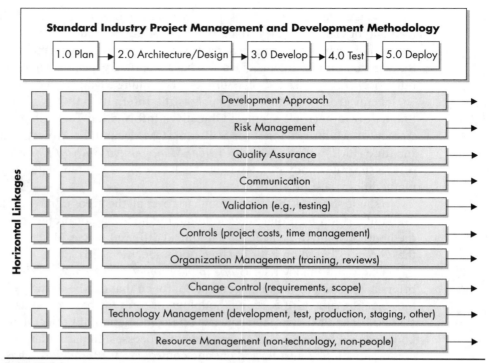

Figure 15.2 Horizontal linkages

The development approach needs to be revisited at the conclusion of the rescue intervention so that lessons learned can be incorporated into the organization's best practices. The following questions need to be asked at this time:

- Was the original development approach the right one for this organization?
- Did the project team apply the approach correctly?
- What advantages would a new approach provide?
- Are other project teams in the organization willing to adopt a new development approach?
- How much more development is the organization going to undertake? Does this justify the investment in rolling out a new approach?
- How much is the organization willing to invest in a new project approach?

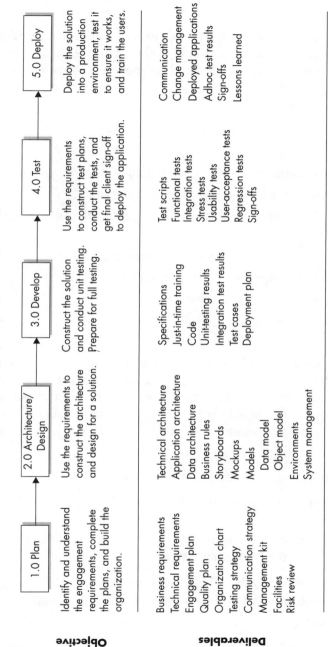

Generic "Running an Engagement" Methodology

	1.0 Plan	2.0 Architecture/ Design	3.0 Develop	4.0 Test	5.0 Deploy
Objective	Identify and understand the engagement requirements, complete the plans, and build the organization.	Use the requirements to construct the architecture and design for a solution.	Construct the solution and conduct unit testing. Prepare for full testing.	Use the requirements to construct test plans, conduct the tests, and get final client sign-off to deploy the application.	Deploy the solution into a production environment, test it to ensure it works, and train the users.

Deliverables	Business requirements
	Technical requirements
	Engagement plan
	Quality plan
	Organization chart
	Testing strategy
	Communication strategy
	Management kit
	Facilities
	Risk review
		Technical architecture
		Application architecture
		Data architecture
		Business rules
		Storyboards
		Mockups
		Models
		  Data model
		  Object model
		Environments
		System management
			Specifications
			Just-in-time training
			Code
			Unit-testing results
			Integration test results
			Test cases
			Deployment plan
				Test scripts
				Functional tests
				Integration tests
				Stress tests
				Usability tests
				User-acceptance tests
				Regression tests
				Sign-offs
					Communication
					Change management
					Deployed applications
					Adhoc test results
					Sign-offs
					Lessons learned

Source: *High-Value IT Consulting*, McGraw-Hill Osborne, 2003, Purba & Delaney

Figure 15.3   Generic "Project Management and Development" methodology

Risk Management

This section presents some of the questions to consider regarding the risk management experience in the overall project. Clearly, the risk management process was not successful in the original attempt at the project and needed to be changed for the rescue operation. This is an evaluation of the effectiveness of the revised approach.

- How well were the lessons learned in the project rescue assessment phase applied in the project rescue?
- Was the organization capable of adopting the lessons learned?
- What types of risks were not originally identified?
- How well did the risk management process work across the different project phases?
- Which risks became reality during the project rescue?
- Were the mitigation strategies effective?
- What could have been done better?

Quality Assurance

There likely was a tremendous rush to rescue your organization's troubled project, and if everything went according to plan, a quality assurance team was in place to maintain the prescribed level of quality within the project deliverables. Here are some questions to ask to help align the future quality assurance process in the organization and also to identify any weaknesses that may have pervaded the rescue intervention:

- How important is quality to the organization?
- What quality tradeoffs were made to meet the deadline? (Hopefully the answer is none.)
- How can we increase the investment available to maintain a high level of quality in all the project deliverables?
- How effective was the quality assurance team?
- Which role provided the best support for quality assurance?
- What problems were encountered in the quality assurance process?
- What improvements can be made to increase the process efficiency?
- Are any formal quality assurance processes, like those offered by ISO, appropriate for the organization? Who needs to champion this in the future?

The Quality Assurance Institute (QAI), Six Sigma, Total Quality Management (TQM), Taguchi, and Quality Function Deployment (QFD) provide best practices in this space.

Communication

Communication is an omnidirectional experience on projects. Pretty much everyone needs to communicate with everyone else throughout all the project phases. This also needs to be done while maintaining controls over what is communicated, when it is communicated, and how it is communicated.

Here are some questions to help evaluate the communication experience during the project rescue and to help improve the future standards around this key horizontal linkage:

- Did anyone complain that communication was poor? Who was left out of the loop? Which roles complained?
- What did team members say about the communication process? Was it clear? Was it effective?
- Was information captured and communicated in a timely manner?
- Were the communication deliverables clear? Did people misinterpret them?
- Were confidential materials ever accidentally distributed? What was done to ensure that this does not happen again?
- What improvements can be made in the future?

Validation

With all the parallel activities being pursued in the different phases, iterative validation becomes imperative. By this we mean that deliverables need to be constructed and tested on an ongoing basis—despite the fact that there is also an entire phase dedicated to testing. Here are some questions to help evaluate the validation process that was used in the project rescue:

- Were the test phase results a surprise?
- How many showstopper problems were identified during the testing phase?
- What type of feedback was received from team members who were required to test their own deliverables?
- What type of feedback was received from the test groups?
- Was there a risk that the implementation was going to be delayed because of too many problems being identified in testing?

- How many problems were identified before the testing phase?
- How well did the test bed work? What improvements were suggested by the team members?
- How well did the ongoing validation processes work with the quality assurance requirements?

Controls

Control processes are relevant to all types of organizations and at all times. In the specific instances of projects, processes need to be defined for controlling such things as project costs and timesheets. The *PMI Body of Knowledge* defines an extensive number of control processes. Here are a set of questions to evaluate the effectiveness of the controls used in the project rescue:

- Were the actual budget numbers modified after reporting, because of newly found financial items?
- How close were the budget forecasts to the actuals?
- How many times were budget or time submissions submitted late?
- Are the financial policies (e.g., expense reports, timesheet submission) well defined? What exceptions were needed to make things work?
- What are the team members saying about the controls?
- Did the controls negatively impact the project timeframe? How so?
- Which controls can be eliminated?
- Which new controls are required?

Organization Management

The organization will evolve after the project rescue is completed. The project rescue team will move onto other initiatives, either inside or outside the organization. Additional skills may also need to be transferred. You also want to make sure that the project organization has an opportunity to recover from the workload of the rescue initiative. Here are the questions to ask at this time:

- Is the project team ready to handle the next project phase?
- What is the cost of retaining the rescue manager as a quality assurance resource on a part-time basis? How about other members of the rescue team?

- What training is required by members of the project team?
- Are additional mentors required?
- What new resources are needed?
- What additional skills are needed by members of the organization?
- How have we acknowledged the efforts of the project team?
- Have the project team members been given time off to recover from the difficult workload they endured?
- What is the attitude of the team members? Are they positive? Are they ready for more challenges?
- Have we been careful to avoid blaming members of the team for having to launch a project rescue in the first place?
- How is the performance review process perceived within the organization?
- Have all the commitments made to the team members been kept?
- Have we listened to the team members?

Change Control

Change control is needed throughout the project life cycle to maintain consistency in the project scope, objectives, and business requirements. Specific processes and tools need to be implemented at the start of the project to ensure that changes to any of these do not destroy the project's progress. This is an opportunity to evaluate the change control processes established for the project rescue (which would have been stringent), how they were perceived, and how to improve them. The following questions should be considered as you evaluate the change control processes:

- Were the change control processes followed by everyone in the extended project team? Who were the holdouts?
- Were the processes too cumbersome? Can they be streamlined further?
- Did the processes stop work from being accepted that should have been done in the phase?
- How clear are the processes? What do people say about the change control form?
- How effective were the tools? Were they too costly? Were they accessible? How easy is it to get meaningful reports from them?

Technology Management (Development, Test, Production, Staging, Other)

Evaluate the technology management processes for the different environments that need to be supported in the organization, including development, test, production, and staging areas. The assessment needs to be done in terms of the following:

- How effective was the product selection process?
- How effective were the vendor negotiations?
- Were there problems with the vendor service-level agreements?
- What feedback have the product vendors provided in terms of working with the organization? Payment terms? Accessibility? Cultural fit?
- How well do we configure our products?
- Is the financial process related to purchasing products too long? Too short?
- What mistakes were made in the technology product selections?
- Did we select any bad vendors? Have any gone out of business? Which ones have broken commitments to us?
- Which vendors have proven themselves to us? Can we negotiate an attractive ongoing relationship with them?
- How do we validate that the appropriate architectures have been selected?
- How do we maintain the reliability and performance of the architectures in the future?

Resource Management (Non-Technology, Non-People)

Other resources, in addition to managing people resources and technology resources, also need to be managed. These resources include floor space, desks, and other equipment. Here are some questions to consider:

- Are we limiting our effectiveness by the controls in place in this area?
- Were team members able to get the tools they need to do their jobs?
- Is the working environment improving individual performance?
- Are people complaining about our resource management policies? How much time is this taking out of their workday?

- Did the project rescue require modifications to corporate policies in order to be able to deliver successfully? Has this been communicated to executive management? Is it being considered for the future corporate standards?

- What else have we learned in this area from the rescue initiative?

Closing Perspective

This chapter closed the loop for the project rescue initiative. The intensity of a project rescue operation cannot and should not be sustained indefinitely. After a troubled project is rescued, the team needs to return to standard project management principles. This chapter cited the Project Management Institute (PMI) and other industry best practices as potential alignment candidates.

## CHAPTER 16

Post-Intervention
Intervention Questionnaire

Throughout this book, we have focused on the processes and tools used to gain control of a runaway project. After the successful recovery and completion of the project, you should conduct reviews and lessons-learned activities to support the effort to continuously improve your processes. In Chapter 14, we looked at the questions pertaining to the review of your rescued runaway project after its completion. In this chapter, we look at the project rescue process itself.

We employ the concepts of the Deming cycle, or PDSA cycle, a continuous quality improvement model consisting of a logical sequence of four repetitive steps for continuous improvement and learning: Plan, Do, Study (Check) and Act. Using the Study and Act components of the Deming PDSA model that's shown in Figure 16.1, we will employ continuous improvement of the project rescue process by identifying a series of questions that the rescue manager can pose to measure the effectiveness of the rescue process (Study). These questions fall into three categories:

- Rescue initiation
- Rescue execution
- Rescue transition back to the normal technical process

Once you collect the various facts and opinions and apply critical thought to produce your findings, you can then measure the effectiveness of the rescue process and make recommendations on how to change it for the future (Act).

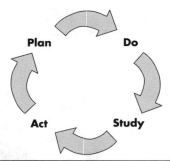

Figure 16.1   Dr. W. Edwards Deming's PDSA Model

Rescue Initiation

In runaway project situations, people always comment on how the project problems should have been detected earlier. The set of questions presented in this section does not focus on problem detection, but rather looks at the timing and effectiveness of the rescue initiation.

Here are some of the questions that the rescue manager should ask related to the project rescue initiation:

- *Was the rescue process initiated as quickly as possible once the project was determined to be a runaway project?* Nerves are already on edge once a project is declared a disaster. Organizations can exacerbate the problem by stalling the start of the rescue process, which can happen because of fear, ignorance, indecision, or any combination thereof. Effective triggers should be in place, and the rescue process initiation should be planned once the project shows signs of failure but before it is formally declared as such. Every day the rescue is delayed is another day of effort and expense shoveled into the black hole.

- *Was the rescue initiation formally communicated to the extended project team?* Throughout this book, we have affirmed the rescue process is a project unto itself. As a project, it should have the same characteristics of a "normal" project initiation. There should be a formal kickoff meeting with all project stakeholders to explain the differences between the rescue effort and the regular project effort. Rescue goals and objectives should be confirmed and the rescue communication plan should be explained. Most importantly, rescue completion criteria—when the project rescue ends and the regular technical process resumes—should be communicated.

- *Was the rescue team staffed with the appropriate personnel?* As with any other project, just having a good process is not enough. You need to have a rescue team that is experienced in the technical process and projects of similar size and scope. The team must also be eager and willing to help get the project back on track. Beware of hidden agendas or negative attitudes on the rescue team, because they will inhibit any successful rescue attempts. You need to understand how the rescue team was selected. Availability should not be driving criteria.

- *How could we have improved the rescue initiation?* This question encourages the extended team members to identify any other enhancements to the rescue initiation process. They should be pressed to identify any issues or concerns that they have not shared.

- *Should we have initiated a project rescue?* This question seems almost rhetorical, based upon the results of the rescue attempt. If the project could not be saved, it's easy to say the attempt should not have been made. Likewise, if the project was successfully rescued, it's easy to say the rescue effort should have been made. But you need to dig a little deeper into the analysis to confirm these simplistic deductions. If the project rescue attempt failed, was it because the process failed or was it because the project was so inherently flawed that it was beyond rescue? If the latter situation was the culprit, why wasn't this recognized when the decision to initiate a project rescue was made? Was the decision politically motivated, because someone was still trying to hide bad news? Now the situation is even worse because more time and expense were frittered away. If the project was successfully rescued, what was the cost? Was the success truly a success or was it a declared success? This very tough question is designed to find out if you threw good money after bad.

Once you have analyzed the answers to these questions, you can make the appropriate improvements and define meaningful metrics (for example, elapsed time between the formal disaster declaration and rescue initiation) for this part of the rescue process.

Rescue Implementation

The implementation phase frequently generates confusion between the rescue implementation and the original project's implementation. Here are some of the questions that the rescue manager should pose to members of the extended project team about the rescue implementation phase:

- *How well did you understand how your role and responsibilities in the project rescue differed from the original project?* This question helps you determine if there was confusion between the roles and responsibilities in the project rescue process and the original project. Follow up by asking the person to explain the differences and how they juggled the two primary roles.

- *What went well with the project rescue effort?* This question gives the team member the opportunity to describe the activities that went well from their perspective. You can get a sense of team strengths and process strengths when similar activities are mentioned by multiple team members.

- *What did not go well with the project rescue effort?* This question gives the team member the opportunity to describe the activities that did not go well from their perspective. If you are conducting a live interview, you need to keep the interview from degrading into a gripe session. Ask what they did to try to remedy the problems. Focus on the process and try to filter out the personality conflicts that may slant the response.

- *What would you change in the recovery process to make it more effective?* This question should enable you to get some great information on how to improve the rescue process. The respondent should have some good insights, especially after answering the previous two questions. Be sure to ask this question after the previous two questions in this list. Probe deeply here. Even reluctant respondents have much to contribute. This question again reminds team members that they have to be part of the solution, and not just the ones who raise problems.

- *How effective was the project rescue communication plan?* This open-ended question gives you insight to the key component of the project rescue process—communications. Keep the questions in context with the communication plan in order to determine the degree by which the plan was executed. Ask the team member if they understood their role in the plan. Follow up with questions about the quality of the communications. Were they accurate, timely, informative, and clear? Would someone not affiliated with the project in any way understand the status of the rescue effort by reviewing the various forms of communications?

Rescue Transition

Perhaps the most ignored phase of the rescue process is the transition phase. This phase marks the end of the formal rescue process as the project is confirmed to be back on track and under the regular management and technical processes. The completion of the rescue effort is not necessarily the completion of the project itself, although they may coincide. Frequently, the rescue process ends with a whimper, which is rather astounding because several people have just completed one of the most stressful, intense periods of their career and there is no formal declaration of success. Understandably, most organizations would be reluctant to stage a huge celebration with the history of the runaway project fresh in mind; however, a remarkable episode has been completed, and that should call for some form of recognition beyond t-shirts and coffee mugs.

There should be a formal transition from rescue mode to "normal" mode. The rescue project should have a formal shut-down just like any other project. The questions for this phase are designed to help you determine whether or not the formal transition took place and, if so, its effectiveness and any long-term effects on the project team members. You hope to never get into another situation like this one, but if you do, you want to have confidence that your team knows how to handle the situation and bring it to a successful conclusion. Here are some questions that the rescue manager should pose to the project team member regarding execution of the transition phase:

- *When did the project rescue effort end, and how did you know?* This question gets right to the key point. Did the rescue manager properly shut down the rescue project and formally communicate the end of the rescue effort to the extended project team? Once again, the communications plan is tested for effectiveness.

- *Where are the project rescue artifacts archived? Do you have access to them?* These questions help you confirm how the formal project rescue shut-down took place. The rescue team members should have access to the final project rescue work products and deliverables for future reference. The rescue manager should confirm that this information is documented in an archive index that shows a brief description of each artifact's content as well as its location in electronic and paper format.

- *What lessons did you learn from the project rescue?* This is another open-ended question that is intended to personalize the project rescue for the team member. For each team member to grow in their experience and career, they must be able to articulate, assimilate, and deploy improvements in the ways they work in the future. Those who are ignorant of history may be condemned to repeat it but those who choose to not learn from it are condemned to perpetual ineptitude.

- *What recognition did you receive for your contribution to the project rescue effort?* Nothing is more disheartening than working hard, achieving results, and going unrecognized. The answer to this question gives you insight to the leadership style and capability of the rescue manager—even if that's you!

Lavish celebrations are probably inappropriate. Save that for the successful completion of the rescued project. But a thank you note for each team member and the unintended victims of the runaway project—their respective families—goes a long way in establishing a sense of accomplishment and loyalty. This is not a totally altruistic gesture. You probably need these same people to complete the rescued project.

- *How did you celebrate the project rescue completion?* Don't be surprised to hear "I got some sleep" as a common answer to this question. The rescue process is mentally, physically, and emotionally demanding. Exhaustion is a common by-product of the rescue process. Give your team some time to pause and recharge; but not too much time, because you don't want your rescued project to start slipping again.

Action Plans

Once you gather all your information, it's time to put it into a series of action plans so that the process improvements are given ownership. Organize your final report or presentation into the following sections:

1. Methodology
   - Who you questioned
   - When they were questioned
   - How they were questioned (individual interview, group session, questionnaire, and so on)
2. Findings and Conclusions
3. Recommendations

The recommendations should be in the form of a Rescue Process Improvement Action Plan. This plan should include a simple project charter and a project plan that delineates the process improvements deliverables to be produced, accepted, and implemented. This last step (Action) is needed to ensure that the good things identified are formally defined and installed back into the rescue process. Make sure the final report or presentation is given to the owners of your technical, management, and rescue processes so the improvements can be assimilated into these appropriate processes, respectively.

Closing Perspective

This chapter provided a series of questions to ask regarding the effectiveness of the project rescue process. It is part of a continuous process improvement method based upon Dr. W. Edwards Deming's Plan-Do-Study-Act model. Specifically, we briefly addressed the Study and Act components of that model. We grouped our questions into three areas: rescue initiation, rescue implementation, and rescue transition. All three phases are important and should go through a continuous improvement effort. Any process improvement methodology will work. If your company uses Six Sigma, Lean, TQM, or another process improvement methodology, use it to test and improve your project rescue process. You hope to never go through this situation again, but if you do, you want to have your rescue processes as refined as possible for your specific situation.

We also briefly touched on the importance of formally recognizing the completion of the project rescue effort and its effect on the rescue team. A project rescue takes its toll on the physical, mental, and emotional condition of the team members. Good, strong leadership is urgently needed, especially in the areas of recognition and celebration of milestones. As leader of the effort, you will most likely receive your share of recognition for rescuing the runaway project. Sharing the wealth will help you to build an energized, motivated, successful, and loyal team.

Intervention Techniques

## CHAPTER 17

Conflict Management, Building Consensus, and Group Relationships

A project cannot be rescued unless there is strong consensus at key levels of the organization. This gives clarity to what needs to be built, how it is to be built, and when it is going to be built, and enables the project rescue team to overcome obstacles as they are encountered so that a successful conclusion can be reached.

Consensus, unfortunately, is difficult to achieve on a project. Combining different personalities from different team members in an already severely strained situation can produce an environment that requires more energy to be consumed in sorting out the people dynamics instead of adding value to the organization.

This chapter examines the key conflicts that can occur during a project, especially one that is being rescued. Relationships are key to overcoming these conflicts. This chapter defines the important relationships between the different roles on an extended project team and explains how these can be leveraged.

Conflicts and Consensus Building During a Project Rescue

Conflict is not necessarily a bad thing, just like stress may not always be a bad thing. Either of these can drive benefits or end in disaster. Unfortunately, probability tends to favor the negative outcome—unless strong controls and careful steering are put in place.

It is sometimes argued that conflict is healthy. But the idea that conflict drives some sort of beneficial decision-making or innovation is as wrong as assuming that a positive work environment always produces results. Conflict happens on projects whether we want it to or not. Our objective is to control and guide its impact and not allow it to run a negative course. Conflict is a state that is neither good nor bad. It's only a starting point.

Reasons for Conflicts

There are many reasons for conflict within a project team during a project rescue initiative. Three basic questions tend to drive all the different types of conflict in a project salvage operation at some level, as follows (see Figure 17.1):

1. Where are we going?
2. How are we getting there?
3. What am I getting out of this?

Answering these questions to every team member's satisfaction is an effective way to start building consensus. An additional set of questions can be formulated to augment these to drive out more detail. Figure 17.2 uses two broad motivational categories, professional and personal, to frame these questions.

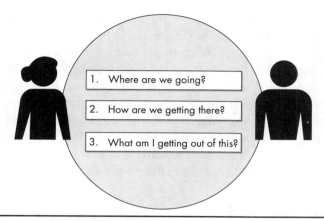

Figure 17.1   Basic drivers of conflict in a project rescue

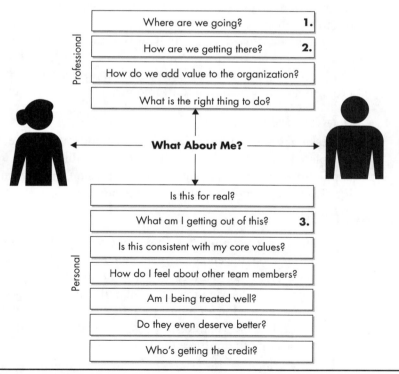

Figure 17.2   Sources of conflict

The questions in the professional motivational category highlight the fact that most professionals are interested in adding value to the organizations that employ them. This offers an important opportunity to find common ground, regardless of other differences that separate team members. It can also generate a powerful bond during a tight timeframe as long as progress is being made.

The questions in the personal motivational category can be further divided into additional subgroups. The "What am I getting out of this?" question is a natural consideration for every human being. The question asks for clarity around what is available in terms of rewards, and also what needs to be made available to gain the focus and loyalty of different resources.

Types of Conflicts to Expect

The questions from Figure 17.2 can be used to derive the types of conflicts that can afflict projects that are involved in a rescue intervention. The project rescue initiative simplifies some of the discussions around these conflicts. The choice for the extended project team is to resolve their differences and succeed together or fail together.

A willingness to overcome conflicts is certainly a major ingredient for being able to do so. This section also examines situations where willingness is not enough. Conflict can exist because of uncertainly, confusion, and frustration, as a disillusioned project team may be trying to overcome a nearly impossible situation.

Professional Motivations

Professionals are motivated by the need to add value to their organization and to complete assignments successfully. Potential disruptions to these goals spawn conflicts that are driven by uncertainty, confusion, and the frustration to do a better job. Team members from all parts of the organization need to buy into the answers to these questions:

- **Where are we going?** This is potentially a big source of conflict. Without clarity about the end goal, team members will argue their perspectives, which can easily lead to a free-for-all. The executive sponsor needs to be fully engaged in ensuring that relevant and realistic end goals are established and communicated, with input from the stakeholders. For the project rescue, the constraints on what is still possible need to drive the end goals. This is an opportunity to reinforce the rescue statement of work.

- **How are we getting there?** If left unresolved, this would be the biggest source of conflict on any project. Team members bring their own perspectives to the process. It is difficult to prove whether a certain direction is the right or wrong one to take. Too often, this does not become evident until the project gets into trouble. The rescue manager and the executive sponsor are the drivers for determining the answer to this question, with the collective input of the team. This is an opportunity to use the rescue work breakdown structure as the answer to "How are we getting there?"

- **How do we add value to the organization?**   This can also become a source of debate, especially in terms of trying to identify the precise level of the impact. A gross margin of 20 percent is better than 5 percent, but what if we could get 50 percent? How dejected does a member of the team become if they are told that 25 percent is not good enough? In the context of the project rescue, value is delivered in several ways. Completing the revised objectives from the project rescue planning phase is the first way. A successful conclusion will also raise the morale of the organization, which is the second value add of the rescue intervention. Furthermore, the experiences gained in the rescue initiative can be used to enhance the capabilities of the organization going forward.

- **What is the right thing to do?**   The final question is also comforting in its intent. Team members want to do what's right for the organization. However, this question also opens up a lot of debate because of the many different answers that are possible. Team members may ask if changing direction is the right thing. Are the objectives too narrow? Could we be doing more? The executive sponsor and the rescue manager need to work with the team to address these questions in a project review workshop after a successful rescue. Without the success, there is no right answer.

Personal Motivations

Aside from a desire to add value to the organization, people are also driven by personal motivations. There is a lot in play here, and this motivational area is more complex than the professional one. The interaction of backgrounds, history, core values, and drivers is difficult to predict, and produces different results in individual candidates.

Some people may be driven by the need to acquire power, others by compensation, and still others by the desire to learn something new or different. Individual team members may be taking a short- or long-term view. There may be medium-term requirements. There may be requirements that the employee may not even be aware of, but which could become a reality before the project rescue is completed—further complicating the status quo.

Several other factors further complicate this situation. For example, a team member may not be upfront about what they really want. They could change their mind, or they may no longer trust what they hear.

Personal motivations can be confused with greed. Some believe that employees who ask about what's in it for them are being disloyal, unprofessional, or difficult. This is not true for the most part. These questions are fundamental to our basic motivations. The objective is for everyone involved to do the right thing for the organization and the people delivering the work.

The following list identifies some of the questions that employees asking themselves or other team members. Addressing these as part of the rescue planning process can take them off the table and get the team focused on saving the project:

- **Is this for real?** The team may question whether the current approach is another knee-jerk reaction—perhaps similar to past attempts that failed. This lingering doubt may only result in drawing a tepid response from them, and could be self-defeating from the very start of the rescue. The executive sponsor needs to convince the team that the rescue intervention is fully sanctioned, backed, and supported. This must be done by making decisions around a revised scope and objectives. Any tools that are needed must be provided to the project team. The rescue manager must be seen as empowered, rather than just another temporary player who is not allowed to make a decision.

- **What am I getting out of this?** This is the fundamental question on everyone's mind, whether they ask it or not. This is true even in the most altruistic cases where the answer may be "whatever's good for the organization." In most cases, though, management should provide incentives for a successful project rescue. These incentives may include recognition (e.g., some type of plaque or trophy to commemorate the event), monetary bonuses (e.g., tiered to different outcomes), celebrations (e.g., ongoing team events), and a career path (e.g., promotions or lateral moves at the end of the initiative). Management needs to listen to individual team members to set up incentives that encourage positive results. Management should also not be afraid of recognizing special circumstances. For example, a team member may want to work from home two days out of the week in exchange for working longer hours.

- **Is this consistent with my core values?** Team members that are being asked to behave in ways that conflict with core values will also feel a lot of conflict. In a project rescue, there is no time to make any adjustments in this area. The core values of the team members must be factored into the part of the solution they are providing.

- **How do I feel about other team members?** Some people can work with anyone. Other people find it difficult to work with someone they dislike. Having put clarity around the destination and the route to get there, management needs to leverage the incentives package and reason to overcome conflicts in this area. If this is not effective, the rescue manager needs to act as the bridge between employees who are in conflict.

- **Am I being treated well?** Team members can misunderstand the urgency of a project rescue and become very sensitive about how they are being perceived by others in the organization. Some will complain that they feel they are being singled out for past mistakes. The rescue manager needs to reiterate, communicate, and demonstrate complete objectivity in pointing out mistakes and errors. Team members will not provide their best value if they feel they are being mistreated or unfairly blamed.

- **Does the company deserve any better than the problems they're currently experiencing on the project?** This is a very negative, cynical motivation. Some team members may privately feel that the negative project outcome is deserved by the organization. This could be as payback to the organization for past perceived or real slights. In some cases, the reaction may be a withholding of information. The continuum extends to the point of vendettas that could drive deliberate problem creation. This behavior is also not limited to any specific role or seniority. The rescue manager needs to be on the lookout for this type of conflict and needs to act swiftly to resolve it. If a combination of incentives and professionalism are not enough to turn the situation around, perhaps the resource needs to be replaced on the team.

- **Who's getting the credit?** Getting credit is just another type of incentive, but one that can have powerful consequences. A project team in trouble can be accommodating, but once the danger is past, individuals may begin to care more about receiving credit for their work than the end result. The rescue manager needs to be aware of this and needs to ensure that credit is allocated as a team or not at all.

Basic Consensus Building

A project is not a true case of consensus building because there is a reporting hierarchy that affects the relationships. In some ways, the hierarchy simplifies consensus building because team members can generally be open to guidance from their manager without personal inhibitions or ego.

In other ways, the hierarchy makes the situation more complicated because individual team members may not be as forthcoming. This reduces their level of output, and you may never even know it. Telling team members what they need to do, without demonstrating that their feedback has been considered, will discourage them from offering valuable input in the future.

Consensus needs to be built around the different project relationships, as you'll see later in this chapter. This is a difficult and time-consuming process. This section examines some of the high-level considerations for achieving consensus, before getting into the details.

Looking for the common ground is the first step in this process. Among the questions presented in the previous sections, the one that needs to be answered unequivocally and completely is "Where are we going?" A clear answer that can be documented and clearly explained around several dimensions needs to be given; otherwise, there is little likelihood of a successful rescue. A complete answer to this question must address the following dimensions:

- What the end result looks like.
- How much we can spend in getting there.
- When we need to get there.

This is another opportunity to emphasis the project charter or Statement of Work.

After establishing a common reference point, the basic consensus building strategy is to find other common ground between the key team relationships. After reiterating and confirming this, the next steps are to work on temporarily bridging the differences. The bridges could be permanent, but this is unlikely to be the case and is not necessary for the rescue intervention. It would help if some of the bridges could be designed to stand, so that execution of future projects is smoother.

Consensus Building Techniques

Building a bridge between different positions can be easier with the assistance of a facilitator, especially when peer-to-peer relationships are involved. The project rescue manager is the obvious choice in terms of identifying and facilitating the resolution of weaknesses in the other relationships on the project. Individuals could take the initiative and resolve their own differences. This requires mutual consideration and can be successful on enlightened teams.

The temporary culture and negativity on a troubled project, though, make it difficult for this to happen. Using a facilitator is the preferred strategy for the rescue. Producing a list of lessons learned to guide future initiatives is also a goal here. The executive sponsor can champion relationship improvements between the rescue manager and other stakeholders and senior members of the project team.

There are several techniques that can bridge differences. Any approach involves a certain amount of "give and take" to arrive at the right drivers. These techniques are best used in combination with each other, in the following order:

- **Reason** This is an appeal to the professional motivations that drive team members. It is reasonable to resolve the conflicts for the organization's sake.

- **The carrot** Reason alone will only get you so far. The argument offered here is that a successful project rescue will help the organization and the result will be realization of the incentives put on the table.

- **The stick** This is an implicit part of every strategy. A lack of success in the rescue will mean some type of natural negative consequences. Penalties could also be involved, but this will have negative long-term consequences if they are seen as being retaliatory and unfair. For example, team members may accept that there will be a loss of revenue and hence no bonuses. However, if people are going to be fired despite their best efforts, the result may be temporary hard work but a loss of loyalty and potentially a lack of quality. Employees will also leave the organization at the first opportunity.

Professional Motivations

Using the questions related to the professional motivations, Table 17.1 provides some suggestions for building a consensus and the challenges that need to be faced in removing related conflicts.

Motivation	Suggestions for Consensus Building	Challenges
Where are we going?	The clarity and depth need to be at an appropriate level for all members of the team.	Establishing the right level of detail is difficult when trying to document this direction. While a stakeholder may believe that a description is clear, it may not be for the team members doing the work.
How are we getting there?	Get input from the team members and use a workshop with strict rules to define an approach that has buy-in from the individuals in the group.	Overcoming difficult opinions that may still exist. The rescue manager needs to drive the decisions in this case.
How do we add value to the organization?	Focus on the success of the project rescue as being a significant contributor.	Keeping focus.
What is the right thing to do?	Focus on adding value to the organization.	Are we doing enough to improve the project?

Table 17.1 Building Consensus Around Professional Motivations

Personal Motivations

Using the questions related to the personal motivations, Table 17.2 provides some suggestions for building a consensus and the challenges that need to be faced in removing related conflicts.

Motivation	Suggestions for Consensus Building	Challenges
Is this for real?	Prove that the organization is committed to the rescue by empowering the executive sponsor. Demonstrate that the difficult decisions are going to be made going forward.	Disassociating this rescue effort from past attempts that were half-hearted or not supported.
What am I getting out of this?	Publish a clear incentives statement. Build a written plan with each team member to describe their role in the rescue, their personal goals, and the incentives.	Targeting incentives at the right levels.
Is this consistent with my core values?	Get feedback from each team member while building the personal plans.	Getting team members to speak openly.
How do I feel about other team members?	Focus the team on rescue objectives. Respect their personal preferences while not impacting the initiative. Remind people that they do not need to like someone or agree with them to work together.	The intensity of the emotions can be overwhelming in this area. Particularly difficult team members may need to be separated for the good of the rescue. Additional effort will be required to fill in the gap as a result of this type of transfer.
Am I being treated well?	Use the personal plan and incentives package to demonstrate commitment to individual team members. Listen to their issues and problems—both professional and sometimes personal. Follow up.	
Do they even deserve better?	Track the initial milestones to see who is producing and who is not. Of those that are not producing, determine whether this question is the root cause.	Getting the most value from a team member who feels this.
Who's getting the credit?	Distribute credit or blame as a team.	Managing promotions and bonuses equitably.

Table 17.2 Building Consensus Around Personal Motivations

Relationship Management

Every person added to a project geometrically increases the number of human relationships. Figure 17.3 shows these relationships. Starting with Person a and Person b, there is one relationship identified by the line marked A. Adding Person c adds the two additional relationships identified as B, for a total of three relationships. Adding the fourth person adds the relationships marked C, for a total of six relationships.

Each of these team members is, of course, a unique individual that can bond or clash on any number of different personality characteristics. They also need to be true to their own core values.

Key Relationship Groups

Figure 17.4 shows the key relationship groups that are important contributors to a project rescue initiative. This assumes that all the team members are competent in

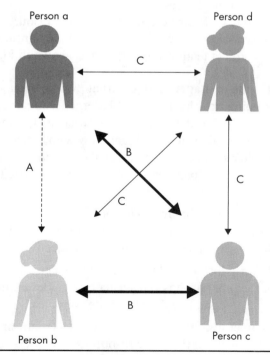

Figure 17.3   Geometrically increasing relationships

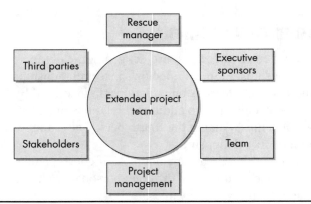

Figure 17.4   Key relationship groups

their roles; otherwise, they should be removed from the project or be closely mentored. Members of these groups are all important for salvaging the project. The rescue initiative cannot be successful without all of them. Let's talk briefly about each of these roles.

There may be lots of different individual resources in the project team, but for the purposes of a rescue initiative, several key groups that collectively form the extended project team can be labeled as shown in Figure 17.4 and defined next:

- **Rescue manager**   An external project manager that is experienced in rescuing troubled projects. "External" could mean external to the organization or external to the project being rescued. The rescue manager could also be the original project manager, now with a mandate to save the project. This would require a fresh start with the executive sponsor to forget about allocating blame for the previous problems. This role concludes with a successful project rescue.

- **Executive sponsors**   One or more executives (usually one) who own the project resources and the project results. They typically own the budget for the project. They report to senior executives in the organization.

- **Team**   Includes all the roles and responsibilities that are not included in one of the other groups. This usually includes all the people doing the hands-on work to complete the project deliverables.

- **Project management**   The members of the project team who are responsible for managing the other resources. Members of this group may remain on the project after the rescue is complete. They report to the rescue manager for the duration of the rescue, even if informally. The rescue manager would not normally have any direct power over their long-term compensation or promotion, but will have influence.

- **Stakeholders**   A group of business owners that is affected by the results of the project. Stakeholders may be providing some portion of the project budget. The users of the solution being built generally report to these stakeholders.

- **Third parties**   Anyone involved in the project that is not employed full time by the organization. This includes vendors that provide hardware, software, and tools. It also includes companies that may be providing resources for the project initiative. Increasingly, it includes offshore companies that play a key role in delivering processes or products for the initiative to be successful.

Project Relationships

The relationships that have the highest impact during a project rescue are shown in Figure 17.5. The figure further prioritizes the relationships, identifying the ones that are key, important, and somewhat important. These relationships must be secure for the project rescue effort to move forward successfully.

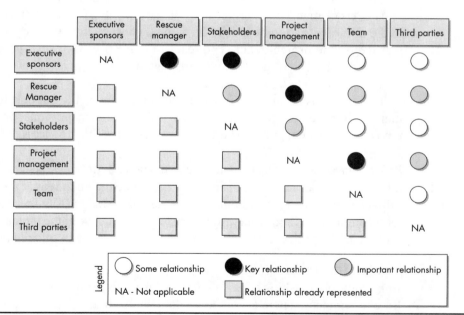

Figure 17.5   Key relationships

Key Relationships

There are four key relationships in the extended organization, as described in the sections that follow.

Executive Sponsor — Rescue Manager   This is the most important relationship to the project rescue. The executive sponsor handles the business side, while the rescue manager handles the delivery side. Their mutual trust and agreement are needed for making the types of decisions that are necessary to salvage a troubled project.

Executive Sponsor — Stakeholders   The executive sponsor is a representative of the other stakeholders. In many, but not all, cases, the stakeholders report to the executive sponsor. These groups must deliver a consistent message, otherwise the project team will not have clarity about what it is trying to build. Weaknesses in these relationships are major contributors to project problems.

Rescue Manager — Project Management   This is a complicated relationship. The rescue manager may be seen as an interloper. There may be the perception that credit for success will go to the newcomer, while some type of blame or stigma will be associated with the original project management team.

The rescue manager's biggest strength is being able to bring a fresh perspective to the initiative, and to be able to leverage the work already done and the lessons learned by the project team. The rescue manager cannot salvage the project independently. The original project management team needs to be fully engaged for the operation to be successful.

This relationship must be based on an agreement of full support for the rescue manager for the duration of the rescue. The rescue manager must position the full project management group to be equal partners in the future success of the initiative.

Project Management — Team   The rescue manager's influence is only as great as allowed by the executive sponsor. This influence may be great at the start of the initiative, but it will start to taper off as the rescue begins to take shape. Longer-term commitments and relationships must continue between the project management group and the project team. Ongoing trust is imperative in this relationship.

Important Relationships

Important relationships are also highly relevant to the rescue initiative, but just a little less intense. There are six key relationships in the extended organization, as described in the following sections.

Executive Sponsor — Project Management   The relationship here may have soured because the project attempt was not successful and needed to be rescued. They may be placing blame on each other. The reality is probably somewhere in the middle. The rescue manager must take on the responsibility of bringing these sides together. The relationship between the executive sponsor and project management will be key as the rescue is completed and you move into other phases of the project.

Rescue Manager — Stakeholders   While the key relationship is between the rescue manager and the project management, additional information and goodwill can be gained from the stakeholders. Stakeholders, as their name suggests, hold a stake in the rescue manager being able to deliver business value. This will motivate them to share information and resources more readily with the rescue manager.

Rescue Manager — Team   There may be hard feelings between the team and project management due to the stressful project environment. The rescue manager needs to establish a trusting relationship with the project team to satisfy their personal and professional motivations. At the same time, the rescue manager needs to help improve the relationship between the team and the management group. The latter is better positioned to reward team members long term, so it is in the team members' best interest to improve their relationship with the more permanent side of management.

Rescue Manager — Third Parties   Third parties play an important role in all contemporary projects. This relationship must be established to fully leverage the infrastructure of all relevant third parties. They need to be available to move the project forward, and a strong reach into the third-party organization increases the number of resources available to the rescue manager to move the process forward successfully.

Stakeholders — Project Management   This is an important relationship over the long term. Stakeholders will probably have a strained relationship with the project management group because of the problems in the project. There may be a lot of finger pointing. Neither group may appreciate the challenges being faced by the other. The rescue manager and the executive sponsor need to smooth out any differences as the project rescue starts to deliver value.

Project Management — Third Parties   The project management group needs to build on the relationship established by the rescue manager with third parties. Again, there probably are existing but strained relationships between these different groups that need to be repaired.

Some Relationship

These relationships are relevant, if not important, for sharing information between groups. They should be encouraged. Importance is in relation to the rescue. The project can still be successful if these relationships are not flourishing. There are five key relationships in the extended organization, as described in the following sections.

Executive Sponsor — Team The executive sponsor should build a relationship with the project team, but this is not mandatory in the short term. Workshops or group meetings can be used to bring these groups together to share information and values.

Executive Sponsor — Third Parties Third parties will want to build a relationship with the executive sponsor. There is a natural attraction to the power exhibited by the latter. However, this relationship is not key to the rescue process and should not interfere with the other, more important ones.

Stakeholders — Team The importance of this relationship is similar to the relationship between the executive sponsor and team. It is desirable, but not urgent. It can be established gradually.

Stakeholders — Third Parties This relationship is similar to the relationship between the executive sponsor and third parties. It is desirable, but can be gradual. Third parties generally benefit more from a special or close relationship with stakeholders than directly from the results of a project rescue effort.

Team — Third Parties Relationships with some third parties may be best established with specific members of the project team. For example, a contract system administration group should develop a relationship with the operations manager rather than the rescue manager.

Closing Perspective

Conflict is a part of every human activity, and the results can be negative or positive depending on how the process is managed. This chapter looked at the types of conflicts that can arise during rescue initiatives based on the corporate culture that has been established and the stresses resulting from a project in trouble. Several proven techniques for building consensus were also discussed. The chapter also examined the key relationships that need to be protected, and how they can be protected, to move an intervention forward successfully.

CHAPTER 18
Additional Tools

The best technique for intervention is prevention. In this chapter, we look at five additional management techniques to those covered in the previous chapters that you can employ during project startup and execution. We look at processes that help you keep your project on track and create audit trails for when projects get out of control. These tools can be used before a project begins or during project execution.

Functional Requirements Management

A key to any successful project is to have clear, defined requirements. Functional requirements management is the process of defining and refining the business functional requirements of the proposed project and managing the development, testing, and training process to ensure that these requirements are ultimately met. You start the process at the top, by gathering strategic goals and objectives from senior management and decomposing them down to the work level. Once the work is completed, it becomes a bottom-up process to assure that the goals and objectives have been met. The process of successfully defining, executing, and managing a project's scope is dependent on thoroughly gathering and documenting the project's functional requirements. The fulfillment of each functional requirement is paramount to the overall success of the project and acceptance of the final product.

Different methodologies have different standards for producing functional requirements. However, most methodologies allow for additional artifacts to support the method's standard requirements document. Presented next are two supporting tables that help you trace requirements back to business goals and objectives. Table 18.1, Project Goals and Objectives, is a centrally located list that should be available to each member of the extended project team via read-only access. This is a valuable reference tool because it confirms and communicates the project goals and objectives and is the basis from which all subsequent project phases are rooted.

Table 18.2, the Requirements List, is also a central repository. This table shows how requirements tie back to the project goals and objectives and also lists the test script that proved the requirement. Notice that a goal may be satisfied by more than one requirement. Likewise, a requirement may address more than one goal or objective. Together these tables provide a quick, easy to read, easy to understand reference of the project's functional requirements. They provide a good appendix to your formal requirements document.

Project Goals and Objectives				Date:		
				Project Name:		
				Completed By:		
#	*Goal/Objective/ Success Factor	*Priority	*Originator	Where Satisfied	How Satisfied	Status
1						
2						
3						
4						
5						
...						
N						

* = Filled out at Executive Interview Session

Priority: Must Have, Highly Desirable and Nice to Have

Status: FC – Full Compliance; PC – Partial Compliance; OOS – Out of Scope; TBD – To Be Determined

Table 18.1   Project Goals and Objectives

Requirements List				Date:	
				Project Name:	
				Completed By:	
Goal#	*Goal/Objective/ Success Factor	Req.#	Requirement Title	How Requirement Satisfies Objective	Test Script #
1		12			
1		17			
2		9			
2		12			

Table 18.2   Requirements List

Goal#	*Goal/Objective/ Success Factor	Req.#	Requirement Title	How Requirement Satisfies Objective	Test Script #
3		1			
4		4			
4		5			
4		6			
...					
N					

Table 18.2   Requirements List *(continued)*

Change Management

Every project will change from its original intent. This procedure, therefore, provides a process based upon experience, which permits effective management of change. *Change* refers to any change or adjustment to approved deliverables or to the project charter (which may have been amended by previously approved change requests). Change is not merely alteration to scope, cost, or date. Modification to any portion of the project charter is considered change, thus assuring effective management of expectations.

A project change procedure controls, at the task level, work effort expansion resulting from technical process inclusions or omissions due to scope, specification, or design errors, team miscommunication, or technical implementation difficulty. This procedure can be used to record, manage, analyze, and control any event, action, or omission that will increase the estimated time to complete any project task. This includes adding new tasks to the project.

Types of Change Requests

Changes come in all shapes, sizes, and origins. This section groups change requests into three general categories—scope change, variance change, and informational change—for organizational purposes only. There is no need to try to fit a change request into one of the categories.

Scope Change

Scope change means something previously approved is being altered. This most often happens when someone identifies a way to improve or change deliverables that deviates from the project charter. The change request, with its impact to date and cost, helps the project sponsor or executive sponsor determine if the change is worth implementing. There should be a scope change request for something that was never budgeted for nor a contingency made available. In short, these change requests are for those situations that are really outside the scope of the project charter.

Variance Change

A variance change may be required when actual activity differs from that which was planned. This is typically seen when the actual effort for a task differs from the estimated effort. The cumulative effect of many variances may require a change request to re-baseline the project. However, sometimes the net effect of positive and negative variances is approximately zero. Prudent judgment is required in this area to determine when a change request is required.

Another example of a variance is lost time. Lost time is not planned. It exists if and only if the team is idled and cannot work on any other tasks because of an external delay or any event that prohibits it from continuing to work on the project. Assigning the team members to other project tasks while the team waits for the delay to be resolved does not constitute lost time. Lost time can have a disastrous effect on project costs and deadlines because it is impossible to forecast and therefore requires constant control and analysis. Lost time task items should be placed in the project plan with a zero budget. This indicates that there is no expectation of lost time, but if it occurs, it will show as a negative variance in the plan.

Because variance changes are usually a combination of many small items, the project manager should record and track events that may later be traced to project delays and lost time. If incurred, lost time should be posted to the project plan and reported on the project status reports and at project status meetings.

In some cases, variance changes should also be processed on those rare and legendary occasions when the project manager recognizes that the project will be significantly under budget because of productivity gains within the team.

Informational Change

Most people associate change with an impact to effort (hours), cost (budget), or schedule (date); however, change may not impact any of these components. Informational changes are just as important as other types of change because they reset or change expectations from those set through the project charter. An informational change request can occur for changes in organizational structure, roles and responsibilities, and process changes that were previously defined in the project charter. For example, if an organizational change causes additional layers of review and approval of deliverables, a change request would need to be created to define the new approval process.

The Change Request Form and the Change Management Process

In this section you see how the change request form is directly linked to the two-phase change management process. The form's primary function is to be the repository of all information related to a change request. The form also provides a snapshot of the change request's progress in the change management process. Figure 18.1 show an example of a project change request form that can be used for a two-phase change management process.

The following steps outline the key activities needed to perform a two-phase change management process. The reason this process is called a "two-phase" process is that there are two points of approval or rejection that allow the process to continue or stop respectively.

1. Anyone may submit a change request. The originator completes the information that describes the change and why it is needed and then submits the form to the project manager. The first section of the form captures the general information about the change request. This information should be used in the change log, similar to the one shown in Figure 18.2, to document the progress of the change request in the change management process through disposition. The next two fields describe the change request and the business or technical reason for requesting the change. All of this information should be complete before the change request is submitted.

2. An appropriate person estimates the effort needed to investigate the change request and documents the hours and cost of just the investigation of the change in the Estimate to Investigate section.. The project plan should contain a change investigation task with the change budget hours as the baseline. If you exhaust the change investigation hours, you should submit a change request for more change investigation hours or else you would have to unilaterally refuse all further changes—a ludicrous tactic.

3. The project manager and the project sponsor decide whether or not to approve the change investigation or reject the change at that point.

4. If the change investigation is approved, a project team member should be assigned to investigate the change and complete the rest of the change request form with the results of the investigation. That person should document any effects on the logical scope, deliverables, project organization, schedule or

cost (hours and dollars) that deviate from the current approved version of the project charter. Additionally, the investigator should document the effects on the project if the change request is rejected.

Project Change Request Form				
Project Name:		**Date of Request:**		
Change Name:		**Change Number:**		
Requested By:		**Presented To:**		
Description of Change:				
Reason for Change:				
Estimate to Investigate:		**Hours:**		**Dollars:**
Project Sponsor				
☐ Approved	**Signature:**			
☐ Rejected	**Title:**		**Date:**	
Project Manager				
☐ Approved	**Signature:**			
☐ Rejected	**Title:**		**Date:**	
Effect on Logical Scope:				
Effect on Deliverables (including a list of any affected deliverables):				
Effect on Organization:				

Figure 18.1   Project Change Request Form

Effect on Schedule (including Estimated Completion Date for this change):

Effect on Project Cost:				
Item Description	Hours		Dollars	
	Reduction	Increase	Reduction	Increase
Total Net Change in Cost:				

Effect of NOT Approving this Change:

Reason for Rejection (if applicable):

Project Sponsor			
☐ Approved	Signature:		
☐ Rejected	Title:		Date:

Project Manager			
☐ Approved	Signature:		
☐ Rejected	Title:		Date:

Figure 18.1 Project Change Request Form *(coninued)*

5. The project manager and project sponsor (and the executive sponsor if the change has a severe impact on the project) should review the change request and supporting documentation and decide whether to approve or reject the change. If the change is approved, the appropriate changes should be made to the project charter, project plan, and any other affected defining documents (such as the requirements document). The project plan should be re-baselined to incorporate the change. If the change is rejected, the reasons for rejection should be documented on the change request form.

6. The change log should be updated and the change request should be filed in the project notebook. All opened and closed change requests should be documented on the weekly project status report and mentioned in the weekly project status meeting.

Project Change Log

Change #	Change Name	Date Submitted	Decisions Approved/Rej		Net Change		Remaining Change Budget	
			Project Name:					
			Original Change Budget:				**Hours**	**Dollars**
							500	$87,500
			Tech	Bus.	in Hours	in Dollars	in Hours	in Dollars
0							500	87500
1	Change 1	5-Jul-04	A	A	20	$2,000	480	$85,500
2	Change 2	13-Aug-04	A	R			480	
3							480	
4							480	
5							480	
6							480	
7							480	
8							480	
9							480	
10							480	
11							480	
12							480	

Figure 18.2   Project Change Log

Risk Management

The goal of risk management is to identify project risks and plan mitigation actions in collaboration between the technical team and the business organization. *Risks* are probable events that could increase the project's schedule, costs, or effort, or adversely impact overall customer satisfaction. The goal is to identify these shared risks, predict the likelihood of the risks occurring, quantify the impact should they occur, and develop a plan for addressing each risk. Most importantl, the goal is to establish agreement between the business organization and the technical team that they need to work together to manage risks as they arise during the project. The project manager should be proactive in assuring that risks are analyzed and that action is taken to mitigate the risk. If you can anticipate an event, then you should be able to weigh the consequences and develop actions to minimize negative impacts.

Risk Assessment Model

The Risk Assessment Model shown in Figure 18.3 is a spreadsheet that provides for the documentation of the risks and computation of the change budget (or risk budget). The risk assessment method computes the risk budget as a percentage of

RISK ASSESSMENT WORK SHEET	30-Jan-02								
PROJECT ESTIMATE IN DAYS =>	1900.00	Risk	700.00	Worst Case	2600				
RISK CHANGE BUDGET =>	54.02%	378.1 =		Cost w/Risk	2278.1				

RISK VARIABLE	Probability of Occurrence (1% to 100%)	Consequence (1 to 10)	Relative Impact	<CBI%	Risk	Mitigation strategy	Probability of effectiveness <CBI	<CBI	Risk Budget
1 Data center will burn down	100.00%	4	4.0	9%	61.12	Install fire control systems	25.00%	-2%	45.84
2 Business needs will change	100.00%	5	5.0	11%	76.40	Freeze Req Def	50.00%	-5%	38.20
3 CIO will leave	80.00%	6	4.8	10%	73.35	Identify new CIO candidates	40.00%	-4%	44.01
4 Interface/app locations are not defined	60.00%	3	1.8	4%	27.50	No mitigation	30.00%	-1%	19.25
5 Event5	30.00%	9	2.7	6%	41.25	Mitigation Strategy 5	80.00%	-5%	8.25
6 Event6	67.00%	8	5.4	12%	81.90	Mitigation Strategy 6	70.00%	-8%	24.57
7 Event7	89.00%	3	2.7	6%	40.80	Mitigation Strategy 7	46.00%	-3%	22.03
8 Event8	78.00%	9	7.0	15%	107.27	Mitigation Strategy 8	45.00%	-7%	59.00
9 Event9	89.00%	5	4.5	10%	68.00	Mitigation Strategy 8	90.00%	-9%	6.80
10 Event10	89.00%	9	8.0	17%	122.40	Mitigation Strategy 9	10.00%	-2%	110.16
		61	45.8	100.00%	700.00			-45.98%	378.11

Figure 18.3   Risk Assessment Model

effort of the difference between the project estimate and the worst-case estimate. The assumption is that this difference is a function of all risks.

In Figure 18.3, the project estimate is 1900 hours. The worst-case estimate is 2600 hours. The difference is 700 hours (at risk). The ten risk variables represent 100 percent, or 700 hours. Each risk is represented as a percentage of the total (Data Center will burn down = 9 percent of the total risk, or 61.12 hours). The fire control systems have a 25 percent probability of effectiveness, representing a 2 percent reduction of the 9 percent, or down to 45.84 hours. The sum of the reduced hours at risk represents the risk budget.

The following list defines the various column headings shown in Figure 18.3:

- **Risk Variable**   Up to ten risk variables may be listed in this column.

- **Probability of Occurrence**   The probability of occurrence (as a percentage) is specified in this column.

- **Consequence**   The relative consequence is indicated in this column as a value between 1 (the lowest) and 10 (the maximum).

- **Relative Impact**   This is a numerical representation of the combination of the probability and relative impact of the risk. The sum represents the total magnitude of all the risks.

- **+CB%**   The fields in this column are computed fields representing the percentage of the total risk per risk variable.

- **Risk**   The fields in this column are computed fields representing the actual number of hours per risk variable of the total number of hours at risk.

- **Mitigation Strategy**   The fields in this column indicate the mitigation action to be used to manage or prevent the risk.

- **Probability of Effectiveness**   The fields in this column represent the probability of total effectiveness of the mitigation action upon the risk variable.

- **-CB%**   The fields in this column are computed fields representing the percentage reduction expected of the mitigation action.

- **Risk Budget**   The risk budget is a product of the percentage difference between (the probability of risks and the probability of the mitigation actions) and the effort at risk, or the difference between the project estimate and the worst case.

The risk assessment procedure should be performed monthly under the direction of the project manager in conjunction with the project sponsor. Newly identified risks should be added to the risk assessment model, and risks no longer applicable should be dropped from the risk assessment model.

The Risk Management Process

The risk management process consists of four steps that guide the team to identify the risks, assess the risks, plan the mitigation strategies for each risk, and update the risk management tool for subsequent risk management sessions.

Step 1: Identify Risks

Review the risks developed during the funding process to understand what risks were known at that time. This set of risks will have changed, but it is the baseline from which to start risk assessment in this phase. Determine which of those risks no longer exist and identify new issues and obstacles that may produce undesired outcomes. Review the issues log for items that should be represented as risks.

Risk elements may be introduced from many areas. Consider the assumptions made when developing the project charter and the project plan. The goal is to convert all critical assumptions into specific, "shared" risks. Once the risk factors for the project have been identified, they should be documented in a risk assessment model spreadsheet similar to the one previously shown in Figure 18.3.

Step 2: Assess the Risks

Each risk should be examined and quantified in terms of cost, schedule, and quality. Some risks may impact both the cost and schedule, and some risks may impact all three. How much a risk will impact the project may be derived from historical project data, industry norms, personal past experience, or the estimation model.

The risks need to be assessed and assigned a percentage chance of occurring. For instance, if your business is in a hurricane region, a work stoppage due to a hurricane is highly unlikely in the winter (hurricane season is June through November), so it would receive a low chance of occurrence during the winter months, but it may be assigned a high chance of occurrence in August, September and October. Conversely, not being able to get enough time from your subject matter experts almost always happens, so it would be assigned a high percentage chance of occurrence. If you prefer the high/medium/low technique, assign 80 percent to high, 50 percent to medium, and 20 percent to low.

Step 3: Plan Risk Mitigation

State the actions that are needed to mitigate negative consequences or to maximize positive benefits. By deciding in advance how to manage each risk, the probability and impact of the risk can be reduced. One of the key elements of project management is to address risks proactively. Thus, mitigating actions can eliminate risks by uncovering acceptable alternatives. Risks may be mitigated, or bounded, in many ways:

- **Contingency planning** Defines an action plan to be executed if an identified risk event occurs.

- **Alternative strategies** Risk events can often be prevented by choosing an alternate strategy—using a method or technique that is already familiar to most of your technical team versus one that is not.

- **Assumptions** Bounding and communicating those bounds can do much to reduce risk. For example, limiting the deliverable review process to at most two iterations bounds the risk of infinite review—failure to obtain approval.

- **Ready staff** Carrying extra staffing to shore up critical path tasks, or to be ready to take over in the event of a project team member leaving, reduces the risks associated with estimating underruns or attrition.

- **Staff qualifications/capabilities** Using overqualified staff in some positions (or staff members with multiple talents) means you may have additional flexibility to respond to risk triggers when they occur. For example, if the project has a tester who can also function as a team lead should the team need additional team leaders during a peak period, the project manager has a ready resource.

- **Risk sharing** In some cases the business and technical organizations may opt to share certain risks—such as environmental (physical space) failures. By sharing the risk, the project manager may have additional resources to draw on to put the project back on track. It's usually a good idea to build teamwork management through risk sharing.

- **Organization** Risks may also be reduced by changing the organization or reporting structure for resources assigned to a particular project. Key personnel may be "loaned" to the project for its duration. This technique helps eliminate the risk of poor participation by key functional personnel.

For each risk, the criteria for change should also be defined. The mitigation plan needs to have someone responsible for driving the effort to minimize or eliminate the risk. Progress against the mitigation plan should occur through status reports and subsequent risk management sessions. The amount of time and resources associated with risk mitigation needs to be included in the project plan. Each risk and its associated mitigation strategy should also have a clear trigger event that is predefined. In most cases this may be obvious, but it's best to declare the trigger event that launches the mitigation action.

Step 4: Update the Risk Assessment Model

Produce a simple report that includes a statement of high-probability risks, estimating assumptions, and impacts/mitigation actions. This report is an effective tool for communicating the risks and ensuring that all parties understand and agree to risk impacts and mitigation action plans. Update the risk assessment model to include the current high-probability risks.

Perform this process before you start your project, to develop a consensus on a change budget consistent with the project risks. When developing the change budget, keep in mind that risks are not necessarily additive. The project manager and project sponsor should use prudent judgment in establishing a change budget that is consistent with the risk assessment model.

Change Budget

The project manager and project sponsor should establish the actual amount of a change budget in accordance with your company's risk-aversion philosophy. The risk-based change budget is a dollar percentage of the original estimate that should be set aside to cover the negative impact of risks identified in the procedure. The change budget represents the net change of all positive and negative impacts (in other words, dollars at risk). The establishment of a change budget assures that funds are available to continue the project when faced with an increase in cost due to the negative impact of an identified risk. Each month, as tasks are completed, their attendant risks can no longer impact the project. Therefore, the change budget can be expected to decrease to zero as the project moves toward project completion. The actual amount of the change budget may be set to whatever amount the executive sponsor feels is consistent with your company's risk-aversion philosophy. However, the risk assessment model provides a method to quantify this amount as a function of the risks, mitigation, and project estimate (budgeted cost).

Issue Management

Issue management deals with the capture, reporting, and escalation of issues identified throughout the life cycle of a project. The objective of this procedure is to capture, log, and track project issues from initiation through closure. The timely management of issues is extremely important to the delivery of a successful project. The elements to timely issue resolution include early identification, communication to all affected parties, and vigilant management through closure.

Definition

An *issue* is a potential change. It is any question or concern that arises that may impact cost, schedule, or project quality. If left unresolved, the issue will become a change to the project.

Three important points to remember about issues are

- Issue identification is the responsibility of every team member.
- Issues can be incidents of a risk. Review the risk assessment model to identify mitigating actions when addressing these issues.
- Issues can arise at any point during the project.

Capture

Issues should be captured, retained, and tracked through a repository (Issues Management Log, similar to the one shown in Figure 18.4) that will retain all issues, including historical information. Each issue should include, at a minimum, the date the issue is captured (logged); the name of the person initiating the issue (originator); a description of the issue; the actual or potential impact of the issue on the project; the issue priority; the name of the person the issue is assigned to for resolution (owner); the target date for resolution; the issue status; a description of what was done to resolve the issue; links to any documents pertaining to the resolution; the issue closure date; the subject matter expert; and, when required, an escalation age and date.

Prioritization

Issues should be prioritized using a mutually agreed upon method between the business and technical organizations or by using the following guidelines:

- **Priority 1**   Must be resolved within 24 hours
- **Priority 2**   Must be resolved within 48 hours
- **Priority 3**   Must be resolved within 72 hours
- **Priority 4**   Must have a resolution date that is agreed upon between the originator and the owner of the issue

Issues Management Log

As of: 9-Sep

Issue #	Escalation Impact (H,M,L)	Priority (1, 2, or 3)	Originator	Status	Owner	Issue Description	Date Logged	Resolution Target Date	Resolution	Resolution source document link	Date Closed	SME	Escalation Age (Days)	Escalation Date
1	H		Tom Smith	closed	Robert Johl	State sales tax cannot be properly applied without the use of a commercial software package.	4-Jun-04	4-Oct-04	Purchase and install VerTAX		21-Jun-04	Bill Smith	0	
2	H		Tom Smith	open		Accounting has conflicting charts of accounts across business units.	22-Jul-04					Bill Smith	50	
3						Issue 3							0	
4						Issue 4							0	
5						Issue 5							0	
6						Issue 6							0	
7						Issue 7							0	
8						Issue 8							0	
9						Issue 9							0	
10						Issue 10							0	
11						Issue 11							0	
12						Issue 12							0	

Figure 18.4   Issues Management Log

Reporting

Issues should be reported and tracked. Following are some useful guidelines:

- Issue management should be an agenda item in the weekly status meeting.
- All issues are reported on the weekly project status report.
- All issues are maintained and updated on the central repository (issue log).
- The status and disposition of all issues are updated weekly.
- Issues presented on the weekly project status report include all open issues and those closed since the last status report.
- A current issue log is maintained and filed in the project notebook each week.

Escalation

Escalation is used to resolve project issues in a timely manner following an agreed upon escalation path. A delay in resolving an issue may result in the generation of a change request. The actual procedure for escalation is left to the project manager and the project sponsor. Issues may be escalated based on aging (length of time since received), missing a target date, or severity of impact to the completion date or budget.

Table 18.3 shows the issues escalation scale, including roles and notification periods based on high, medium, and low impact to the business. The highest point of escalation normally is the Project Steering Committee. The escalation roles should be identified in the project charter roles and responsibilities sections as well.

Closure

Closing issues is very important, whether they are resolved or converted to changes. Following is a set of guidelines for closing issues:

- An issue is reported as closed when the action taken by the owner is satisfactory to the originator.
- Only the originator may close an issue.
- The issue originator who is advising closure should send a memo or e-mail to the project manager.
- The project manager should keep a copy of all closure advices in the project notebook.
- All issues are maintained for historical purposes in the issue log.

Roles		Notification Period (Days)		
Business Team	**Technical Team**	**Low**	**Medium**	**High**
Project Sponsor	Project Manager	>3	>1	0
Executive Sponsor	Program Manager	>10	>5	>3
	Project Steering Committee			>15

Table 18.3   Issues Escalation

Acceptance Management

In every project, the executive sponsor, project sponsor, or designee documented in the project charter should officially approve and accept deliverables, change requests or milestones that have been performed along the way. Acceptance along the way helps to mitigate risks by closing tasks that can be affected by a risk. By providing the business organization opportunities to review work performed, any miscommunications can be caught early and managed. The project manager should meet with the project sponsor and executive sponsor to review the completed work. The executive sponsor should then approve the work, confirming that it was completed as agreed upon in the project charter. There are several different times when a formal acceptance and approval should be sought and obtained:

- When a deliverable is completed
- When a change request or a group of change requests is completed
- At the end of every phase or milestone
- At project completion

Project Acceptance Procedure

Most technical methodologies define a formal acceptance procedure. Unfortunately, that process is often ignored and default acceptance or the "no news is good news" criteria is used, creating conflict, misunderstanding, and miscommunication between the business group(s) and the technical group. Make sure acceptance is a deliberate, formal process, to avoid the inevitable finger-pointing blame game that will ensue by ignoring it.

The following process can be used if your organization does not have a formal acceptance process:

1. Based on the project charter and project plan, the project manager should create a Deliverables Acceptance Log, listing each deliverable and milestone that requires the project sponsor's or executive sponsor's approval upon completion. This log should be part of the project charter and the acceptance process should be described during a formal project charter presentation.

2. As change requests are submitted, they should be added to the Deliverables Acceptance Log in chronological order between the predefined deliverables and milestones.

3. The project manager should complete a deliverables acceptance form for each deliverable, each milestone, and each change request. The form should describe in detail the deliverable, milestone, or change request and should provide space for the project manager and the project sponsor or executive sponsor to sign off. Any supporting documentation should be attached, such as testing forms, screen prints, e-mails, or reports.

4. If more than one change request is completed within a given period of time, they can be grouped on one form if it makes sense to do so.

5. These forms can be completed either at the time each deliverable, milestone, or change request is added to the Deliverables Acceptance Log or at the point in time when signoff is required.

6. At the close of the project, a project completion (or final) acceptance form should be completed, indicating that all expectations were met and accepted per the project charter (as amended by authorized change requests).

7. The Deliverables Acceptance Log and all completed deliverables acceptance forms should be kept in the project notebook in the section labeled "Acceptance."

8. When work is completed for a deliverable, milestone, or change request, the project manager should meet with the project sponsor and executive sponsor to review the performed work. This review session (walkthrough with all necessary parties) can be incorporated into the planned status meetings or it can be a specific acceptance meeting. If the work is satisfactory, the project manager and the project sponsor or executive sponsor should approve and accept the work.

9. All deliverables should be approved by the project manager and the project sponsor or executive sponsor.

10. Deliverables that have been submitted for approval should be tracked on the Deliverables Acceptance Log, which is maintained in the project notebook.

11. The deliverables acceptance form should be signed and returned to the project manager as specified in the project charter. The form should be marked accepted or rejected. Acceptance means that the deliverable fully meets expectations. Acceptance or rejection of deliverables by default or by conditional approval is not allowed.

12. Deliverables that are not accepted within the time period specified in the project charter should be added to the project status report and the project issues log until they are resolved. Any outstanding deliverables should be reviewed at weekly status meetings. Late acceptances can result in a noncompliance change request.

13. If a deliverable is rejected, a detailed description of why it was rejected should be included on the form. If required, a meeting can be held to discuss the deliverable in detail. All errors and omissions should be detailed in the rejection.

14. One resubmittal should be permitted to allow the deliverable to be modified and to address the items that were specifically rejected. If additional resubmittals are required, the change procedure should be invoked.

15. Negotiations between the business organization and the technical organization management should begin if disagreement arises as to the action to be taken or the extent of corrections needed to satisfy the executive sponsor with regard to a rejected deliverable. All attempts should be made to resolve the issue at the lowest management level possible. When necessary, escalation to the next higher management level should take place.

Closing Perspective

This chapter looked at five tools that you and your team can use before and during a project to help prevent a runaway project. These tools are common, ordinary, simple tools that have been tested under fire and produce consistent, successful results. Projects get in trouble when project managers and project sponsors do not use these tools, either because they lack knowledge or experience; or they deliberately circumvent the processes because they believe the tools are a waste of time. Ironically, the latter situation tends to occur when projects start to fall behind and the project management team looks to "cut corners" to get back on track. They bypass the very tools that will help them get back on track!

Though there are many, many more tools and processes to help you manage your project, we chose these five because they are easy to use, cost nothing to implement, and are very effective. Requirements management helps you keep track when requirements start to change or additional requirements creep into the project. Having a single, easy-to-read chart of requirements and how they trace back to the business goal and the supporting testing keeps the extended project team focused. Change management allows you to control changes to your project and put the deliberate decision to make the change into the hands of the appropriate decision maker. Failure to manage change is the number one killer of projects. Risk management allows you to take a holistic view of your project and the external forces that may affect it. Proactive risk management with good risk mitigation strategies helps keep you from being surprised by some external factor. Issue management gives you a proactive approach to handling those items that could force change if left unattended. Finally, acceptance management provides a formal process to approve work as it happens. It mitigates the "big bang" acceptance or acceptance by indifference.

## CHAPTER 19

Virtual Database of Experiences and Techniques

This chapter uses a broad approach for collecting and summarizing case study information in order to make the lessons more readily usable on new initiatives. We have examined different projects that have been rescued, to extract key issues and results, and have summarized these in separate categories to create a virtual database of valuable lessons learned.

The names and incidents in this chapter are taken from different contributors and have been generalized to protect privacy. Readers are encouraged to send to us their own lessons learned for inclusion on our web site and/or future editions of this book. We will include your name in an acknowledgements section but will not relate it to your submission, in order to also protect the privacy of the information you submit (please send e-mails to spurba@rogers.com). Please let us know if you wish to remain completely anonymous, in which case we will not include your name in the acknowledgements section either.

Each case study segment is described in terms of a situation, a diagnosis of the situation, how that solution was identified and applied, any results that were achieved, and some additional thoughts in hindsight.

People

People-related case studies are divided into the groups previously identified for the extended project team. Projects that go well do so because of the hard work and talent of the people in a project team. However, people are also the conduits or sources of problems. The potential issues are all over the board, including a lack of ability, an excess of ego, too many commitments, bad decision-making, and strained relationships.

Project Sponsors

Executive project sponsorship, or lack thereof, is a significant recurring problem across projects. But who can point this out to the people in charge? The sponsors are paying for the project and hold the authority. Sometimes, when everyone is searching for another source for the problems being experienced on a project, the true answer is to start at the top.

The causes can be subtle (e.g., an executive who is unaware of a risk factor) or dramatic (e.g., an executive keeps changing the business requirements, much to the chagrin of the project team). Not catching onto this cause may end up costing the organization real money and real problems. Examining this potential source should be a matter of course in every project rescue—regardless of the egos or hierarchies involved. But this can best be done with the full, active support of the executive.

Sponsor Looking for a Specific Answer

An executive sponsor and business owner hired an external project manager to assume leadership over an initiative that was not producing results. The client was in the process of building a web portal with hooks to back-end financial applications. Deadlines were described as tight, relationships were tense, and something needed to be done.

- **Diagnosis and solution implemented**   Interviews with the different team members in the organization and a review of the project charter revealed that the project objectives were unclear. There may have been other problems, but unless the project objectives were first clarified, the project could not succeed. The solution required revisiting the requirements phase, despite executive pressure to continue. This required the executive to mandate a new project direction.

- **Results achieved**   The project team refocused efforts to capture the business requirements. The stressed internal relationships were repaired.

- **In hindsight**   There could have been other problems in the project, but without the infrastructure of clear business objectives, the project would never be successfully delivered. The team would go from one problem to another, spending more money than it needed to.

Revolving-Door Sponsors

The client was a major automobile manufacturer. The relationship between the client and the consulting company was strained due to miscommunications, late deliveries, and the quality of the interpersonal relationships. During a major release, the executive sponsor was promoted and moved to another part of the organization. A new executive sponsor was appointed.

- **Diagnosis and solution implemented**   The appointment of a new executive sponsor was actually a good opportunity to overcome past barriers. The previous and new sponsors were debriefed on some of the existing issues, but the new sponsor was open to making an independent assessment on the quality of work. Being new to the project, the new sponsor also needed to gain some traction. So did the project manager, who provided a walkthrough of all the project deliverables. Their mutual needs enabled them to agree on a direction and, as important, commit to overcoming future obstacles in getting there.

- **Results achieved**   The project release was implemented one week late (on a six-month project duration) but within the original project budget.

- **In hindsight**   The relationship between the executive sponsor and the project manager was key to salvaging this project.

Sponsor Not Fully Engaged

The project was with a major financial organization. The objective was to produce a new financial application to rate risks that the organization was assuming when handing out loans to its client base. The requirements were not clear and the technology was new to the organization. A rescue manager was hired to salvage the project. The blame was placed on the technology.

- **Diagnosis and solution implemented**   The executive sponsor was actually too far removed from the project to realize that the team was not really sure about what it needed to build. The analysts were making decisions for the business stakeholders. The development team was busy learning the new technology. The milestones were nonexistent. No tools were available to measure progress. The solution involved working with the project director to agree on the objectives of a six-month pilot project that would validate a cross section of the functionality.

- **Results achieved**   Several of the team members were reluctant to try the new approach. They were confident the original approach could still work, but were too busy to provide a detailed project plan showing how to complete the project. The team opted to follow the new direction that was laid out and described in detail. The pilot was completed within the time and budget allocated. The first successful delivery in well over 18 months allowed the project director to solicit additional support from the executive.

- **In hindsight**   This is a key lesson to keep in mind on all projects. Team members often defend an approach without providing the detailed implementation steps. The rescue manager does not have the luxury to trust an approach without being able to confirm the detailed plan. In this case, the pilot approach allowed the details to be described, explained, and understood. The project director became more engaged on the project from a day-to-day perspective. This allowed decisions to be made, while forcing the project team to commit to results.

Sponsor/Project Manager Conflict

In this project, the executive sponsor and the project manager both worked for an organization that protected their position, so neither was concerned about their employment status. However, neither liked working with the other and many significant decisions were not being made where it required their cooperation. The project team started to feel the misdirected anger, and milestones were being missed.

- **Diagnosis and solution implemented**   Given that the two key people on the extended project team were at odds and, in fact, taking it out on the rest of the team, there was no one with the immediate authority to make a difference in this conflict. Several team members tried, and were either demoted or transferred off the project. After the project failed, it was restarted with an external consulting team taking the lead role, but still reporting to the original project sponsor and project manager. This consulting team was able to implement the solution. The key to its success was implementing a proven methodology, adding more experienced resources, and enforcing stringent controls.

- **Results achieved**   While the external consulting organization succeeded in implementing the solution, the process was still rife with cultural clashes and politics. It was not a smooth implementation, but was probably the best one possible given the dynamics of the client organization. In particular, the rescue manager and the client sponsor had very different approaches to people management. The client sponsor let the rescue manager drive until success was assured and then swapped him with another project manager.

- **In hindsight**   The combination of executive/project sponsor and project manager is critical for a positive outcome on a project. Even in this case, although the project was implemented on time and budget, the budget was built with the overhead of managing the strained relationship.

Sponsor/Rescue Manager Conflict

In this example, a project was considered to be in serious trouble when several key milestones were missed in succession. A rescue effort was launched to save as much of the initiative as possible. An external project manager was given the rescue manager role. When they started to redevelop the project charter and timeline, the rescue manager and executive sponsor disagreed on the project plan, objectives, and technology.

- **Diagnosis and solution implemented**   The problems that drove the original project attempt to the edge of disaster started to repeat again. The new approach was not being successful because of some underlying considerations. By implementing a methodology, the rescue manager succeeded in highlighting the causes of the problems that were being felt, but was not able to change them without a commitment from the executive sponsor to do things dramatically differently. The executive sponsor was left to decide whether to fulfill the original project objectives, but with more support for the original project team, or to follow the revised, more comprehensive direction.

- **Results achieved**   The rescue manager demonstrated that there was no panacea available to solve the organization's problems. The executive sponsor opted to follow the original direction, but empowered the original project manager.

- **In hindsight**   This is another example where an executive sponsor's view of how a project should be conducted wins out for better or worse.

Project Team

Unlike even the most complex technology architectures, the dynamics of the project team are the most difficult to forecast. We can learn from the specific outputs of various inputs. But keep in mind that the personalities and specifics of the situation do not guarantee the same outcome as in the case of technology alternatives. It is important to have a process in place when dealing with project team issues.

Avoiding Details

In this example, members of a project team were willing to work 18-hour days to deliver a project release successfully. Unfortunately, this passion also exhausted members of the team, so that they started to miss the small details. An executive to whom the project team reported noticed the situation and decided to work with the project team until the current release was successfully in production.

- **Diagnosis and solution implemented**   The offer of help from the executive was appreciated by the project team because there were no negative connotations associated with it. By attending the three times daily status meetings, the executive was able to ask the detailed questions that identified several problems that would have delayed launch of the project by several days and would have resulted in a cost overrun.

- **Results achieved**   While the project team did most of the work, the positive support of the executive created an environment in which several showstoppers were identified and corrected before they became a problem.

- **In hindsight**   Had the executive remained aloof, or had not asked precise questions about the technical environment, several showstoppers would not have been noticed until the system was going to launch. At that time it would have been too late to deal with the issues, the project launch would have been delayed, and the client would have lost a great deal of confidence in the development team.

Team Member with Competing Personal Interests

In this project, one of the key architects had personal commitments that made long workdays and weekend work impossible. The architect had information about the application that was critical for a successful launch. The architect's knowledge and skill sets made the threat of dismissal irrelevant.

- **Diagnosis and solution implemented**   No amount of discussion would increase the commitment of the key architect. The rescue manager decided to work closely with a subordinate of the architect. This allowed the subordinate to build up a knowledge base and, more important, ask the architect for help. The architect, while still committed to the outside activities, was more accessible to his direct report.

- **Results achieved**   The subordinate played a key role in learning the architect's skills and helped to successfully deliver the project. This also helped relieve dependency on a key resource. The project was launched successfully.

- **In hindsight**   The architect was willing to help a direct report, but could not be persuaded to work extra hours by management. The architect viewed helping the direct report as a form of mentoring or nurturing. The architect viewed working extra hours at the behest of management as a betrayal of core family values.

Hostility Among Project Managers

In this project, which involved many different offices from across the United States, the managers of the different teams were blaming other groups for a lack of solid achievements. After nine months of no major progress, an external rescue manager was brought in to help facilitate a solution.

- **Diagnosis and solution implemented**   The project's objectives were complex, which made an early success unlikely. The geographic distance between the offices, and the fact that some offices were the product of different mergers and acquisitions, created an overall defensive atmosphere. The external rescue manager, with no axe to grind, was able to work with the different groups to remove blame from consideration and to revise the objectives to provide the badly needed successes in an incremental fashion.

- **Results achieved**   The project was delivered in three significant releases over an 11-month period.

- **In hindsight**   The strong personalities of the project managers, who had an average of 100 or more direct reports, made cooperation difficult because blame was felt.

Hostility with Third Parties

In this project, an existing project team was merged with an external consulting team at the start of the project. The two groups continued to act as separate entities, even to the point of open hostility during team meetings.

- **Diagnosis and solution implemented**   After the project came to a point of near disaster, both groups were open to another project manager from another part of the organization coming into the picture and helping to solve the problems. At this point, fear of project failure started to outweigh the other factors.

- **Results achieved**   The new project manager, with no baggage, was able to provide a solution that the extended team could follow. Deliberately not blaming anyone, and actually stating that no one was going to be blamed, was the catalyst that made cooperation possible.

- **In hindsight**   This is another example where people problems and jealousy cost a company avoidable expenditures.

Not Making Difficult Decisions

In this project, the client management, absolutely brilliant and demanding professionals, was reluctant to make any difficult decisions on an Internet community project for a world-class organization. The delay was due to a lack of confidence in the content being produced because of the bad structure of the project deliverables. There was a complete disconnect between the consulting project team and client management.

- **Diagnosis and solution implemented**   While the specific content could be debated, as could the personalities of the various people, decisions were not being made because a base that both groups could agree on was not being built. The solution was to bring in another project manager to help the two sides bridge their differences. The new project manager was selected based on academic and professional credentials that would overcome any questions of credibility. This started to remove the tension on the project team, allowing agreements in the infrastructure to be realized, thus allowing the more important decisions to be made.

- **Results achieved**   The project was completed to the satisfaction of the client.

- **In hindsight**   The client's culture demanded certain standards to be met. The project team was not experienced in delivering to the level of prescribed rigidity. The credibility of the rescue manager allowed both teams to overcome the differences.

Contract Manager Not Making It

In this example, two consulting firms teamed up to do an assessment of an organization's processes. After half the project duration had elapsed, the client sponsor approached the account managers to complain about the lack of progress and direction on the initiative. This was actually a surprise to the account managers from both consulting firms.

- **Diagnosis and solution implemented**   The designated project manager did not have the strategic skills to define the big picture. A decision was made to move the part-time quality assurance manager into a lead role. It was felt that he was the right person because of his experience in rescuing troubled projects in the past. This was preceded by a frank discussion with the client sponsor to demonstrate an understanding of the project's situation and what would be needed to recover it.

- **Results achieved**   The client sponsor felt that it would be easier to recover the current project rather than try it again with a different team. This allowed the new organization's structure to focus on the issues, resolve the issues, and successfully complete the project. However, the project went over budget, which had to be absorbed by the consulting company to maintain the client relationship.

- **In hindsight**   In the first half of the project, there was a general sense that things were not proceeding smoothly. However, no one followed up. Only a major milestone in the second half of the project caused a reaction. It would have been better to have an earlier milestone to identify this type of situation, to reduce the amount of expenditures.

Personality Examples

The examples in this section highlight some of the personalities traits that different members of the extended team will exhibit during a project rescue.

Rescue Manager Taking Control

In this example, four rescue managers were unsuccessful in assisting the turnaround of an ERP project for a large retailer. The fifth rescue manager reviewed the history of the project and experiences of the predecessors to build a new approach.

- **Diagnosis and solution implemented**   The lessons learned demonstrated the need for a hands-on approach for the rescue. The new direction was successful, but the rescue manager left a lot of the internal resources feeling threatened about their positions.
- **Results achieved**   As the solution moved forward, the rescue manager made a conscious effort to withdraw from day-to-day activities.
- **In hindsight**   This is an example of the very strengths that are required to solve a set of problems resulting in a different set of problems. The same rescue manager would probably not be able to repeat the good performance because of a lack of objectivity—real or perceived.

Hostile Project Team

A project team had been working on an initiative for over a year with no tangible results to show the executive sponsors. Progress was not being made. Anyone with new ideas who joined the team from the outside, full time or part time, was met with hostility. They were not allowed to succeed either.

- **Diagnosis and solution implemented**   Many attempts to change the dynamics of the project team were unsuccessful. The solution involved a series of workshops to collectively build the solution to the problem. The workshops had several confrontations that had to be managed by an external facilitator.
- **Results achieved**   The workshops allowed a solution to be designed by the collective project team. The solution was segmented and ownership

was passed to subteams. An external manager acted as the integrator to bring the segments back together.

- **In hindsight** This was another example where team members who were not experiencing success were worried about how their careers would be impacted by letting someone else succeed where they did not.

Protective Project Manager

In this example, a project manager was highly protective of two junior developers. The work quality of the subteam was impacted. The project manager continued to defend the performance of the two junior developers even though the quality of their products was the lowest in the organization. Strong messages to improve their performance were delivered to the junior developers by the project manager, but noticeable improvements were not observed.

- **Diagnosis and solution implemented** The loyalty of the project manager topped other considerations. The project manager was willing to deliver difficult messages, but was reluctant to take the next step. The project manager was a strong performer in other areas. The project manager's director made the decision to let the two developers go, with notice. The project manager was asked to deliver the message.

- **Results achieved** The two developers were not surprised to be let go and soon found employment elsewhere. The project manager did a good job once the decision was made.

- **In hindsight** The project manager was clearly wrong in allowing the developers to continue in their role. This was reflected in the project manager's performance as well.

Project Management Seizing Control Back

A project was being successfully rescued, when members of the original project team started to take control back from the rescue manager. This went to the point of changing financial authorizations and the business requirements. This attitude was a significant contributor to the problems that brought the project to the verge of disaster in the first place.

- **Diagnosis and solution implemented** While the project was rescued successfully, the client team was clearly nervous about losing credit on an ongoing basis. The rescue manager had already planned to start relinquishing control and opted to do so a little bit sooner.

- **Results achieved**   The project was successful, but some of the original attitudes that resulted in problems started to return.

- **In hindsight**   External rescue managers may want to build directly into the project plan a transition out period. Care should be taken to ensure that this does not lead to a misunderstanding of a lack of commitment.

Stakeholders Not Assertive

In this very large financial project, the stakeholders had strong demands, but were not assertive in getting them implemented. Furthermore, the stakeholders would always back down in front of the project managers during status meetings when a lack of progress was being discussed.

- **Diagnosis and solution implemented**   Everyone was trying to be appreciative and to perform well on their jobs. However, communication between the different project teams was not effective. A rescue manager was needed to work closely, sometimes confrontationally, with each of the project teams to identify integration strategies with the products of the other groups. The confrontations were not allowed to linger for any extended period of time.

- **Results achieved**   The revised strategy salvaged the project so that it was delivered incrementally.

- **In hindsight**   More assertiveness would have helped the project be delivered under budget.

Third Parties and Their Own Metrics

In this project example, a client was employing several different third parties, including some offshore companies, to deliver an ERP solution with heavy customization. Some of the third parties were competitors and driven by metrics or goals that were not in the best interest of the client.

- **Diagnosis and solution implemented**   After missing several deadlines and hearing one vendor blame the other repeatedly, the project management eventually reached a level of frustration where it was willing to close down the project. It took calls at the president level to establish the appropriate level of cooperation.

- **Results achieved**   While the solution was implemented, the frustration felt by the client team resulted in several vendors being dismissed.

- **In hindsight**   Too many vendors were given too much authority to act on their own. The service level agreements did not adequately address the cross-vendor cooperation that was needed to be successful.

Process

With so many changes in the business environment, technology, and world environment, processes are one of the first areas to be neglected. Proven processes become obsolete quickly. This removes the discipline to use them. Organizations begin to improvise and lose the benefits of repeatability, reuse, and best practices.

Methodology

Methodologies and frameworks provide prescriptive approaches for achieving specific goals. There are many different variations and approaches available to organizations.

Unclear Requirements

In this project, the team documented every requirement that the business users wanted. Changes were documented and propagated through the requirement deck. The approach was so thorough that after six months, not a line of code was still written, but half the budget was consumed.

- **Diagnosis and solution implemented**   The solution that worked was to build a prototype interactively with the business users. This allowed an agreement to be reached on the requirements within a week, as both sides were more willing to accept some uncertainty because they could agree on the substantive details.

- **Results achieved**   The prototype was accepted as the business requirements. The project was delivered in several phases.

- **In hindsight**   The strong emphasis on the documentation was driven by fear of uncertainty and a fear of getting started.

Incorrect Methodology

A large financial institution hired a senior consulting team to do a postmortem on a project that had not been successful. The question was to find out what went wrong. Was it the technology? Was it the management team? Was it the requirements?

- **Diagnosis and solution implemented**   A series of interviews and the project documentation revealed the source of the problems being experienced by the project. It was a financial application that would have required at least two months of solid testing. It also required a number of other controls to be built. A rapid application development methodology that did not have this level of detail was used. It was not appropriate for the task.

- **Results achieved**   The postmortem results drove the selection of more appropriate methodologies for the organization.

- **In hindsight**   An appropriate methodology provides a checklist that can be used to confirm the validity of a direction being followed.

Testing Started Too Late

In this complex project example, none of the subproject teams were ready for the testing phase as per the project plan. As a result, the testing phase was pushed out toward the nonmoveable start date.

- **Diagnosis and solution implemented**   Testing of whatever functions were available was started immediately. Although this required duplication of effort, finding some of the problems early allowed them to be fixed before the formal test phase started.

- **Results achieved**   Even though functions were marked as complete, the testing phase showed integration problems that delayed implementation.

- **In hindsight**   Never mark something complete unless it has been fully tested.

Not Enough Time from the Beginning

In this example, a project missed deadlines repeatedly and went into production eight months later than originally planned. The budget was also exceeded.

- **Diagnosis and solution implemented**   A postmortem showed that the project could not be completed in the timeframe that was allotted. This resulted in new decisions that created additional problems.

- **Results achieved**   The lessons learned were shared with the chairman of the large financial institution.

- **In hindsight**   It would have been better to reduce the functionality to meet the shorter timeframe that was available. It would have been cheaper and would have allowed other departments to deal more appropriately with their customers.

No Measurable Milestones

A project team was not able to produce any positive results even after a year of trying. There were no noticeable confrontations or other personal issues on the project team.

- **Diagnosis and solution implemented**   A rescue manager reviewed the project and determined that there were not enough milestones to push the team into making firm decisions.
- **Results achieved**   The approach called for a pilot implementation in three months. This was met.
- **In hindsight**   People can be very busy doing value-added work that leads nowhere.

Only Testing a Subset

A project team was spending all its time testing subsets of a larger application as it was being constructed. The testing was being done in isolation with very little information sharing. Each of the subteams felt that the project was proceeding well, but had no idea of the problems that were not being identified between modules.

- **Diagnosis and solution implemented**   Fortunately, this situation was diagnosed early enough to allow the approach to be changed. The problem was that the separation of the subsets meant that a lot of work and testing would be done. However, the pieces would not have fit together when the virtual silos were integrated.
- **Results achieved**   Instead of testing silos, a test bed was implemented to test the application from one side to another during development.
- **In hindsight**   Offshore development initiatives can fall into this trap every easily.

Approvals

Getting that final user approval to complete a project is mandatory and satisfying. This section discusses some collective experiences in this area that complicate what could otherwise be a pleasant experience.

Oversold Functionality

The marketing team sold to the client a solution that was not fully built up. Some functionality was built, but significant portions needed to be customized or completely rewritten for the client's requirements. The timeline was built using optimistic assumptions.

- **Diagnosis and solution implemented**   This approach resulted in several problems. Extra work needed to be done to complete the solution, which required a lot of unplanned work from the project team. This resulted in morale problems. At the same time, the client lost confidence in what it was being told. The good news was that the client still trusted the vendor, but the lack of confidence caused the client to question every deliverable that was produced. This extended the timeline.

- **Results achieved**   The vendor ended up spending many times more than it expected to in order to get signoff. This essentially required a lot of rework and extra work on the part of the vendor so that the project ended up making no profits. Interestingly, the results had both negative and positive aspects for the client. The client received a workable solution at a lower price than it would have paid if the scoping had been done correctly. However, this was offset by a great deal of frustration and missed deadlines.

- **In hindsight**   It's in everyone's interest to sell based on what is really available.

No One to Sign to Launch

The testing team completed the acceptance process at 4:00 A.M. It was expected to finish at 9:00 P.M. the night before. The business sponsors had given up and gone to bed. The expectations for the project team were to have the system running live in the production environment by 9:00 A.M.

- **Diagnosis and solution implemented**   No one with the authority to sign off on the test results was available by the time testing was completed. The project manager made the decision to call the executive sponsor at home, but could not find the number to call—the cell phone went to the answering machine. The project team decided to start the launch process but keep some of the switches off until someone with the proper authority was found.

- **Results achieved**   The executive sponsor gave approval to proceed at 10:00 A.M. It took a few hours for the application to be available in production. This was about half the time that a full launch would take. It was not a complete success or a complete failure.

- **In hindsight**   Every project launch requires a contact sheet and someone authorized to launch 24×7.

Sponsor Not Fully Engaged

In this example, extensive acceptance test results were prepared for signoff, but the sponsor was not ready to give final approval. They just were not aware of all the details and did not feel comfortable taking this risk.

- **Diagnosis and solution implemented**   It took a few extra days to get approval to launch the solution into production.
- **Results achieved**   The project was launched late.
- **In hindsight**   Project sponsors who appear to be distant during the project life cycle need to be briefed face to face on what is expected from them.

Technology

Although technology can be complex, it is more predictable than human personalities. However, rapidly evolving technology is a growing complication to project success. Technology problems typically occur because of misunderstandings, lack of planning, lack of testing, or a lack of validating that a selected design is correct.

Contingency

Who wants to think about contingencies when a system is going to be launched with great fanfare and significant added value to the organization? On the other hand, who wants to disrupt business because someone forgot to set an environment switch?

Insufficient Planning

A mission-critical application was tested and launched into production. The servers were fault tolerant to ensure maximum online availability. Unfortunately, one of the servers crashed due to a hardware failure during the first day of operation. The resulting load on the server that was still operational caused performance to decline significantly. Additional servers were not available for several days.

- **Diagnosis and solution implemented**   This scenario had not been considered. It took four days for another server to arrive and be configured. Complaints from online customers were dealt with through customer service.

- **Results achieved**   The application was brought back up almost a week later. Customer service had to work hard to deal with the resulting issues.

- **In hindsight**   Identify the cost of the contingency strategies and allow the executive sponsor to communicate the amount of effort that is tolerable in the event that unexpected problems impact a launch.

Insufficient Measurement Tools

A project was launched with strong disaster recovery planning. A hosting center was prepared to take over if the system crashed. However, tools were not available to identify conditions less than all-out disaster, when various contingencies would be introduced.

- **Diagnosis and solution implemented**   Monitoring tools were purchased and implemented. Contingency processes were defined for different situations that could arise.

- **Results achieved**   Although management felt the lack of monitoring tools was a major exposure, the contingency plans were not required.

- **In hindsight**   Monitoring checkpoints should have been part of the deployment plan.

Performance

The performance of different transactions in a web-based application is dependent on many factors that are difficult to predict or control. Internet-based architectures need to be built with more flexibility than their counterparts in the past. For example, a particularly successful e-business site could conceivably have a hundred million hits in one day—or it could have just a few.

Runaway Success

A web-based application was launched after stress testing for twice the expected volumes. The launch coincided with a great deal of advertising, so ten times the expected number of users ended up coming to the site in the first day.

- **Diagnosis and solution implemented**   The system response time was very poor and remained that way for several days while the servers were reconfigured with more memory and CPUs.

- **Results achieved**   The response time reached a normal level with the hardware upgrades.

- **In hindsight**   It would have been useful to work with a hosting company to deal with spikes in user volumes.

Major Transactions Too Slow

A claims application demonstrated strong performance in most transactions; however, some frequent transactions that were used by users were not put through a stress-testing process.

- **Diagnosis and solution implemented**   The application required additional tuning of the frequently used transactions.

- **Results achieved**   Money that would have been required to upgrade the hardware was saved by focusing only on the frequent transactions.

- **In hindsight**   Doing the stress testing sooner would not have had a material impact on the outcome of the project.

Payment Issues

An organization's process for paying its vendors and suppliers has an impact on the quality of service it receives. The payment process can also impact the type of information and access to special programs that vendors may have to offer.

Vendors Not Paid in Time

Vendors delivered the software at a huge discount and agreed to several payment periods. Payments were made late and only after repeated requests. Another wave of negotiations were needed for the next set of software licenses that were required for implementation.

- **Diagnosis and solution implemented**   The rescue manager was required to rely on personal friendships to get a high discount percentage.

- **Results achieved**   Although the software was acquired at a large discount, other information and programs offered by the vendor to their regular clients were withheld.

- **In hindsight**   Delayed payments can cost more than the interest saved.

Word of Mouth

Again as a result of delayed payments to some vendors, other vendors became reluctant to present their products. They were certainly willing to sell their software at full cost and a large upfront payment.

- **Diagnosis and solution implemented**   The project team needed to call on a lot of personal favors to get cooperation from the vendors again.
- **Results achieved**   Time that could have been spent on project development work was instead spent on vendor management, trying to recover good will that was lost.
- **In hindsight**   This was not a good use of time and also damaged employee morale in the process.

Closing Perspective

This chapter provided a virtual database for the types of problems that may be faced on different types of projects. The information was collected from a variety of sources but was changed to make the lessons generic in nature.

Index

INTERNATIONAL CONTACT INFORMATION

AUSTRALIA
McGraw-Hill Book Company
Australia Pty. Ltd.
TEL +61-2-9900-1800
FAX +61-2-9878-8881
http://www.mcgraw-hill.com.au
books-it_sydney@mcgraw-hill.com

CANADA
McGraw-Hill Ryerson Ltd.
TEL +905-430-5000
FAX +905-430-5020
http://www.mcgraw-hill.ca

**GREECE, MIDDLE EAST, & AFRICA
(Excluding South Africa)**
McGraw-Hill Hellas
TEL +30-210-6560-990
TEL +30-210-6560-993
TEL +30-210-6560-994
FAX +30-210-6545-525

MEXICO (Also serving Latin America)
McGraw-Hill Interamericana Editores
S.A. de C.V.
TEL +525-1500-5108
FAX +525-117-1589
http://www.mcgraw-hill.com.mx
carlos_ruiz@mcgraw-hill.com

SINGAPORE (Serving Asia)
McGraw-Hill Book Company
TEL +65-6863-1580
FAX +65-6862-3354
http://www.mcgraw-hill.com.sg
mghasia@mcgraw-hill.com

SOUTH AFRICA
McGraw-Hill South Africa
TEL +27-11-622-7512
FAX +27-11-622-9045
robyn_swanepoel@mcgraw-hill.com

SPAIN
McGraw-Hill/
Interamericana de España, S.A.U.
TEL +34-91-180-3000
FAX +34-91-372-8513
http://www.mcgraw-hill.es
professional@mcgraw-hill.es

**UNITED KINGDOM, NORTHERN,
EASTERN, & CENTRAL EUROPE**
McGraw-Hill Education Europe
TEL +44-1-628-502500
FAX +44-1-628-770224
http://www.mcgraw-hill.co.uk
emea_queries@mcgraw-hill.com

ALL OTHER INQUIRIES Contact:
McGraw-Hill/Osborne
TEL +1-510-420-7700
FAX +1-510-420-7703
http://www.osborne.com
omg_international@mcgraw-hill.com

Sound Off!

Visit us at **www.osborne.com/bookregistration** and let us know what you thought of this book. While you're online you'll have the opportunity to register for newsletters and special offers from McGraw-Hill/Osborne.

We want to hear from you!

Sneak Peek

Visit us today at **www.betabooks.com** and see what's coming from McGraw-Hill/Osborne tomorrow!

Based on the successful software paradigm, Bet@Books™ allows computing professionals to view partial and sometimes complete text versions of selected titles online. Bet@Books™ viewing is free, invites comments and feedback, and allows you to "test drive" books in progress on the subjects that interest you the most.